MIDDLE CLASS DREAMS

MIDDLE CLASS DREAMS

*The Politics and Power of the
New American Majority*

STANLEY B. GREENBERG

TIMES 𝕋 BOOKS

RANDOM HOUSE

To Luisa DeLauro

LIBRARY OF CONGRESS CATALOGING-IN-PUBLICATION DATA

Greenberg, Stanley B.
    Middle class dreams : the politics and power of the new American majority / Stanley B. Greenberg. — 1st ed.
        p.   cm.
    Includes index.
    ISBN 0-8129-2345-6
    1. United States—Politics and government—1993— 2. Macomb County (Mich.)—Politics and government. 3. Middle class—United States—Political activity. 4. Middle class—Michigan—Macomb County—Political activity. 5. Clinton, Bill, 1946–   . I. Title.
    E885.G74   1995
    320.973—dc20   94-31603

Manufactured in the United States of America

9 8 7 6 5 4 3 2

First Edition

. . . .

AUTHOR'S NOTE

I started out a year and a half ago to write a book about America's middle-class revolt against politics. Bill Clinton was the center of that story, as his campaign captured the forces of change to bring down the older order and as his presidency offered the promise of a new kind of politics. In the process of writing the book, I began to realize just how profound was the revolt. The 1992 election was not just about George Bush or even the national Republican ascendancy. It was a revolt against the whole party order, forged over a century, that no longer allowed ordinary citizens to feel part of a community and no longer allowed people to feel confident about the future. The 1994 election carried forward the revolt, this time with the Republicans leading the charge against a corrupted politics. Some look at 1994 and see but another turn of the partisan screw. But for me, it was just further confirmation of the historic scale of the public's disaffection and determination to find something new. How the parties and candidates fare in 1996 will depend on how well they understand the character of this tumult.

I wrote this book from a not very disinterested vantage point, the Clinton presidency, where I have had the honor to work for the president of the United States. I toyed with writing a first-person account of these times but quickly abandoned the idea as inappropriate and too self-important. Such reflections are better suited to a time when the Clinton project has played out to what

v

I hope is a successful conclusion. Even as I have finally written this, in the third person, the reader will find no backstage revelations about the Clinton campaign or the Clinton White House. The alleged warring factions will remain hidden. I offer no blow-by-blow account of the administration's key legislative battles. And finally and thankfully, this is not an exposé of Bill Clinton—how he ticks, makes decisions, treats people, campaigns, or works.

Instead, this book is about the historic forces that surround Bill Clinton's rise to the presidency and the longer term changes they reflect. To be sure, he helped create this moment, but the forces at work are bigger than the president himself. They set the stage, the roles, and the tests that will define his presidency and test the new Republican leaders in the Congress. These are not ordinary times; the party political order has collapsed, and the citizenry is dispirited, alienated, and fragmented. At the same time, however, voters are looking for some new social compact that will allow them to rebuild a sense of community and progress. If there is to be a Clinton Era, it will be because Bill Clinton understood this moment and capitalized on it.

I wrote this book out of a sense of urgency, lest the country lose this opportunity to remake its politics and recapture what has been lost. The day-to-day news and the day-to-day struggle to govern have crippled the political imagination and reduced our public life to a series of small and tawdry dramas. It is difficult to peer through the morass of details, problems, battles, and scandals to see the more elevated challenges before us. It is difficult to see that the short-term poll numbers and even the results of midterm elections are but reflections of something deeper. I wrote this book so that all the characters in this drama—the people, the politicians, the social critics, and the press—may better understand what is really happening and what is really at stake.

To escape the daily grind of presidential politics, I tried to reexamine our current circumstances from a number of more distant perspectives. First, I worked to set the historical stage—

to understand what was really at issue in the last presidential election and whether it constituted an historic break that could change the course of our politics. Second, I immersed myself in a single suburban community, Macomb County, Michigan, far from Washington, D.C., where I could see more clearly how changing national political forces play out in the lives and politics of middle America. And finally, I listened closely over a number of years to ordinary citizens in various circumstances all across the country. Such people have taught me that voters share a common sense about what is right and wrong in our society, how leaders have failed their obligations, and what meaning is possible in politics. Their sense of loss and their hopes set the terms of debate for our politics.

This book was written in the full glare of events that changed the balance of political forces in the country. While the core arguments about the breakdown of party traditions and the social contract remained unchanged, I made significant revisions to extend the analysis to address the new challenges facing our politics.

My point of departure for this book was not 1992 or 1994, but 1985, when I first went to Macomb County. I had been invited by Michigan's Democratic leaders to help figure out why this Democratic bastion in the suburbs had turned away from the party and why so many of its union supporters were now self-identified Reagan Democrats. It is still not clear to me, in retrospect, why they turned to me. I was a somewhat obscure academic, teaching at Yale University about comparative politics, race relations, and South Africa. But in 1982 and 1984, I had advised and conducted polls for Bob Carr, who won election to Congress in a newly reapportioned Michigan seat, replete with blue-collar suburban areas.

And from what they could tell, I appeared to be a good listener. As an academic researcher, I had traveled to places like Birmingham, Alabama, Johannesburg, Belfast, and Tel Aviv, even Detroit, conducting extended, free-flowing interviews, trying to build stories from people's tales. I wrote about politics in poor neighborhoods and about industrialism and race discrimination, but always beginning with the individual—always with an understanding of how people interpret their own lives and roles in a changing world.

Though the party leaders and I were only dimly aware of it at the time, another factor drew me to Macomb: I was not easily put off by the racial worries and prejudices of working-class communities. For years, Democratic and union leaders had set a moral example on civil rights, and many had stood in the front ranks of the March on Washington in 1963. But Macomb County was lily-white and had fought bitterly to stop school busing. It was no longer possible to avoid the contradiction, though few dared face the issue, lest the fragile Democratic coalition explode on them. As a professor, I had spent many years trying to understand the struggles of workers coping with a divided society—in places like Alabama before the civil rights era, South Africa, and Palestine before the creation of the state of Israel. In these places, some unions explicitly ignored race and ethnic lines and brought workers together despite their profound differences. But many other unions, some led by socialists and communists, made different choices. The Mine Workers Union in South Africa struck repeatedly to win an all-white labor policy that would protect white miners from undercutting by rural African migrants. The Steelworkers in Alabama negotiated segregated ladders of promotion that confined blacks to the dirtiest jobs and gave whites a monopoly of skilled positions. If not necessarily the right moral choices, they were reasoned and understandable ones, I had argued, in the context of a divided country.

I was little conscious of these issues when I began work in Macomb. But the Michigan Democrats allowed me to listen to voters who were genuinely anguished with their growing insecurity in the workplace, their unlikely association with Republicans, and their uncertain place in a Democratic vision. My final report described how racial sentiment had disfigured white middle-class perceptions of the Democratic party, government, and the American dream, and it urged a new middle-class discourse that could accommodate both black and white. The report caused something of an uproar but, for better or worse, set me on my current course. A number of national party leaders sought to cut the discussion short, but others took notice, including Rick Wiener of the Michigan Democratic party, Ken Melley of the National Education Association, Al From of the Democratic Leadership Council, and Arch Gillies of the World Policy Institute, who supported my early work. Bill Clinton, was busy in Arkansas, but he took notice too.

♦ ♦ ♦ ♦

This book is not so much about President Bill Clinton as it is about his times. But he had the vision and tenacity to help create this moment, and he has the inner strength and sense of history he will need to change our country's course. Some look at the Clinton White House and see unruliness. I see a president who is passionate and engaged, who respects ideas, who enjoys and depends on intellectual combat, who thirsts for understanding, who listens, who has a deep compassion for people, who makes sound judgments, and who has the courage to take on momentous challenges. I want to thank him for allowing me this vantage point, for respecting my contribution, and indeed for encouraging me to write this book.

The president and the country are fortunate to have Hillary Rodham Clinton, and I have been privileged to watch and work with her. She is both a passionately private person and a passionately public one who confounds those who insist she be typecast. I have seen both her tender and tenacious sides. I have seen her protect her family and protect the president. She is very much a part of the moment.

I was given the opportunity to write this book because of the sense of purpose and sense of history that guided the Clinton campaign. There were good people involved, top to bottom, but the inspired leadership of James Carville and the battle-tested camaraderie of the primary campaign and the "war room" carried all of us to a new level, sweeping along George Stephanopoulos, Mandy Grunwald, Paul Begala, Frank Greer, and all those young and not-so-young people who gathered in Little Rock every morning to change America.

This book was immeasurably changed by the good judgment of those who took the time to read and criticize the manuscript. Although I may not appear to take criticism well, the book does reflect the work of Diane Blair, David Bonior, Ron Brownstein, Al From, Paul Gewirtz, David Lauter, Bruce Lindsey, Samuel Popkin, Marla Romash, Theda Skocpol, George Stephanopoulos, and my family of loyal political scientists, Ed Greenberg and Anna Greenberg.

My colleagues at the various incarnations of Greenberg Research—particularly Al Quinlan, Joe Goode, and Celinda Lake—protected me from all sorts of distractions and helped create an intellectual climate that made this book possible. So many loyal and good people at Greenberg Research have worked to push our inquiry to a higher standard.

Along the way, a number of organizations and candidates supported focus-group and survey research independent of this book that I was able to use and cite in the course of my writing. I want to thank them for indulging my academic instincts and allowing me to probe for something deeper. They include the Center for National Policy (on understanding the economy), the Advocacy Institute (on Congress and special interests), the Democratic Leadership Council (on Perot and independent voters), the World Policy Institute (on American identity), the Michigan House Democrats and Michigan Democratic party (on Macomb County), the National Education Association (on party perceptions), Americans Talk Issues Foundation (on attitudinal consistency and government reform), the Campaign for New Priorities (on a changing world and domestic investment), and the Academy of Florida Trial Lawyers (on responsibility).

A number of candidates retained me to think strategically on their behalf and unintentionally helped advance my education and my respect for voters. I want to thank Senators Chris Dodd, Joe Lieberman, and Jeff Bingaman, Ambassador Andy Young, Vice President Al Gore, Ambassador Walter Mondale, Congressmen David Bonior, Bob Carr, Bob Matsui, and Bruce Morrison, State Senator Peter Welch, Speaker Bob O'Donnell, and State Comptroller Bill Curry—for believing in me.

A number of research organizations opened their doors and shared information freely, including the Library of Congress, the National Archives, the Institute for Social Inquiry of the University of Michigan, Mullins Library at the University of Arkansas, the National Committee for an Effective Congress, Voter Research and Surveys, Cambridge Reports, the Louis Harris Data Center at the University of North Carolina, Opinion Research Corporation, and the Gallup Organization. A number of people helped me fill in gaps in my understanding or attain critical material, including Mark Halperin of ABC News, John King of the Associated Press, Ed Bruley, Congressmen John Dingell and David Bonior, Al From, Dick Morris, Jay Mazur, Greg Hawkins, and Diane Blair.

Alan Wolf, my research assistant, organized all the databases and spent the last year tracking down the impossible. He was aided by Neil Shipley, Brian George, and Todd Louis.

My administrative assistant at Greenberg Research, Cristina Yablonsky, was in full command of my professional life. She juggled the uncommon pressure of the White House, South Africa, and the book—always with extraordinary grace and strength and good judgment.

Bob Barnett played a gifted George Bush in the campaign's mock debate, but he was even better as an agent. He warmed immediately to the book and made sure that I found my right niche in the publishing world.

My editors at Times Books, Peter Osnos, Paul Golob, and Geoff Shandler, believed in this project yet always pushed me to think bigger and about the future. They helped me escape the day-to-day events and understand the historic moment that motivates this book.

It is customary to acknowledge one's parents for bearing you, one's spouse for proofreading, typing, and baby-sitting services, and the children for being quiet. I will thank my children Kathryn, Anna and Jonathan for growing up and taking on challenges that matter and my parents for serving dutifully as proud cheerleaders and defenders. My wife, however, does not conform to the stereotype, nor did she do a lot of proofreading. Rosa DeLauro is a member of Congress and my best friend and partner, who gives all this meaning.

I dedicate this book to Luisa DeLauro. More than sixty years ago, in 1933, she wrote in New Haven's Tenth Ward Democratic Club newsletter: "We are not living in the middle ages when a woman's part in life was merely to serve her master in the home, but we have gradually taken our place in every phase of human endeavor, and even in the here-to-fore stronghold of the male sex: politics." Though she worked behind a sewing machine in a sweatshop so her daughter could have something better, she has also served thirty years as ward leader and member of the Board of Aldermen, using her untiring spirit to help people. We carry on her work.

Stanley B. Greenberg
Washington, D.C.
December 1, 1994

CONTENTS

MIDDLE CLASS DREAMS

1. THE CRASH

THE 1992 election was a crash—not just of George Bush's presidency but of our modern political history. The election confirmed the collapse of the dominant political traditions that had organized American politics for nearly a century—a Democratic party standing for the common people and a Republican party associated with a business-led prosperity. These enduring party images had given a sense of purpose to national politics, and without them ordinary American voters were left scared, both of their own cynicism and anger and of their isolation from forces bigger than they. The crash of 1992 left people without a social compact that would permit them to feel trust in the civic order and stall the forces of dissolution.

The crash was reflected in the 1994 election as a disconnected citizenry acted once again on its growing alienation. This time, voters turned away from the spectacle of a Democratic Congress and a Democratic-dominated national politics that seemed trapped in pointless partisan battle, dominated by special interests, and slow to address the needs of ordinary citizens. Thus, even more of our political history lay shattered.

That Bill Clinton won the presidency with only 43 percent of the vote and that Republicans two years later captured the House and Senate has led some to imagine that not much happened in 1992—no new Democratic majority, a lot of people "mad as hell," and for many Republicans just a hapless George

Bush who broke his "read my lips" pledge not to raise taxes. The Republicans would soon be returned to power.

But Richard Nixon had received little more than 43 percent of the vote in 1968, and that election marked the end of the New Deal Democratic majority as more than 57 percent voted against the Democrat and to bring down the curtain on racial liberalism. In 1992, 62 percent voted against the legacy of Reagan Republicanism, and Bill Clinton assumed the presidency much as Richard Nixon had, as a wrecker of the old order and a potential builder of the new. But in 1992, so much more lay in ruins. Indeed, the 1994 midterm election was not about the Republicans. It was about the profound failure of our politics.

It is hard to appreciate the scale of the crash because so much of what we read and see every day in the news, so much of what we hear from the commentators and pundits, is itself part of the wreckage. Our view of political reality is obscured by a bewildering amount of news. Some of it centers on the tawdry as reporters stampede one another rushing to uncover the latest act of political misuse or misappropriation, the latest perk, the latest hint of sex. Some of it centers on the rush for immediate meaning—polls that tell us about public thinking before the public has had time to think and analysts who proclaim each event or election a harbinger of the future (and like weather forecasters, pay no price for being wrong). Some of it centers on the presidential trail itself, which creates news wherever it leads—from the golf courses and town halls to summit meetings and state dinners.

The news is not necessarily political reality. As Walter Lippmann observed "news and truth are not the same thing"—"the function of news is to signalize an event, the function of truth is to bring to light the hidden facts, to set them into relation with each other, and make a picture of reality on which men

can act."[1] Distracted by detail, magnitude, immediacy, and titil-
lation, we often fail to recognize the real character of our era
and the fundamental changes going on underneath; the clutter
limits our ability to imagine what America's future politics
might look like.

In 1964, Lyndon Baines Johnson's historic landslide election
and the demolition of Barry Goldwater seemed to portend the
demise of conservative Republicanism. Johnson swept into
Republican bastions across the country, and Goldwater was left
holding a handful of unreconstructed Deep South states. In the
aftermath, editorial writers and commentators declared that the
"two-party system [is] at present lying in ruins," and Goldwater's
"conservative cause" had "wrecked his party for a long time to
come."[2] But the drama of the news was hardly the real drama,
for underneath, political loyalties were being dislodged and new
forces were emerging. Within two years, an explosively angry
electorate had begun to turn its back on the Democrats, and in
1968 Richard Nixon had capitalized on Goldwater's appeal to
white southerners with a "southern strategy" that won the
White House for the Republicans.

In 1977, Jimmy Carter abandoned his presidential limousine
for the inaugural parade and walked the mile and a half down
Pennsylvania Avenue to the White House. At a time when the
country was shaken by the Watergate scandal, here was a man of
character: peanut farmer, submarine officer, born-again Christian calling for a "a new spirit amongst us." The new president
would affirm his pledge "to stay close to you, to be worthy of
you, and to exemplify what you are." The Carter presidency, it
was believed, would restore trust in government. In the end it
only accelerated the public's disillusionment. To this day, many
Americans still describe Carter as "honest, too honest." They
better understood the potent underlying forces that had nearly
elected Gerald Ford despite Watergate and the Nixon pardon

and that enabled Ronald Reagan to mount his revolution in 1980. A budding tax revolt, rising inflation, and racial polarization were bringing to life a reality and a future different from those anticipated at the time.[3]

In 1991, George Bush bombed Baghdad, taunted Saddam Hussein, and chased the retreating Iraqi army across the desert. In the process, he chased away nearly all the Democratic challengers, who declined what *U.S. News and World Report* called "the likely suicide mission of running against George Bush."[4] Six months later more than 70 percent of the electorate gave the president high marks for managing the country's affairs. These were the "facts," but hardly the reality. Those who depended on them misjudged the future. They missed the rising disenchantment with official Washington and with Reaganism's failing bounty and loose ethics. And they missed the public's longing for a government capable of attacking the country's long-term problems. There was something new and powerful brewing underneath.

In 1994, with Republicans picking up 8 seats in the Senate and 52 in the House, it should not be surprising that the commentators of the day have rushed forward with some dramatic projections. Newt Gingrich called it "a historical tide, not just a partisan election." Senator Bob Dole told a reporter that the election represented "a vote of no confidence in the Clinton agenda, which means we need to develop a whole new one." For Senator Phil Gramm, it "has the potential to be a permanent realignment." David Broder wrote that the results recall "ominous historical antecedents," and he proceeded to construct an electoral college map that gives the unnamed Republican presidential nominee 316 electoral college votes just for starters.[5] But these immediate and literal interpretations of events are no less subject than the earlier interpretations to the historical forces that are shaping our modern political reality.

Today those who would understand the new political realities once again have to maneuver through the news, aided on their way to and from work by the radio commentary of a Rush Limbaugh or a Howard Stern or, on Sunday mornings, by the weekly gatherings of pundits. If the evening news is insufficient, there are the tabloid-style newsmagazines, like *Hard Copy* and *Inside Edition.* The Clinton presidency has generated a lot of news, mostly negative, according to those who keep track of such things. The $200 haircut closing a runway at L.A. Airport (which did not happen, but no matter). Gays in the military. Whitewater and commodity trading. An admired First Lady battling for kids and health care, lobbying Congress—but does she wield too much power? Bosnia. U.S. marines being dragged through the streets of Mogadishu. The president before a joint session of Congress on the state of the nation. The agenda—the deficit, the economy, health care. The Clinton town meeting in Moscow. The Gore-Perot debate on *Larry King Live.* NAFTA. D-Day. The emperor and empress of Japan. Paula Jones. Interest rates down. Interest rates up. Rosty indicted. Three strikes and you're out. Midnight basketball. Pork. The president's health care proposal is dead in Congress. State President Nelson Mandela. GATT delayed. Haiti. Iraq. Middle East peace. Unemployment down to 5.8 percent. Republicans take control of the House and Senate. Newt Gingrich. GATT deal. Poll ratings down. Poll ratings up.

But what is the political reality underneath? The events, crises, and personal stories naturally demand our attention, but they also obscure our understanding of what is really happening to our politics. They cloak rather than reveal the powerful forces at work in our society. The underlying truth is that we are living through a period of fundamental change, when political convention has crashed and political leaders are struggling to invent something new. To understand the character of our politics, one must escape the day-to-day news and look carefully at our history, at our communities and neighborhoods, and to the American people themselves.

TWO PARTY ERAS AND TWO BETRAYALS

Modern America has been shaped by two dominant political visions of the nation's promise: a top-down view that placed its faith in a business-led prosperity and a bottom-up view that championed and advanced the common person. The top-down view held that business leadership and entrepreneurial values would bring change, growth, and a general well-being. The bottom-up idea held that people had to be protected or assisted so they could prosper as the country changed and that their rising standard of living was the measure of the nation's success. Each vision represented a kind of compact that honored certain values and behavior and created certain obligations that in turn allowed ordinary people to order their lives and maintain their faith in the country.[6]

These worldviews were forged during two great-party eras, each launched in economic depression and each dominated by a central organizing principle. The Great Republican Era lasted over three decades (1896–1928), beginning with William McKinley and ending with Calvin Coolidge; it elevated the prestige of business and industrialists and advanced the idea that if business prospered, so would the United States. The Great Democratic Era also lasted over three decades (1932–64), from Franklin D. Roosevelt to John F. Kennedy; it saw the commitment to the common person move to center stage, and it promised a national responsibility to promote work and raise living standards.

These great-party eras left vivid images in the consciousness of most Americans, and these images were passed down as truths. The images are timeless, transcending geography and circumstance. Whether you speak to a black father on the South Side of Chicago or a young professional from the commuting world of north Jersey, a businessman at his city club or a street person in his doorway, you will hear that Democrats are for "the common man," "the middle guy," "the little guy," or "the little people." The Republicans are "more business oriented"; they "stir the economy from the corporate level." This simple distinction is an elemental truth across the land.[7]

According to this received wisdom, which reveals itself in any focus-group discussion with ordinary voters, the Democrats begin with the common people, whom they seek to protect from adversity. They stand up for producers who work with their hands, but are vulnerable to the whims of more powerful forces in society. Democrats are seen variously as nurturing and combative as they seek to expand the welfare of average Americans. Theirs is a party that "cares," has "a sense of fairness," is "more distributive to all the people." It makes a commitment to "social reform," to "more opportunities for the middle class as far as education, jobs, and housing." "It sounds a little old-fashioned," one voter observed, "but I think of the Democratic party as more caring of the average Joe. And the average Joe is the backbone of the country, the taxpayer."

The Republicans, in the popular imagery, believe business and industry are the dynamic forces in society, "creating jobs and economic growth." Republicans are modernizers who understand money and the economy, and their work promoting business "helps everybody"—at least "everybody who wants to become part of the labor force." One woman described the chain to a more general bounty: "from economics comes the jobs, comes the places to shop, comes the backbone or the spine for the development of a town, a community, a county, a state."

The great-party eras crystallized the Republicans' identity as the party of business and the Democrats' image as the party of common people, both trying to be expansive enough to win over the middle ground. For a century, our leaders have struggled to make their case to those caught in the middle—William Jennings Bryan's "common man," Franklin Roosevelt's "forgotten man," Richard Nixon's "forgotten American," Bill Clinton's "forgotten middle class."

Over the past thirty years, as the great-party eras waned, we have witnessed two bold attempts at party renewal, both of which failed and both of which embittered those caught in the middle. Lyndon Johnson's Great Society brought an explosion of programs to protect people and advance opportunity in a political world turned upside down by the civil rights issue. But by narrowing the definition of "common people" to the most disadvantaged, his bold initiative distorted the Democrats' bottom-up vision, making it into something constricted and racial. Johnson's expansive moral formula rallied the country at a time of crisis, but as a political formula it could not embrace the middle class. This attempt at renewal crashed in 1968, leaving the national Democratic party marginalized and middle America feeling betrayed. The broken contract produced an unprecedented explosion of political distrust.

On the Republican side, Ronald Reagan in 1980 sought to renew the vision of a business-led prosperity, elevating once again the productive role of American business and the creative power of American enterprise. He opposed taxes and government regulation. He sought to persuade working-class America that its interests and values were best represented by a Republican government. But during his term in office, growth faltered for ordinary citizens, and profits turned to excess, extravagance, and greed. With Americans feeling betrayed again, this attempt at Republican renewal crashed in 1992. The Republican victories in 1994 were impressive but merely political, reflecting no greater confidence in the party or top-down Reaganism.

The party images, passed down as truths, had become tarnished, now seeming like inherited wrongs. Ordinary voters believed that the Democrats, motivated by a "bleeding heart" and a desire "to do good," encourage a frenzy of demands to meet untold needs. Democrats overreach, "go overboard with spending," "go over the brink," and end up taxing the very people they are supposed to champion—the common people. And yet the Republicans, in trying to be "big-business oriented," end up helping "the people that already have the money." In practice, Republicans have produced unequal results and economic stagnation and in the process turned profits into greed: "The Republican party appears to be very greedy and seemed to be very narrowly passing legislation and doing things for business"; "Republicans say, 'Start with the big money-making corporations, and start from there.' A person can't survive with the trickle effect."

Little wonder most Americans came to believe something was fundamentally wrong: the Democratic party no longer championed the common people, and the Republican party no longer enriched the many. A party that is supposed to help people turns out to hurt them; a party that understands how business can promote growth instead promotes only greed. But this was not just a failure of political parties; it was a crash of the dominant ideas, forged over a century, for organizing a modern society and achieving prosperity. It was a crash of the dominant and inspiring visions that gave Americans confidence.

Instead people feel abandoned. They face the struggle to support a family, secure a home, and provide for their children—absent any faith that the leaders know where they are taking the country or how to ensure a better future. Voters feel betrayed, doubly betrayed.

THE DISSOLUTION

The Republican presidential vote in 1992 sank 16 percentage points from George Bush's performance in 1988 and 21 points from Ronald Reagan's in 1984, the high point of the Republican ascendancy. Bush's 16-point collapse, as the political scientist Walter Dean Burnham points out, has been exceeded only three times in U.S. history; Hubert Humphrey's 1968 collapse of 18 points was one of them. These crashes are bookends for this period of betrayal and dissolution. For Bush and the Republicans, their winning of just 37.4 percent of the vote ranked as the second worst performance by an incumbent over two centuries and marked the fall of Reaganism.[8]

The Republicans in 1992 had lost their hold on working-class and lower-middle-class America, including most of those Americans who had earlier walked away from the Democrats. Bush held on to just 28 percent of the Democrats who voted for him in 1988 and 24 percent of those who still identified themselves as Reagan Democrats. Among voters with an income between $15,000 and $30,000, Bush lost to Clinton by 45 to 35 percent, a 15-percentage-point swing away from the Republican performance of 1988. This shift had devastating consequences. Bush lost every state but one when he lost this lower-middle-income stratum.[9]

The Republican top-down coalition no longer had the coherence and shared ideas that could accommodate both the wealthy at the top and the working middle class, which was angered by its excesses. Without an expansive vision cementing the middle to the top, there could be no Republican ascendancy. The Party could clearly re-emerge as a voice of alienated politics but without a top-down vision, not as a force that could change the country's political direction.

Ross Perot's astonishing third-party performance—gaining 19 percent of the vote—was further testimony to the breakdown of the dominant political order and the power of the double betrayal. Perot caught the pieces in this crack-up, particularly younger voters, non-college-educated younger men, disaffected and more secular Republicans, and independents. He ran very well in the Northeast and the West (reaching 30 percent in Maine and 27 percent in Nevada), where the Republican collapse was most pronounced, but did poorly in the Deep South, where the Republican coalition largely weathered the storm. Perot's performance is thus a direct measure of the fault lines that have split open the national Republican party and exposed the bankruptcy of the political order.

In this fractured political world, Bill Clinton won with 43 percent of the national vote—about equal to Nixon's total in 1968 as noted above and somewhat better than what Woodrow Wilson in 1912 and Abraham Lincoln in 1860 achieved in multicandidate fields. Clinton won by exposing the contradictions in top-down Republicanism, winning decisively among lower-middle-class voters and splitting the suburbs across the country. He ran a campaign, according to one study, in which the decisive issues were living standards, the role of government in health and education, and the question of abortion. Civil rights, which was important up until 1988, dropped sharply in significance.[10] The Democrats were no longer a party hopelessly bedeviled by race, blocked from building a multiracial bottom-up coalition. In a two-way contest, absent Perot, Clinton would have won the traditional majority among African Americans (90 percent) as well as a fraction short of a majority among whites (49.4 percent) and 55 percent of the lower middle class earning up to $30,000.[11]

But 1992 was not a two-way contest, and Clinton had not yet forged a new majority, just as the Republicans' national majority after 1968 would only follow Nixon's successful assault on the old order. As the 1994 midterm elections suggest, the Democrats' new majority still stands in waiting.

Misreading the Crash

Before the 1992 campaign began, commentators and prospective Democratic presidential candidates alike said the crash could not happen. Bush's high poll numbers dampened their political passions and obscured their view of the political forces at work. Blinded perhaps by the headlines of the day, they failed to sense the wreck ahead: a Republican ascendancy increasingly implausible to the middle class and a party order increasingly distant from the citizenry.

Two major books published in 1991 describe a Democratic party in crisis and destined for defeat. Their titles leave little to the imagination—Peter Brown's *Minority Party: Why the Democrats Face Defeat in 1992 and Beyond* and Thomas and Mary Edsall's *Chain Reaction: The Impact of Race, Rights, and Taxes on American Politics*—and together these books leave the Democrats shrouded in almost unrelieved gloom. They say almost nothing about the crisis of the Republican party or the crisis of the Republic.[12]

Each book begins with race, civil rights, and the upheavals of the 1960s, taking for granted the images and political divisions forged during those times and assuming that contemporary politics remained dominated by the "betrayal" of the Democrats' bottom-up history. Each tells of the widening gulf between the party and its white working-class supporters, who reacted against the urban riots and busing, as well as the growing Democratic elitism, permissiveness, and seeming indifference to the value of work. The Democrats made "choices," the Edsalls write, "that render problematic, at least for the foreseeable future, the restoration of a nationally competitive coalition representing the interests of those in the bottom half of the income distribution."

The Edsalls also argue that the Republicans had successfully used the "overlapping issues of race and taxes" to forge a populist conservatism and "break the underlying class basis of the

Roosevelt-Democratic coalition." The Republicans had won over white working-class and lower-middle-class voters who felt "besieged in the preserves they had built, in their homes, neighborhoods, jobs, schools, and unions." The Edsalls believed the Republicans had succeeded in bringing the affluent and the workers together into a stable coalition variously described as "an ideological common ground," a "cross class alliance," "a sustained policy majority," an effective "joining [of] the interests of business and moderate-income whites," and finally, "a merger of ideological interests."[13]

In fact, the opposite was almost certainly true. In another acclaimed book from the pre-campaign period, *Why Americans Hate Politics,* E. J. Dionne Jr. describes the core contradiction of the party order of the 1960s: "The new conservative majority that has dominated presidential politics since 1968 is inherently unstable since it unites upper-income groups, whose main interest is smaller government and lower taxes, and middle to lower-income groups, who are culturally conservative but still support most of the New Deal and a lot of the Great Society." The diverse elements of the Republican coalition found common ground in some areas—the reduction of social spending on the poor and the reversal of affirmative action—but they agreed on little else. This was hardly a "merger of ideological interests." They disagreed on cutting back the regulatory state, on reducing government spending, on holding down the minimum wage, on Social Security, on trade, and much more.

It was the specter of a crack-up that led Republicans back to the race and cultural issues during the Bush years. If these fires could be stoked, Republicans could keep populist social conservatives from acting on their class instincts and from looking for other ways to advance their interests and secure their values. The Republicans' resort to race was no measure of strength; it was the measure of an unstable Republican coalition. The "conservative malaise," as Dionne describes it, "explains why George Bush ran such a persistently negative campaign in 1988" and why he seemed so intent on resurrecting the "cultural" issues in 1992. But the middle ground would not be muddied. Voters broke free of the old categories and assumptions, and now the wreckage of the old party order lies before us.[14]

The Corrupted Congress

The voters' disappointment in the national parties was part of a more general disaffection with American political institutions that now stood above the ordinary citizen. These institutions no longer seemed guided by ideas that people could have faith in. They no longer seemed grounded in principles and obligations that would promote community. The *Times Mirror* national survey of the new political landscape describes the "sharp increase in alienation, cynicism and general discontent with the political system" that was evident in 1992 and that continued to worsen in 1994.[15]

Today much of the anger of ordinary voters centers on the Congress, which has emerged as a symbol of personal greed crowding out democratic representation. This image of Congress contradicts people's idealized concept of what members of Congress and U.S. senators are supposed to be doing in Washington: representing ordinary people.[16] In 1990, a bare 12 percent of the people thought most members of Congress "pay a good deal of attention to the people who elected them," compared with 42 percent in 1964. Just before the 1994 midterm elections, just 18 percent approved of the way the U.S. Congress was performing.[17]

The congressional pay raise and the bank and post office controversies produced a voter revolt because they challenged in the starkest possible fashion what congressional representation is supposed to be: instead of going to Washington to work for the people, members of Congress were going there to work for themselves. "I wish I could vote myself a raise; that's all I can say right here," said one survey respondent at the time; another observed, "It seems odd that these guys can get a $40,000 pay raise; these are the same guys that voted against [raising] the minimum wage from $3.35 an hour." These members of Congress find themselves rising above the people: "They're already up on this pedestal, and when they go on these trips and they get put in these nice hotels and people are waiting on them hand and foot . . . they are being pampered. It's like they're not really there to speak to the people." And one voter summarized the sentiment: "They're not humble any more."

Many observers looked and saw an electorate "mad as hell." In their book *The Confidence Gap,* Seymour Martin Lipset and William Schneider review the rising alienation since 1965 and describe a "collapse of confidence," a public "cynical and mistrustful" of its leaders. Popular commentators are drawn to a similar conclusion: in Rush Limbaugh's words, "Something is terribly wrong with our government"; in Martin L. Gross's bestselling work, *The Government Racket,* "Something is *fundamentally* wrong in Washington."[18]

The Revolt Against Politics

The off-year election of 1994 was a voter revolt against politics and thus a continuation of the process of dissolution, not a renewal of the party order. People voted against the Congress, politics, and big government—all seen to be under the control of Democrats and all out of touch with the lives and needs of people. The TV advertisements of the Republican National Committee urged voters to "Send the Clinton Congress home." While Republican leaders unveiled their program for the new

Congress, it had little to do with the elections. Republicans ran against the Democratic-controlled Congress and Democratic government. Their call for a balanced budget constitutional amendment, term limits, tax cuts, and welfare reform were all clubs to batter the state. And voters got the message. In most surveys after the election, voters said they were voting against "politics as usual"—the partisan bickering, crooked politicians, parties that don't work together, a government that is out of touch with the people.[19]

In the election, Democrats held their own among high school graduates and won voters earning up to $30,000 a year, though not as impressively as two years ago. Their losses came in the middle strata that contain the voters most uncertain about the course of our politics. Democratic congressional candidates lost by 6 points (53 to 47 percent) those people who struggle for an education beyond high school but never get a four-year degree; two years ago, Democrats had won that group by the exact same 6-point margin. They lost voters by 2 points (51 to 49 percent) in households earning $30,000 to $50,000, after winning them by 4 points two years ago. They took big losses with white men, losing by 24 points this year (62 to 38 percent), compared to 2 points in 1992.[20]

But in the end, both parties stood in a kind of disreputable parity. Republicans had managed 51 percent of the vote in the congressional elections and middle-class voters were clearly split between the parties. While the Democratic party image was badly tarnished, as we shall see later, the bigger story was that both parties stood at historic lows with the public.

Voters cast their votes against a corrupted politics. But corruption takes on meaning—bringing about alienation, and eventually, a reinterpretation of the political order—only when the dominant ideas have failed and lost their hold on the people. For most of the last century, the top-down and bottom-up visions of America gave people confidence in America's purpose and direction, assuring them that the nation was governed by sensible principles and values and that the leaders understood how to make life better. The petty corruption of big-city bosses was tolerated because the voters felt that the bosses were on their side. But the failed renewals of the Great Society and Reaganomics shattered public confidence in the country's leadership and direction and left people to their worst interpretations of political life.

The lies, the perks, the bounced checks, the waste, the sweetheart deals, the privileges, the indifference to popular opinion—all stirred outrage when the country's leaders could no longer show ordinary Americans the way forward. And no amount of muckraking, ethics investigations, campaign reform, or term limits will restore the public trust. Political distrust is rooted not in corruption but in a larger failure of ideas.

TOWARD A NEW CONTRACT

Bill Clinton allowed Americans to crystallize their discontent with the old ideas and failed policies. He forged his broad solution for bottom-up politics in the backwoods of Arkansas in 1974 and impressed it on the nation in 1992. It was a "people first" appeal that champions the middle class and its values and proposes public-sector investments to restore the country's economic growth. He attacked a government that had failed ordinary citizens while proposing to use government to attack the country's problems. He called himself a "new kind of Democrat" who sought to bring people's values back to government and to restore hope in economic progress. His appeal to the middle class, along with Ross Perot's protest against a corrupted politics, brought the whole edifice crashing down.

The question now before the country is whether anyone can lead the nation after the crash. Clinton has served as president, and either he or somebody else will win the presidency in 1996, but winning is not enough. The stakes have been raised. As Bush discovered, clinging to power in these times may be a treacherous course that produces only further alienation and fragmentation. Trying to push our encrusted political institutions to act may also prove perilous, as we saw in 1994. Can any leader or any political party remake our politics and restore the public's faith, or is the country doomed to deepening alienation and despair? Are we doomed to live with "the news" as political reality?

Perot or some successor may play in the rubble of party failure and build on the rage that betrayal has wrought, but Perot is in no position to build something new or forge a new social contract. In 1992 he articulated the people's loss of ownership of a government that was careening toward fiscal disaster. He used the symbols of the national debt and the imperial Congress to make himself the depository for this loosened political discontent. But Perot is only a symptom of the political decay, not a voice for some new order.

The Republicans have buried all traces of George Bush and are seeking the best route to a renewed Reaganism. But there is only a small audience in the country for its claims, which are part of the wreckage of 1992. Along with George Bush, voters buried the idea that prosperity should be built from the top down. In the 1994 election campaign, Republicans never mentioned their "Contract with America" to revive the Reagan years in any of their national TV advertising and virtually no Republican congressional candidate mentioned it either. A prominent group of Republican pollsters told their campaigns, "We can't afford for this fight to be 'trickle-down economics' versus a new direction. Instead, the contrast should be new (term limits, dramatic congressional reform) versus old (no change in Congress)." And the

"Contract" pointedly never included a rollback of Clinton's tax increases on the wealthy. Even as voters went to the polls to throw out an unprecedented number of Democrats, more voters said they preferred to go forward with Clinton's economic program than to go back to Reagan's.[21]

If the Republicans are to offer business and the wealthy a new scope for enrichment, this time the bounty for ordinary people will have to be real. Until then, Reaganism will have no more claim on the public imagination than the Great Society. Both are now caricatures of the party traditions that helped guide the nation; both are now scorned by the nation.

Bill Clinton and the Democrats are battling to forge a new contract with middle-class America and thus remake the party order and pull the country back from the abyss. As the Democratic candidate for president, Clinton repudiated the old party assumptions, forged over three decades of failed renewal; he walked away from the party order that emerged from the 1960s. Race, crime, taxes, and spending no longer doomed his prospects, as they had those of the Democrats before him. Clinton offered a renewed bottom-up vision to downscale and middle-class America, both black and white, liberated to a large extent from the divisions and demons of the 1960s.[22]

Yet powerful forces —including political institutions that resist being remade and an economy that may no longer offer so much promise—are at work to stop Clinton and the Democrats from succeeding. A pervasive pessimism and a shortfall of political imagination and political capacity could leave the Democrats thinking small before this historic challenge, yet the country insists on being hopeful that President Clinton can succeed.

The Republicans face the challenge of taking their 1994 election victory over corrupted politics and turning it into something that people can have faith in. Republicans can continue to fuel the anger with Congress and government and further undermine the public's confidence in government's ability to do anything productive. There is clearly a formula in all that for winning elections, though not so clearly for lifting the country's spirits. They have the burden of convincing people that there is a Republican idea for ensuring a generalized prosperity and rebuilding a sense of community.

The struggle around the Clinton presidency represents America's struggle after the crash to give birth to a new politics. It is fueled by an aspiration for a new contract in new times and perhaps for renewed dreams.

◆ ◆ ◆ ◆

This book tells a sweeping story about modern America, but it starts in a small place in suburban Michigan called Macomb County. Bill Clinton went there often, as did George Bush and Ronald Reagan, because winning Macomb represents a kind of mastery of our history. The voters there believed in the country's promise; they took their contract with the New Deal right to the suburbs and bought a piece of America. In 1960, this was the most Democratic suburb in the nation, but the riots, the anti-busing battles, and the transformation of the Democratic party changed all that. The residents of Macomb felt betrayed and voted en masse for Ronald Reagan. But in time, he betrayed them too.

These middle-class suburbanites are conscious of being caught in the middle, doubly betrayed by those who would govern from the bottom up and those who would govern from the top down. The old politics has failed them. What they really want is a new political contract—and the freedom to dream the American dream again.

As Bill Clinton moves into the heart of his presidency, the people there are watching, so that is where we begin.

2. MACOMB COUNTY IN THE AMERICAN MIND

MACOMB County—it seems a quite ordinary place to have attracted so much attention. Our politics used to gravitate to places like Cadillac Square in Detroit, where perhaps a hundred thousand blue-collar families would gather at the end of summer to cheer on their would-be leaders. Harry Truman opened his underdog 1948 campaign there to the first signs of real political life. John Kennedy came in 1960, sitting atop a suitcase in an open convertible. With Walter Reuther at his side, he told this labor crowd to elect an administration "which has faith in a growing America."

Then there was the garment center in New York City, where union leaders and politicians would march arm in arm down Seventh Avenue, confident that working America, spilling out of the shops onto the sidewalks, waving, would send them off to lead. In 1960, a quarter of a million packed in between 35th and 40th streets to hear John Kennedy summon the nation to a "new frontier." Broadway and Hollywood were there in force— Melvyn Douglas, Janet Leigh, Henry Fonda, Shelley Winters, Myrna Loy, and Tallulah Bankhead; Billy Eckstine's big band kicked off the festivities with "The Star-Spangled Banner." In 1968, an exuberant Hubert Humphrey looked out on the sea of working people packed into those five blocks, and he clung to the local politicians and union chiefs, trying to take some of that history and laborers' sweat to the polls.

Or more simply, there was 219 North Delaware, Independence, Missouri: the home of Harry and Bess Truman. That is where anxious candidates like John Kennedy and presidents like Richard Nixon and Lyndon Johnson came to pay their respects and show they could stand in the shoes of a common man who had led the nation.

Republican aspirants have found their way to these centers of American life—to the Main Streets across the country. Nixon drew almost a half million people to Michigan Avenue in Chicago in 1968, but there was greater comfort in the towns of perhaps two thousand, like Deshler, Ohio. Nixon emerged on the platform of his railway car to the sight of the grain elevator and an aging crowd that somehow managed to share his anger about the rising crime rate in the United States.

In an earlier day, the people—750,000 of them—traveled to Canton, Ohio, to see Republican William McKinley campaign from his porch on North Main Street. The crowds and reporters trampled the flower beds and the picket fence, but McKinley came out dutifully to acknowledge the cheers and attack free silver as a bad deal for laboring people. The pilgrims came in delegations, sometimes one or two thousand each, their discount fares underwritten by a generous and supportive railway industry.[1]

Nostalgia and aging politicians frequently drag our leaders back to these precious places. But the rituals of fall have moved imperceptibly away from the small towns and big cities to ordinary suburbs—across the Detroit city line at Eight Mile Road, to Macomb County. This is the site of the real drama in our political life. This is the site of an historic upheaval that has wrecked the old and promises a new volatile kind of politics.

That is why the *Los Angeles Times* called this suburban county "ground zero" for the 1992 presidential campaign. Bill

Clinton came here three times during that year, starting with a Democratic-primary town meeting on March 12 at Macomb County Community College in the sturdy working-class suburb of Warren, then returning on September 24 and ending with a huge Columbus Day picnic that filled a football field in Sterling Heights. He once asked his campaign advisers whether Macomb had more electoral votes than Florida. George Bush understood the challenge and came twice to this key battleground, telling a Republican-primary audience in Fraser that there was a "boom" in export jobs. Later he dispatched Barbara Bush to an Italian cultural center and Dan Quayle to a tank plant, both in Warren. Bush stood in the gymnasium at Macomb County Community College and taunted his opponents, whom he called bozos; that day Bill Clinton was standing ten miles away, in downtown Detroit, addressing a racially mixed audience but speaking to Macomb: "While Mr. Bush will go to Macomb County today and tell those people that I'm not their kind of person . . . I've got a lot more in common with the people in Macomb County than George Bush ever had or ever will."

In 1988, Michael Dukakis had stumbled into Warren to don a helmet and take an ill-fated tank ride at the General Dynamics factory. His statewide supporters rallied without him on election eve at Clintondale High School. Ronald Reagan came twice in 1984 and in 1988 came back to Macomb County Community College to introduce George Bush to the new center of American politics. This one simple community college has hosted seven presidential candidates since 1984.[2]

The politicians came because of the numbers. In 1960, Macomb County was the most Democratic suburb in America, giving John Kennedy 63 percent of the vote. Lyndon Johnson took the Democratic tally up to 74 percent four years later. Then it all collapsed. John Kennedy was a distant memory by 1984, when Ronald Reagan won an extraordinary 67 percent of the vote. Macomb was now the national home of Reagan Democrats and the working material for a new American political alignment. In 1992 the Republican presidential vote plummeted 24 points from Reagan's high-water mark. The Macomb County battleground, site of an historic upheaval, was now strewn with this political wreckage: 43 percent for George Bush, 38 percent for Bill Clinton, and 20 percent for the independent Ross Perot.[3] On this battlefield lay the ruins of the New Deal and Ronald Reagan's America and all the uncertainties of a new era.

The poignancy in this upheaval captures the broader struggle in our political life. These extraordinary electoral swings are the convulsions of hardworking people, union people, who gave their hearts and hopes to the Democratic party and its leaders, who believed in America and its dream, who bet everything on its reality. That is why they took the chance and bought homes in Warren and Roseville. But in the 1960s and 1970s, the leaders who were supposed to fight for them seemed to care more about the blacks in Detroit and the protesters on campus; they seemed to care more about equal rights and abortion than about mortgage payments and crime. The resentment and disillusionment crystallized in a sense of betrayal, and the people of Macomb County rebelled. They became Reagan Democrats, some said, though they were more like refugees from a war who soon grow disillusioned with the resettlement camps. The Republicans had promised them a new deal and a better future, this time under the tutelage of entrepreneurs and job creators. But the rich made out big while the middle-class languished— indeed, struggled—to hold on to their jobs and homes in a changing world. They grew disillusioned with the new Republican bargain, which itself turned out to be a betrayal.

Macomb is an exaggeration, a caricature of America, because it so wholeheartedly identified itself with the currents that swept the nation in the years following the Second World War.[4] Its residents were not just working Americans who made their way to the suburbs. In 1985, almost 40 percent lived in union households, most of them members of the United Automobile Workers, one of the most aggressive unions in the country. Seared into the consciousness of Macomb families are the 1937 UAW sitdown strikes at Flint and at the Kelsey-Hayes wheel plant in Detroit. More immediate and more important were the postwar strikes and contracts that linked the fate of the auto worker to the fate of the industry. By 1955, the union had won a three-year agreement with something like a guaranteed annual wage with supplementary unemployment benefits. The working men of Michigan had battled for a system that put them on salary, giving them security and the money to buy into the American dream.[5]

They found that dream in the houses and yards of Macomb County, to which the white workers began to move in the 1950s. Macomb's population, just over 100,000 in 1949, nearly quadrupled by 1960 and increased by another 200,000 by 1970; in 1980, the census tally stood at 694,600. Home construction boomed: sixty thousand houses were built in the 1950s and continued at that pace for a quarter of a century. The factories moved to Macomb as well: GM's Buick assembly division, Chrysler's stamping plants, and Ford's transmission and chassis division.

These were America's workers, who had managed to carve out an idealized version of the American dream, for which they were grateful. The median household income in Macomb in 1985 was $24,000—$7,000 above the national median—even though a majority of the income still came from manufacturing. Just a third of the people had gone beyond high school, yet four out of five families owned their homes, and nearly two thirds owned two or more cars. Almost everybody—97 percent—was white. With Lake St. Clair and its marinas forming the eastern boundary of Macomb, workers here rounded out the dream:

Macomb County has more boats per capita than any other place in the United States, and its congressman heads the boat caucus.[6]

Little wonder, then, that Macomb's mostly Catholic workers proved loyal to the national Democratic party in the 1950s and '60s, even as other suburban Catholics were tempted by Eisenhower. This was one place where the New Deal's promise was real. These voters gave Kennedy his biggest suburban win and made their support for Lyndon Johnson nearly unanimous. Gratitude to the party and the union ran deep. In 1968, every state representative, every state senator, every congressman was a Democrat. In fact, Richard Nixon's law-and-order candidacy generated little excitement in this middle-American suburb: Nixon received no more votes than Barry Goldwater had four years earlier. But one in five voted for the independent George Wallace—a signal that all was not so peaceful in Mudville.

In Macomb County, there was not a lot of sympathy for the rioters who burned down more than a hundred buildings in Detroit during five days in July 1967. The looting and fires overwhelmed the capacities of the local police as the National Guard and then 4,700 U.S. paratroopers were called in to quell the violence. Forty-three people died in this, the country's bloodiest race riot.[7]

Over the next four years, the people here were consumed with the racial character of their world—the most segregated metropolitan area in America. Barely any blacks—just 5 percent—were able to break into Detroit's suburban ring, affectionately called the doughnut. Then, on September 27, 1971, U.S. District Judge Stephen J. Roth ordered the busing of schoolchildren across the entire metropolitan area in order to integrate the schools of Detroit and its suburbs. All the school districts were directed to develop busing plans, though none was ever implemented, and in 1974 the Supreme Court overturned Roth's ruling.

Even so, the decision caused a firestorm in white suburbia, particularly in Macomb.[8] There were rallies and marches everywhere. Every community sprouted anti-busing organizations, whose anger infused the cultural and political life of the times—from local parishes and union halls to the floor of Congress. After the Roth ruling, the five liberal Democratic members of Congress from the Detroit area signed a joint letter announcing their determination to force a vote on a constitutional amendment to ban busing. Congressman John Dingell, representing Dearborn and River Rouge, sponsored an amendment to bar the use of gasoline to take students beyond their nearest school—producing a heated clash with Congresswoman Bella Abzug of New York. Her accusation that the Detroit-area Democrats were "demagogic or racist" violated protocol and was stricken from the *Congressional Record*.

The largely white Region One of the UAW, encompassing Macomb County, became a conservative Democratic bastion. Its long-time leader, George Merrelli, broke with the liberal leadership of the UAW to oppose busing. The town of Warren was becoming a "conservative cauldron," as one official put it, and had to be split in the 1971 reapportionment in order to keep it from electing a conservative congressman of its own.

In 1972, George Wallace won the Michigan Democratic primary—his first big state win outside the South. Wallace's victory was built in part on his winning a remarkable 66 percent of the vote in Macomb. The AFL-CIO and Teamsters had endorsed Hubert Humphrey, and the UAW backed both Humphrey and George McGovern, but that clearly did not matter much in Macomb. Wallace described busing as "the most asinine, cruel thing I've ever heard of" and called on "the people of this country to recognize that an all-powerful government could take over their unions, businesses, their children, as they are now doing in Michigan on busing." With his rallies overflowing with

blue-collar workers, he railed against the "fat cats" and against
the crime that threatened their communities. Exit polls in metropolitan Detroit found 70 percent identifying "crime in the
streets" as the number-one problem—the catchall for everything that angered Macomb's white middle-class voters.[9]

In November, the full ramifications of the primary vote
came into focus. Macomb voters seemed to give up on the
national Democratic party, which failed to understand them.
They scorned George McGovern in the general election, giving
him just 36 percent of the vote and repudiating his close association with the anti-war upheavals and social welfare adventurism. In 1976, they had trouble warming up to the moderate
southerner, Jimmy Carter, who lost narrowly to a Republican
from Michigan, and they slipped further back in 1980 as Ronald
Reagan won a very respectable 53 percent majority.

But for all these defections, Macomb County voters did not
easily sever their special relationship with the Democrats. At the
base of the ticket, in races for the state Board of Education,
where people know nothing of the candidates and just vote
their gut loyalties, Macomb was casting 60 percent of its votes
for unknown Democrats—right through 1978. In 1982, they
voted a straight Democratic ticket—53 and 56 percent for
governor and attorney general, respectively, but more than 60
percent for the U.S. Senate. They sent a team of pro-UAW
Democrats to the state legislature in Lansing while expressing
complete comfort with their Democratic congressman, David
Bonior.[10]

Most of these voters understood the insecurities that bedevil
those who still work with their hands or depend on manufacture, and they were not going to walk away easily from what
they had forged here. To say no to Democrats was to walk away
from a political culture that had given them decent homes and
yards and dreams. This was no easy walk. All the upheavals and

fires in Detroit and all the new Republican talk of law and order were just not enough to overturn this order.

But the slide, then collapse, of auto jobs and the erosion of union contracts called into question the bigger contract that New Deal Democrats had signed with middle-class America. That home, boat, and safe neighborhood were line items in a special relationship. Every lost job jeopardized the contract. Across the nation, hourly wages of production workers began to drop after 1979, and over the next decade a million and a half manufacturing jobs were lost. Things were especially bad in Michigan. The auto industry, along with the sprawling network of allied shops and services that snake through working America, was desperately retrenching. This was no simple recession. By 1983, unemployment had jumped to 17.6 percent in suburban Macomb. Over 70 percent of the laid-off auto workers lost a third or more of their savings. Median family income started dropping. Population growth ended. The three-decade boom in housing construction just came to a halt in 1980, and so did the Democrats' reach to working, aspirant America.[11]

The 1984 election was a disaster for the national Democrats. Walter Mondale was not some fringe lefty consumed by obscure issues. He was the candidate of organized labor and of every organized interest that found its home in the Democratic party. He was the candidate of the UAW, whose leaders believed Mondale had supported them and now believed they should support him.[12] Mondale had conventional views on defense and was schooled in the anti-Communist liberalism of Hubert Humphrey. But his rhetoric about the social contract had a hollow ring for a middle America that had made its deal with the Democrats. When Mondale preached "fairness," they heard "taxes."

In 1984, the voters of Macomb County turned their backs on the Democratic liberalism that had been so intertwined with the dream they had built and guarded. And this time, the national landslide was a local debacle as well. The crown jewel of suburban Democracy gave just 32 percent of its vote to Walter Mondale and handed over nearly half the seats in its state legislature to the Republicans. The Democratic candidate for the U.S. Senate, Carl Levin, hung on with 49 percent of the vote, but party support no longer ran deep: the gut-level Democratic vote for state Board of Education plummeted to 44 percent. The heart of middle America had scorned almost everything Democratic.

LISTENING TO MACOMB

The local Democratic leaders were stunned. Clearly something special and enduring had been shattered. The headlines were tough enough: in *The Detroit News,* REAGAN LANDSLIDE CAPTURES 49 STATES. ELECTORAL MARGIN HIGHEST IN HISTORY. The surprise was not that Mondale had lost but that three members of the legislature were gone too. These were good people, working people who had stood with union Democracy, but now they had lost to a stockbroker, a realtor, and restaurateur. One of the Republican victors told his victory party that "it appears there is a realignment here, and perhaps the rest of the country."[13] National union leaders had tried to be reassuring, passing around post-election polls that showed Mondale doing just fine with union members—if you think 55 percent is just fine. Statewide the Democrats were hanging on to a slim seven-seat majority in the state house even as some of them huddled with the Republicans to discuss the prospect of electing a Republican speaker. On the other side of the capitol, things were worse: the Democrats had lost control of the state senate by one seat.

Two out of three people in Macomb were now Reagan voters. The heart and promise of an enduring New Deal coalition, forged in a growing suburbia, had been simply cut out. Nobody relished facing the future with a Democratic party built atop minority votes in Detroit and academic liberals in Ann Arbor.

The party leaders then did something odd: they called in an academic and a political pollster—me. They wanted somebody new to come to Michigan, to take a hard look at Macomb, to pose the toughest possible questions and be honest about the future. Use whatever techniques you need, they said, but get to the bottom of Ronald Reagan's thrust into the heart of working America.

At the end of March, I began a conversation with Macomb County's Democratic defectors—people who had identified historically with the Democratic party but turned to Ronald Reagan in 1984. The conversations took place in small, comfortable settings like a hotel room or the back of a restaurant, where like-minded people would feel free to open up and speak their minds: all men or all women, all union folks or all non-union, all working women or all housewives, all white—and all Democratic defectors. The conversation began in March in Warren and ended in April in Waterford Township, just outside Macomb, where a similar history had wrecked the Democratic ascendancy. The Reagan Democrats, as we shall see now, spoke their mind.[14]

The first extended conversation was about vulnerability and betrayal, virtue and honor. The Reagan Democrats had staked their way of life on a bargain with a party that was supposed to stand up for common people. That was the party's purpose and its historic role. Somewhere nestled back in their heads was the party of Jefferson and Jackson, Bryan, Roosevelt, Truman, and Kennedy, the party that identified with their lives and would understand what was happening to them. That party would understand simple things—a mortgage and taxes, family and neighborhood, a good job and a strong America. But Mondale, Carter, and McGovern—whom had they fought for?

These were disillusioned, angry voters, but they were not Republicans. They spoke of a broken contract, not a new vision. Their way of life was genuinely in jeopardy, threatened by profound economic changes beyond their control, yet their leaders, who were supposed to look out for them, were preoccupied with other groups and other issues.

These voters wondered why they weren't the central drama of the Democratic party. They should be honored, not shunned, by a party that was now uncomfortable with, maybe even contemptuous of, their values, their fears, and their simple suburban ways. Their homes in Warren and Sterling Heights symbolized their virtue, not their privilege. They believed they were in trouble, yet the party implied their trouble was less important than the needs of black people, people who, in their minds, lacked virtue. Something was very wrong.

Ronald Reagan enjoyed great popularity here in the aftermath of the 1984 landslide. These defecting Democrats saw in him an essential honesty, a willingness to stand tough for his beliefs and to stand with "small" America against things "big," particularly government. Their affection for Reagan made it possible for them to flee the Democratic house in flames. But our conversations were not about Republicanism. They were about the Democratic betrayal of middle-class America.

Economic Change and Personal Vulnerability

Macomb County voters knew they were in trouble. With the economy contracting and being reconstructed, so were their dreams. Underlying all the political talk was a lot of simple fear. Givebacks and layoffs, foreign imports and robotics, and the sight of industries moving South—these things now dominated their economic world.

Plants were threatening to split for Tennessee or Mexico and leave people with nothing. That threat represented a daily reminder of the people's impotence and their inability to achieve higher standards of living. One man observed, "If we wanted to keep pushing for more and more money, they will close the doors, and they will take the whole shop down South and open up and hire people for half the wage." With foreign interests taking over companies, workers felt that those making the decisions were even more remote and more inaccessible.

These workers felt threatened as well by computers and robotics, technologies that may have been creating new jobs but not ones accessible to them. A group of union members agreed that "the average man" who "pushed buttons on the press" was giving way to the "guy that walks in and sits at the computer, types in the data."

They were threatened by foreign imports and foreign people. The foreign cars were cheaper, built with lower-priced labor (a "buck a day," one woman noted), and thus took away jobs and drove down wages. In their eyes, they were caught in a downward spiral: people get laid off and in turn cannot afford to buy American cars. A union man declared, "We are losing money, and they're importing all these people from Vietnam, Mexico, from everywhere. Here's a bunch of people that can't even speak English, are half-illiterate, came out of an adobe hut, and they are going to compete with us for our jobs?"

People expressed their feelings of vulnerability most poignantly when they were discussing the prospects for their children. The image of children leaving school generated enormous emotion and emerged as important even for those who did not have teenage children. People saw the system as blocked on all fronts: by computers and new technology, by the unions, and by the cutbacks in government support, particularly for college loans. "If something isn't done quickly, this is going to come to a real traumatic head, and my kid is going to be over there scraping the bottom of the barrel," one man declared. "There won't be an education; there won't be a skill because the system closed down fast." With the middle class being denied college loans, the system was perceptibly shifting away from their kids. As one of the older men declared, "What happens is you're creating an elite, those families that can afford to put their children through college. They're going to run the country."

While their vulnerability was growing on all sides, the Democratic party was turning on them. One man lamented being out there on his own:

> It seemed like all of a sudden the Democratic party was turning its back on the Joe Average on the street. He was digging deeper in his pocket, and the interest rates were going up, and inflation was skyrocketing, and we weren't going any place. We were going backwards. We were having less money to spend, the standard of living was decreasing instead of increasing. And I think the average guy just shook his head and says, "Wait a minute. This isn't the way it used to be."

The Middle-Class Poor

These traditional Democratic voters felt squeezed and neglected, pressed on one side by richer people who carried few burdens and paid no taxes and on the other side by poorer black people who are the recipients of free programs and also paid no taxes. These voters were and are the middle class that is quite literally "cramped" and "supporting both ends," the hardest working and most virtuous, yet the least honored.

In its own description, this middle, residual group constituted the middle-class poor. It was the product of a collapsing class structure that placed all of society's burdens on this narrow stratum. One should not underestimate the strength of this identification and the sense of burden. A man from Waterford observed:

It's a hard pill to swallow, but I see a growing despair. At one time, say fifteen or twenty years ago, before Vietnam, we had upper middle class, middle class, lower class—fairly well defined class system in this country. And the last fifteen years—you have seen it grow to upper, upper class, and we are seeing more of the middle class become the lower middle class, and then you have the people that have been pushed off the edge. You have, then, a small minority of wealthy people or businesspeople who are controlling the nation and an enormous mass of people who are just struggling to get by.

They did not factor poorer people into that struggle. The "upper class—they got all the tax breaks," so they were privileged; but so too were "the people that are on welfare." The welfare recipient, a housewife observed, "buys a house and a car; he is just getting all of his money sent in to him; he doesn't have to worry about working for it."

In their view, the middle class carried society and government on its back and was indispensable to the survival of the nation. Though politically impotent, the middle class had historically played a heroic, selfless role. If the middle class refused its obligations, the social order would come to a grinding halt.

If all middle-class Americans say, "That's it, we're boycotting. I'm quitting work so you can't tax me," give it a year. The government would fold because nobody else is paying taxes. The poor can't pay taxes. [The rich] can't pay taxes for the simple reason that they are getting it all back in too many tax shelters. So, all the middle class—if we refused to work, the government would fold. This country wouldn't be.

And yet no one, including the national political parties, seemed to acknowledge the tremendous burden the middle class carries. The Republicans thought mainly about "big business," and the

Democrats concentrated mainly on the minority groups. When asked whose interest the Democratic party best represented, one isolated person responded, "the working man," but everybody else talked unreservedly about the neglected middle class. Indeed, the shared sentiment on this issue among a group of housewives took on all the fervor of a prayer meeting:

> They [the Democrats] do try to give everybody this give-away money, like you said. They are not interested in us because we are the ones that are going to pay for it.

> I really feel it's the middle-class person. We really don't have much representation because Republicans are for big business, and the Democrats are for the giveaways, and we are the ones that pay all the taxes.

> Right.

> And the middle class is going to be eliminated.

> Yeah.

> And who will represent us?

> No one.

> And who paid those taxes but us middle-class people?

> We do.

> We do.

These workers saw themselves as members of a new minority class that was ignored by the government but forced to support social programs that did not benefit them. A male union member put it this way: "Why are we being discriminated against right now? . . . Well, I am going to start calling us a minority."

White Victims, Black Privilege

These white defectors from the Democratic party expressed a profound distaste for black Americans, a sentiment that pervaded almost everything they thought about government and politics. Blacks constituted the explanation for their vulnerability and for almost everything that had gone wrong in their lives; not being black was what constituted being middle class; not living with blacks was what made a neighborhood a decent place to live.

For these white suburban residents, the terms *blacks* and *Detroit* were interchangeable. The city was a place to be avoided—where the kids could not go, where the car got stolen, and where vacant lots and dissolution have replaced their old neighborhoods. The black politicians, like Coleman Young, were doing just fine, they believed, getting rich off special favors, special treatment, and special deals. But Detroit was just a big pit into which the state and federal governments poured tax money, never to be heard from again: "It's all just being funneled into the Detroit area, and it's not overflowing into the suburbs."

These suburban voters felt nothing in common with Detroit and its people and rejected out of hand the social-justice claims of black Americans. They denied that blacks suffer special disadvantages that would require special treatment by employers or the government. They had no historical memory of racism and no tolerance for present efforts to offset it. They felt no sense of personal or collective responsibility that would support government anti-discrimination and civil rights policies.

In each of these discussions, we read a statement about the nation's special obligations to black citizens because of historic discrimination in the United States. The statement was attributed to Robert Kennedy—the last Democratic leader to bring together ethnic white Catholics and black Americans with one ethical vision. But the Democratic defectors of 1985 would have none of it:

That's bullshit.

No wonder they killed him.

I can't go along with that.

I myself think we are all Americans, and we are all under the same amendments and the Constitution of the United States. I don't think anybody should have any preference because he is black or green or purple. . . .

I'm fed up with it, man.

I can't see where they feel like they are still repressed.

I really feel that they have had so much just handed to them. . . . Most of them are abusing it. It's where now—it's almost like a turnaround. They're getting, getting, getting, and the whites are becoming the minority.

I think it's getting old. I want to hear—I want to see a TV commercial that says, "Send money so white people can go to college." It's an old issue.

Almost all these individuals perceived the special status of blacks as a serious obstacle to their personal advancement. Indeed, discrimination against whites had become a well assimilated and ready explanation for their status, vulnerability, and failures. When applying or taking a test for a job or school, blacks had a structured advantage. If blacks failed, standards would be lowered to "get the minorities inside." The tests in any case were rigged, one union member observed.

Well, let's say, for example, two people are going for a skilled job, and there is a test like an apprenticeship test. Minorities, for example, will be given certain considerations, you know, like they might get three points for being a black or Hispanic or Mexican, whereas the white guy doesn't get anything. He starts three points in a hole, and then it goes to education. The white guy takes the test, and he might not do very well in algebra. But they'll give the black guy the answer; so he's going to get that skilled job.

The black cop would always be promoted before the white cop. Indeed, white middle-class children, when they attempted to break into the labor market, would find a black preference operating there too, blocking the way: "My son—he passed the test and went through all the qualifications, but they at that time had to hire the minorities. He lost out."

The government, the participants believed, was party to all this, even in areas where "objective" criteria should have applied. One of the older men related to a receptive group how the government denied him permanent disability because he was not black or Hispanic. Another reported that after his wife died, the Social Security Administration refused to provide benefits for his minor children even though a black woman, applying for identical benefits at the same time, was approved.

Federal government offices, in particular, were seen as a black domain, where whites could not expect reasonable treatment. If you applied for a job at the post office, "you may as well take the application and tear it up" because "there are twenty blacks behind you, but they will get the job." The federal offices, they believed, were staffed by blacks—or "all minorities, blacks, Mexicans, . . . one white"—who act to the advantage of black applicants and customers.

Many sensed that the federal government itself had come down directly and personally to block these workers' opportunities. This was not an abstract or an analytic position; it was a deeply felt personal slight that shaped the individuals' whole perception of the government. One of the union men failed to get a business loan because, he reported, "I was an average American white guy," and his views resonated through the group:

> I have put in for openings, and they have come right out and told me in personnel that the government has come down and said that I "can't have the job because they have to give it to the minorities."
>
> And you see this. You are penalized for what you have worked for.
>
> I am getting to the point where, hey, I got an attitude. . . . I got an attitude toward business, government, and anybody in control, anybody in authority, because they shit all over me.
>
> I know what you are talking about. I tried to apply for a business loan yesterday; they said, "No go. Forget it; you just ain't the right color, pal."

The federal government that had once helped create their world was now wholly biased against them. For the men, particularly those over thirty, the feeling took on a special intensity. When asked who got a "raw deal" in this country, they responded successively and ever more directly: "It's the white people"—"white, American, middle-class male."

The word *fairness* (the touchstone of Mondale's 1984 campaign) had become a pejorative term for special pleading—as one Macomb housewife put it, "some blacks kicking up a storm." It never occurred to these voters that the Democrats could be referring to the middle class, those carrying the greatest burden in society.

Government: A Slap in the Face

These defectors showed nothing but contempt for the "free spending" government that Democrats had fashioned. Government to them was more a burden than an ally in their time of trouble. The government's sending its money to the undeserving was just a slap in the face.

For the middle class, taxes were real money. Taxes were visible and experienced. Pay increases evaporated into Social Security, state and federal withholding taxes. A group of Macomb housewives reported that because of "all the taxes," one "can't save for a down payment," and "you have to go out and give up your week's vacation at work to cover the taxes."

Yet not one Macomb participant in these discussions could identify any appreciable benefit from government spending or, more pointedly, any benefit from the government's handling of their tax dollars. They asked repeatedly: What happens to all our taxes? Their blank and frustrated faces revealed their bewilderment. They could make no link in their minds between their taxes and some visible and valued public spending. The money certainly did not go to the people who need it: not to the hungry and not to the students. "Nobody ever gets to fixing the roads," an older man lamented.

They strongly suspected that the money was squandered, first and foremost in Detroit, which, as we recall, was a pit. "Why aren't our leaders thinking about all of us?" one man asked. "Detroit is not the state of Michigan. Michigan is a lot bigger than just Detroit." The politicians, in addition, used the money to enrich themselves: the housewives suspected they used it "for their little junkets to go away on," or they put it "in their own pockets."

The Democratic party was reduced and narrowed by its association with free-spending government: "too many free programs, too much spend, spend, spend." That concern seemed less one of fiscal responsibility and more one of identity of interests. Whom did the party represent? With whom did it identify itself? There was a widespread sentiment, expressed consistently in the groups, that the Democratic party supported giveaway programs—that is, programs aimed primarily at minorities. This was no longer a party of great relevance to the lives of middle-class Americans. As one man expressed:

> I am kind of a born and raised blue-collar worker. My father is a Democrat and goes all the way back, you know. He might roll over in his grave. I can't take any more taxes; I can't take any more foreign trade like this. Where is the American car on the road? It has to end somewhere.

Another man observed, "The Democratic candidates seemed to be better and more for the working man at that time—fifteen or twenty years back."

Ronald Reagan: The Bridge to Macomb

Ronald Reagan touched these voters because he could represent the nation as a whole and because he stood with "small people." This vote was not about party or ideology or specific policies. In the minds of Macomb voters, Reagan transcended those aspects of election decision making. He elicited affection and pride, insinuating himself into the lives of middle-class voters. Whereas Richard Nixon had only inflamed these voters, Ronald Reagan touched them.

The starting point was a special honesty rooted in a determined consistency. That is what put Reagan in a position to represent all America and with pride, particularly against the backdrop of the Iran hostage crisis and a wavering Jimmy Carter. Reagan's firm conviction communicated strength and unity. Many of these Democratic defectors differed with Reagan on specific policy questions, but the power of this imagery overrode the reservations:

> He got tired of being shit on left and right. It is obvious that Ronald Reagan finally got people to get behind him. He

got ahold of that House and the committees. They are finally telling them, "This is the way we are going to run it."

I don't think he is a man that will back down.

He has guts.

Reagan is straight as an arrow—John Wayne.

Whatever he says he will try and stick by.

Right or wrong.

He has high morals.

Very high morals.

This consistency and pursuit of larger goals created a special relationship with the people and, at the same time, brought pride to the nation. Reagan, by pursuing his goals, by not worrying about the critics and the minor hurts, created a parentlike authority that was transcendent. Several men spoke about Reagan personally:

> The thing of it is as a parent myself . . . I make a decision, and then I have to stick by that decision. Sometimes it may not be an easy decision for me to make. . . . It is the same way with Reagan. He may have to make the decision, but in his heart he has to feel that he is making the right one.

> That is the most important part of being a parent: they are looking at an overall picture, just like we as parents do for our children. They are looking at an overall picture for the nation. We're looking at special interests, whether it be abortion, the arts, lower taxes. We want our needs served. We don't really care a lot about somebody else's needs as long as ours get served first. But he has to look at everyone's needs, and some of those needs are going to conflict—just as in a parent. It is not an easy job.

The imposition of this consistent, strong authority "builds us back as a nation," the men believed. "Where somebody like

Jimmy Carter—you never knew where he stood, and it was always at the bottom of the well."

These voters just looked right through Walter Mondale into the eyes of Jimmy Carter, described variously as "wishy-washy," a "mouse," "lost," a "mother hen," "a wimp" who "fiddled around and fiddled around." He headed a party that was seen as vacillating, disorderly, and weak.

Reagan's strength and universal qualities did not turn to arrogance or stubbornness because he associated himself with average people. Ronald Reagan sided with the small against the big. He was seen to be waging a sincere and determined struggle against big and inexorable forces, particularly against "big government." Reagan may not have slowed things, but, said one voter, "I'll tell you what: I definitely believe that he it trying with all of his heart to do the best he can for this country."

Reagan's attack on big government was not situated in some philosophical objection to regulation or penchant for the market. Macomb voters were in a populist frame of mind. They identified with things small and suspected "big" and "powerful" institutions of any kind—labor and business, government, and both political parties.

Despite a strong labor tradition, unions were distrusted— "big, strong organizations" that should be helping "small people" but were not. Corporations were also roundly condemned as powerful and self-interested; they elicited little admiration as job creators. In the generalized assault on bigness, many respondents seemed to elide unions, business, and government, condensing a whole range of powerful forces:

> The idea was good. They got real big and powerful and out of hand. That's my opinion.

> They kind of lost interest in the people working for them, and . . . It basically boils down to the upper level. . . . It's a business. Now that's what it is.

It's another big brother.

Yeah, I feel they expanded their limits a little too far.

They're a corporation in themselves is what they've almost become.

It's a government. It's a company to them. They just want to see how much money they can make.

At the other end of the struggle was small business, sharing an identity with middle-class America: "people working their butts off to try and make a go of things" yet squeezed by the big companies, "being taken advantage of," "overtaxed," and "struggling." The identity of interests was explicit for one of the younger men: "Small businessmen are picking up—just like middle-income men—a heck of a brunt when it comes to the tax structure in this state."

Reagan's association with their small world bought the Republican candidate an enormous amount of slack from voters who were self-consciously populist. They freely disagreed with Reagan on the subminimum wage, "taking away student loans," import quotas, "the arms race," Social Security ("those people being cut are really suffering"), and the air-traffic controllers' strike. Yet the doubts evaporated before the dominant images of Ronald Reagan: determined and honest, a proud nation for small people. Reagan was able to bridge his own world to the ordinary world of Macomb County.

Conservatism and Republicanism, however, had trouble making it across the bridge with Reagan. These voters liked Reagan yet comfortably called for regulation and state intervention in area after area—college loans for the children of the middle class, strong enforcement of occupational-safety laws for factory workers, tough measures to bar Japanese cars from the American market and foreigners from American jobs, strong action to spur the economy in case of a downturn, government takeover of the utilities.

For a minority of the Reagan Democrats, the Republicans now seemed more expansive, more open to blue-collar voters:

> The Republican party has changed its whole format over the last five or ten years. It seems that they catered to the business- and to the upper-echelon people on a financial basis. And it seems that they expanded their views now, and they are starting to look at every one. . . . And I think that they are doing more for the average guy, whereas before they seemed like they used to funnel all their efforts into the upper echelon.

A few of the men acknowledged the Republican recovery, though unaccompanied by any genuine peace of mind. Republican "good times" start at the top:

> Things seem to be going smoothly right now.

> They traditionally generate more business internally, in the country itself. It is not always good . . . because a lot of it tends to follow itself upwards.

The women too acknowledged the economic recovery, but in the same conditional terms, as put by this younger housewife: "I guess they've brought the economy around for their own advantage. They made it look the way they wanted it to look, but they have done it."

This grudging acknowledgment of economic "facts" was dominated by conventional images of a Republican party out of touch with working America. "I think the Republican party is basically for big business," one of the younger housewives observed. "Whether it's federal, state, local—they support big business more." The men referred to a party that was "elitist." "The Republicans tend to take care of big business first, as a priority," one of the older men pointed out, "because that's who is supporting them." While the Democrats "traditionally" have supported the farmers and the "little guy" in "hard times," the Republicans have been "for big business." And one of the older male participants followed up, "They always have and always will be."

That left Macomb County voters drifting into an anti-party limbo, disillusioned with the Democrats but little interested in Republicanism. This dis-affiliation left most of them detached and alienated, like this man: "Personally, I have very little on either of those, Republican or Democrat. I would say I am neither. I have very low expectations for government people anymore. That's the way I feel."

A DEAD END?

Ronald Reagan was not on the ballot in 1988, but on the Saturday before the election he made a final appeal at Macomb County Community College. He attacked Michael Dukakis for opposing prayer in the schools, appointing "left-wing judges," supporting gun control, and offering a "weak-kneed defense policy." The president was not subtle, labeling Dukakis, "liberal, liberal, liberal." He warned that "all the progress we have made is on the line" and reminded voters that George Bush had fought "to lift regulations off the shoulders of America's economy."

And Reagan was explicit in his historic task of making Macomb's rebellion into a new order: "I want to ask those who some people call Reagan Democrats to join me and come home with me today. Come home to me and to George Bush."[15]

Macomb tilted slightly back toward the Democrats, but not significantly, given its history: 61 percent voted for George Bush and just 39 percent for Michael Dukakis. In the most Democratic and blue-collar areas of the county, like Warren and Rose-ville, the Democrats barely edged up to 45 percent.

The 1988 campaign left Macomb County flat. Michael Dukakis passed through with barely a trace. His misadventures at the tank factory in Warren produced some comic relief, but even that was richer in detail than his image among Macomb's Reagan Democrats. In 1989, in another round of focus groups four years after the first conversations, Macomb voters described Dukakis as "canned," "cold," "wishy-washy," "vague," "nothing," a "nonentity type of thing where he was just up there."[16] They concluded, to devastating consequences at the ballot box, that he simply lacked the experience, depth, and respect to manage this country and our relations with other countries. Michael Dukakis eschewed any populist reach to middle-class America, except for some grudging "on your side" rhetoric at the end of his failed campaign.

There was now a Reagan Democratic state of mind in Macomb County. First, voters remained deeply cynical about the government and Democrats who had devoured their taxes over so many years and had forgotten the middle class. They worried that Democrats would let things get out of control, producing layers of bureaucracy and high taxes. Second, they saw this political world as still profoundly shaped by race. The Reagan Democrats of 1989 believed that the Democrats gave precedence to "special interests" (by which they meant racial minorities and Detroit) over the general interests of the middle class. This perception was seared into the consciousness of these voters and constituted a standing qualification to anything the Democrats wanted to do with government:

> I just have a feeling that the Democratic party is controlled by select, powerful minorities. I don't think maybe they reflect a broad spectrum, but they don't hit the middle. They are missing it.

They have really aligned themselves with the blacks, and it is really coming back to haunt them.

[The Democrats] are the ones that push the recognition of the minorities. And they figure if each minority got a chunk of the pie, that they would be entitled to one hundred twenty-five percent of the pie, which doesn't count anybody else.

This perception of Democratic politics and government led to some crystallized conclusions. First, the Democrats were considered "free spenders" and "spendthrifts" and prone to "giveaway government" and "bottomless social programs" for minorities that do not work, "take advantage" of the middle class, and "want something for nothing." The contrast with the Republicans was becoming more and more vivid: the latter were "anti-spending" and in favor of "lower taxes," "cutting programs," "reducing welfare," being "conservative toward spending," believing in "responsibility and control."

Second, Democrats, driven by special interest demands, were seen as leaderless and "unfocused." "Every little special interest group that comes up . . . tears them apart," they said, expressing a belief that led many of the swing voters to conclude that the Democrats had "bad leadership," "poor leadership," and even "no leadership." The Democrats could not keep things "from getting out of control."

Finally, Democrats appeared to lack any clear set of principles that would build confidence in them as stewards of the economy. Although these voters placed importance on the Democrats' seeming to worry more about the common, working man than the Republicans did, the party's lack of association with prosperity was devastating. An older Reagan Democrat drew this conclusion: "You go back thirty years ago, when the Republican party was for the businessman and the Democratic party was for the small working man, and I think they are equal now." The Republicans were now associated with finance and money, with growth, prosperity, and employment increases, with "economic responsibility" and "economic stability."

Dukakis's candidacy dashed, it seemed, any notion of Democratic renewal in Macomb County. In its "body language" and themes, the Dukakis campaign communicated monumental indifference to the turmoil there. The world had been turned upside-down in suburban Michigan, yet Democrats dared not acknowledge the rebellion and its challenge: that of crafting a vision that encompasses the values, aspirations, and vulnerabilities of middle-class America.

THE CRASH

And yet in 1992, Macomb's doubly disillusioned voters turned their backs on the conservative-Reagan compact, just as they had turned their backs on the liberal–Great Society compact some eight years earlier. The new Republican electoral majority just collapsed. In a very real sense, Macomb's insecure middle class was on its own, struggling to hold on to its way of life, its political world shattered beyond recognition. Neither the Democratic nor the Republican vision had any currency in Macomb County.

Most stunning was the sudden collapse of the Republican majority. Bush plummeted 18 points from 1988 and 24 points from 1984, when Reagan had appeared to seal the deal. In Warren, at the heart of suburban auto manufacture, Reagan had taken the Republicans all the way up to 64 percent of the vote, only for Bush to take them down to a paltry 39 percent; Bill Clinton carried this conservative bastion. But the Republican collapse swept across all of Macomb, even to the more upscale areas, which depend less on manufacturing. In Sterling Heights, where the median income reached almost $50,000, the Bush slide was 25 points: from 71 percent in 1984 to 46 percent in 1992.

Bill Clinton held on to the Dukakis vote in a three-way contest, which is no mean feat. By holding firm at 38 percent—that is, down just 1.1 percent from 1988—he produced a dramatic shift of the two-party vote: he closed 33- and 22-point defeats in 1984 and 1988, respectively, to just 5 points—a virtual dead heat in 1992. He won all the working-class suburbs of any size: Roseville by 10 points, East Detroit by 7 points, Warren by 4, and Mount Clemens by 12. The swing to Clinton was about 4 points greater in the upscale areas as Ross Perot ate further into the Bush vote.

Clinton would have run even better across Macomb had Perot not reentered the race. The exit polls conducted in Michigan for the television networks showed Perot voters choosing Clinton over Bush, 43 to 36 percent, in a straight two-way contest.[17] In Macomb, that would have pushed Clinton up to 49 percent of the vote—a near majority and a new game after a decade of Democratic humiliation.

Ross Perot gained 20 percent of the vote in Macomb, nearly paralleling his national performance. But in Macomb, that 20 percent is part of a larger story: betrayal and disillusionment expressed as utter disaffection.

The 1994 election in Macomb made clear just how contested middle America remains. Republican candidates for governor and the U.S. Senate ran very well, taking 70 and 56 percent of the vote, respectively. Yet Democratic Congressman David Bonior won his portion of Macomb with 62 percent and Democratic Congressman Sandy Levin won his with 50 percent. More stunning was the comeback of Kenneth DeBeaussaert, who had lost his state House seat in the Reagan landslide of 1984 but this time defeated a Reagan Democratic incumbent state senator who had switched over to become a Republican.

There is no new Democratic or Republican majority in middle America. The New Deal dream that had brought working America to the suburbs remains as shattered as supply-side economics. This is a completely new game with new rules, though the players can hardly dispel the images and themes, the old rules, that dominated their consciousness over the past four decades, maybe longer. The story of Macomb is not just about two parties and two prospective candidates contesting the Presidency. It is about two broken contracts and the search for something new that people can depend on.

3. THE GREAT-PARTY ERAS

THE political consciousness of ordinary citizens is rooted in the century-long struggle of our great parties to manage progress and help people in a modernizing America. Through years of political combat, the parties nurtured core ideas about how to organize this emerging industrial nation and give people faith in its future. For ordinary people struggling to hold on to what they had and to make something better, these ideas formed a kind of compact with the nation's leaders.

But this idealized imagery was always qualified in people's heads by a popular test of genuineness: Will Republican efforts to promote business, prosperity, and progress reach downward, making life better for ordinary people? Will Democratic attempts to provide relief for working people impede business growth and progress and thus endanger prosperity? In effect, people were asking whether the compact was real, something they could depend on. The parties' struggle to forge a compact and establish its genuineness has created the ruling ideas and values of each successive era in our modern political history—including the shambles that is our current era. The failure of both parties to pass the test of genuineness has left people feeling betrayed, without a compact and with diminished faith in the future.

When Republicans fashioned themselves as modernizers and champions of a general prosperity, they won the right to rule. The Democrats, by contrast, were seen as backward looking and divisive. At these historic moments, Republican leaders were able to reach down to ordinary people and include them in a Republican vision of growth. By joining together people and progress, they shaped an era—dominating the common sense and conventional wisdom that frame political life. But when the Republicans allowed themselves to become narrow and self-centered, merely representing business, they lost their hold on the country.

In similar fashion, when Democrats successfully championed both people and economic growth, they dominated the day: they set the terms of debate while marginalizing the Republicans as backward looking, mean-spirited, and greedy. But when the Democrats protected people by protesting change, they lost their hold on the country. The common man thanked the Democrats for their entreaties but turned to the Republicans, who offered the prospect of growth and material improvement.

This is why Macomb County is center stage in our political drama, for it represents the battleground where the national parties clash over their essential definitions. The Democrats must reach up to show these middle-class voters that the Democratic formula for joining people and progress offers the best promise for a better life. The Republicans must reach down to them to make the case for their unique formula. This is not a battle for voters and numbers; it is a battle over identity. Thomas and Mary Edsall got this just right when they said that these working- and middle-class voters stand at the "fulcrum of power"—"essential to the ideological coherence of each party."[1]

The stage for this historic clash over definition was set by a history that created the party imagery now rattling around in our heads. Each party came to this scene shaped by a great period of ascendancy and a bleak period of marginality; each tried to regain its glory by seeking a new formula for people and progress, yet each failed to reform itself, leaving the drama unresolved. We are now in a stage of unknown political possibilities.

The Great Republican Era was more than three decades long, stretching from 1896 to 1928, framed by the presidencies of William McKinley and Calvin Coolidge. The upheaval of 1896 set the character of the age and, perhaps more than any other election in our history, shaped the images of the two modern political parties. William Jennings Bryan ran as a Democratic populist, a rural protest candidate fighting for the "little guy" and opposed to modernizing capitalism. Bryan could not escape a pervasive sense of Democratic failure brought on by a debilitating depression under a lackluster Democratic president, Grover Cleveland. William McKinley ran as an economic nationalist and modernizer who pledged to promote a business-led prosperity. The election of 1896 created a self-confident Republicanism—unapologetic about capitalism's bounty and opportunity—prepared to reshape America. Only the split in the Republican party in 1912 and the First World War dampened the Republican ascendance. When Coolidge pronounced that "the chief business of the American people is business," he simply reflected the ethos of this age.

The Great Democratic Era, like its Republican predecessor, was forged in depression and lasted more than three decades, from Roosevelt's election in 1932 through Lyndon Johnson's 1964 landslide. Franklin Roosevelt lifted the spirits of a country in which one in four was without a job. He stood up for the common people, not just to give them greater security but also to ensure a more general prosperity for the country. Roosevelt, Harry Truman, and John Kennedy were modernizers who promoted economic growth and a larger American role in the world. To this day, Herbert Hoover remains a symbol of wealthy Republicanism's political indifference to the suffering and cries of a country in desperate economic trouble.

The Democrats under Lyndon Johnson took bold steps to renew the Democratic vision of the people, giving us the Great Society. Johnson expanded government to protect the elderly from sickness, to renew the rotting cities, to lift up the poor from poverty; he used the moral authority of the federal government to include black Americans in the country's and the party's definition of *people.* But the people, broadly defined, never ratified this experiment, which seemed to be guided by too narrow a view of the common person. In 1968, more than 57 percent of the electorate turned to Richard Nixon or George Wallace, and America declared its verdict on the Great Society.

The Republicans under Nixon and Reagan sought to renew the Republican vision, offering a Republicanism open to the values and needs of average Americans. They cracked open the Democrats' downscale base with the club of law and order and then associated themselves, particularly in the South, with moral and religious sentiments threatened by a Democratic party absorbed in civil rights, women's rights, and the legacy of Vietnam (the political equivalent of sex, drugs, and rock and roll). Under the banner of Reaganomics, Republicans offered across-the-board tax cuts—with the best deals reserved for the wealthy—and a reinvigorated vision of a business-led prosperity. But the prosperity was short-lived and not very general. Bill Clinton exposed the excess and the growing burdens on middle-class America as Reaganism dissolved into Hooverism.

The imagery that dominates our political life today was bequeathed to us by these two great-party eras and these two failed efforts at renewal. Today Democrats and Republicans alike struggle amidst the wreckage left by this history, searching for new formulas for joining people and prosperity. And Ross Perot picks about in the rubble.

THE GREAT REPUBLICAN ERA

The struggle of the two great ideas that formed the modern American political consciousness first fully emerged in the epic electoral battle of 1896. Party historians, of course, are eager to push the lineage of their parties' imagery back into the eighteenth and nineteenth centuries, to founding fathers like Jefferson and Hamilton, Jackson and Lincoln. There are good partisan reasons to take ownership of these national treasures. Each party wants to broaden its appeal by associating itself with the national icons and, perhaps more important, by associating the nation itself with the party's particular view of the world. Thus the founding fathers adorn our parties just as they adorn our national institutions.

There is some reality to all this. Thomas Jefferson, arguably the first Democratic president (though known formally as a Republican in his day), idealized the common man and sought to build a nation from the bottom up. He wanted a nation of "freeholders," who, in working the land, would constitute a "chosen people." Jeffersonianism came to represent the struggle for equal rights against the privileges of special classes and monopolies. Andrew Jackson wanted to take the government out of the hands of the "rich and powerful" and give it back to the "humble members of society." Like Jefferson, he sought to open up the public lands in the West at low prices to generalize freeholding—a democratic imperative for a country that wanted to lay its foundations in the common people. Jackson himself was a war hero, a vulgar and intemperate man, and immensely popular with the rabble whom he allowed to overrun the White

House on his first inauguration day. (One unsympathetic observer wrote, "It was like the inundation of the northern barbar-
ians into Rome, save that the tumultuous tide came in from a
different point of the compass.") The better classes scorned his
ways but, even more, his assault on the Bank of the United
States, where concentrated power was employed (in his words)
"for selfish purposes." His opponents attacked him for "appealing to the worst passions" and "endeavoring to stir up the poor
against the rich."[2]

The Federalists and their heirs, the anti-Jackson Whigs, were
impatient with the rabble and eager to promote commercial and
national progress. Although the link to modern-day Republicanism is only partial, the Whigs were counterpoised to Jefferson and Jackson—and they sure sounded like Republicans.
Hamilton wanted to build a new nation, first by establishing its
standing with financial interests and creditors and then by creating the conditions for commerce and manufacture. Hamilton's
purpose was straightforward, to "unite the interest and credit of
rich individuals with those of the state." This was top-down economics. Henry Clay's "American system"—based on managing
the national debt, protecting industry, and supporting internal
improvements—aimed at fostering growth and a general prosperity. Abraham Lincoln, the first Republican president, was a
modernizer of the first order, breaking the back of a reactionary,
landed class in the South and making possible the emergence of
a dominant industrialism based on free labor.[3]

This partisan history is quite real and animated: it brought
forth a massive mobilization of the electorate and the development of party organizations. But the period has little to do with
the pictures in our heads today. The nation, not the two political parties, owns the first century of our history. Jefferson, the
frontier, and the Union belong to all of us. The Declaration
of Independence, the Battle of New Orleans, the Gettysburg

Address—all are national treasures situated in our national consciousness. From our vantage point today, these were all about building a nation, not party politics.

Their legacy affects our politics, to be sure. Just look at the line that runs across southern Ohio, Indiana, and Illinois or through the hill counties of northern Alabama, and you will still find the electoral divide that separated North and South. In pockets of the South, the real Democrats are still the party of white supremacy. But for most Americans today, these are legacies without meaning. We long ago made the decision to go with the winners in these party battles that no longer engage us. The Republicans' war to save the nation is today a profound statement of national unity. Jefferson, Hamilton, Jackson, and Lincoln are not party figures. They are nation builders.

But nearly all our national leaders since the Civil War remain partisan figures because their battles remain ours. They may have led the nation in war or through depression, but they are associated with an unresolved conflict over how to manage our modern industrial society. That is why the election of 1896 is so important—"the hottest," Frederick Lewis Allen wrote, "perhaps, in the whole history of the United States."[4] It is the starting point for *our* struggle to define our country.

The modern parties were seared into the modern American mind in 1896 because they battled for a modern America. This was a time of historic change in the way people lived and worked; it was a time of change in who owned what in society, in who held political power, in who was esteemed and who was ordinary. This was a period of profound insecurity and new-found glory, of impoverishment and enrichment, of high-profile winners and many losers, depending on your vantage point. This was a battle to define the behemoth called the United States of America. And in 1896, the top-down view won, giving us the Great Republican Era.

Between 1880 and 1910, the United States emerged as a manufacturing and industrial society. National wealth increased 275 percent, and the manufacturing of finished products by 250 percent. The steel industry introduced the Bessemer and open-hearth processes; conveyors and hoists became standard in manufacture; shoe production was taken over completely by machines; refrigeration changed meat packing and created a food industry. By the end of the period, before the First World War, the moving assembly line made possible the mass production of automobiles.

The technological transformation was more than matched by the social upheaval. Urbanization and industrialization jumped in the decade of the 1880s, slowed somewhat during the depression years of 1893–97, but started up again after 1900. A country that was only a quarter urbanized in 1880 (28.2 percent) was approaching an urban majority by 1910 (45.7 percent). The rapid transformation of America was driven by ever bigger enterprises that found new ways to organize themselves—as corporations to reduce risk; as holding companies to achieve greater stability; as marketing organizations to increase market power; and as trusts and monopolies to reduce competition. Corporate power increased at the expense of agriculture and labor.

Between 1870 and 1900, farmers found themselves in a vise, pressed on the one side by declining prices and on the other by new monopolies in marketing and transportation that pushed their costs up. More and more farmers found themselves surviving as tenants rather than as freeholders; a crushing debt and sharp downturns in prices produced a rising desperation across the Great Plains and the South. With massive immigration in the 1880s through the first decades of the next century, industrial workers struggled to maintain wage levels. By 1910, a fourth of all children between ten and fourteen years of age were at work full-time. The use of federal troops or state militias to crush the national railroad strike (1877), the steelworkers' strike in Home-stead, Pennsylvania (1892), and the Pullman Company strike (1894) sent the nation a message about the character of modern government.[5]

The stage for the political battle between McKinley and Bryan was set by the panic of 1893 and the depression of the '90s, which raised the stakes for everybody. The depression lasted at least until 1897, and industrial output did not fully recover until after 1900. By June 1894, 192 railroad companies were in receivership, representing a quarter of all the rails. Unemployment reached 17 to 19 percent in 1894. By some estimates, 2 to 3 million people were out of work; 100,000 of the unemployed walked the streets of Chicago. Farm incomes and prices hit their lowest point in 1896. And this was a country without a real system of relief and without any real experience with a modern industrial economy.[6]

The Failure of Politics

Party politics from the Civil War era was at a dead end. Confident entrepreneurs, waves of immigrants, and the new laboring classes were busily remaking America. The country's cherished freeholders, daunted by the pace of change and the new power centers, grew increasingly desperate and disillusioned. Yet politics was stuck in gridlock and consumed by issues from the past.

The Republicans and the Democrats were still fighting over the issues of the 1860s and '70s—the Civil War, the secession and readmission of the southern states, Reconstruction, the former slaves and the former rebels, and the fraud that characterized the post–Civil War elections. With the still-fresh memory of a half million war casualties, the passions ran high. The battle to rule grew even more heated as Republicans sought to exploit the "Negro vote" in the South while trying to restrict the flow of

Democratically inclined immigrants to the North. The Democrats, in turn, attacked the corruption that infused every post–Civil War government and established itself as the party of white supremacy in the South.[7]

Yet for all the noise, the parties were deaf to the battles of the new industrial world. There were few pages in either party's platform devoted to subjects like wages, trusts, and monopolies. The electoral politics of the age was increasingly irrelevant to the emerging grievances and preoccupations in the cities and on the farms. The established political order showed little interest in opening up a debate between the new winners and the new losers. It was largely silent about the new capitalist machine that was transforming America and plowing under the many who could not keep up.

The Democrats managed some bottom-up rhetoric and, indeed, opposed the expansion of a federal government formally allied with the economic elites outside the South. This was a period of extraordinary corruption: massive land grants to the railroads, suitcases of cash carried onto the floor of numerous state legislatures, and sometimes the Democrats rose up to decry it. Samuel Tilden and Grover Cleveland spoke of the rich and powerful taking over government and, in the latter's words, leaving the ordinary citizen "struggling far in the rear" or "trampled to death beneath an iron heel." In the tradition of Andrew Jackson, Democrats in the post–Civil War period resisted big government and spending. They opposed corruption, public works, and tariffs, all of which allied powerful economic interests with big government.

But this view of government left the Democratic party's leaders impotent and the party itself divided before the cries of farmers and urban workers. Cleveland was known for exposing waste and vetoing pension bills, but he refused to address the needs of debt-ridden farmers or the emergent factory and mine workers or the threat from the growing monopolies and trusts.

He showed little interest in the railroad regulation or monetary reforms that would have angered eastern financial interests. Even the depression of the 1890s brought no response from Cleveland, except his acceding to business demands for sound money, the use of federal troops to crush the Pullman strike, and putting the Socialist organizer Eugene Debs behind bars. There was no new Democratic program for facing the economic change sweeping America.[8]

In the end, neither Democratic nor Republican leaders considered challenging the ascendance of industry and markets. They were consumed with other issues and largely content to set these questions aside. There were populist challengers within the Democratic party, like Governor Ben Tillman of South Carolina, who promised to "stick my pitchfork into his [Cleveland's] old ribs," but Cleveland held firm as a "gold Democrat" and to the bipartisan establishment consensus on sound money.[9]

The parties fought bitterly on the old issues, but to a stalemate. No political party was dominant or genuinely in control as the economic crisis overran the country. The Republicans had emerged on top after the Civil War, but theirs was an artificial hegemony made possible by the exclusion of the former rebel states. In 1876, the Republicans probably stole the disputed presidential election, though they had to give up on Reconstruction as the price for the White House. In 1880, the Republicans won nationally by just 7,000 votes, and the Democrats, under Cleveland, won in 1884 by just 63,000 votes. In the decade of 1878 to 1888, congressional voting left the two parties at almost perfect parity. In 1889, Republicans held 168 seats, just two more than a majority. This was not an era for great initiatives, even with political rebellion brewing on the prairie.

The elections in 1890 and 1892 produced some of the most extraordinary electoral swings imaginable as the public readied itself to break open this system and create something new and modern. With signs of gridlock and defections in the West, the

Republicans were swept out of the House in 1890, losing an astonishing 78 seats and leaving the Democrats with a majority of 235 to 88. William McKinley lost his seat in Canton, Ohio; the populist William Jennings Bryan won election to Congress from Lincoln, Nebraska. The Democratic sweep presaged Cleveland's return to the White House in 1892.

But the Cleveland Democratic party refused to respond to the populist revolt or to the depression that followed the 1892 elections. In effect, Cleveland refused to allow the Democratic party to emerge as a bottom-up party responsive to the struggles of its day. In the 1894 midterm election, voters showed their willingness to abandon the Democrats, as the Republicans gained 117 seats in the House—the biggest electoral collapse ever. The stage was set for Bryan and McKinley and the first modern-party era.[10]

Poised for Top-Down Rule

While the Democrats under Cleveland refused to grasp their opportunity, the Republicans were poised to emerge as a dominant top-down party. They freely waved the bloody shirt, touting their history as the party that had won the Civil War and brought the nation back together, but the Republicans were now ready to go beyond the theme of national savior. They created a massive system of Civil War pensions, thus cementing the loyalty of large portions of downscale America. The pension joined the party's role in saving the Union with its solemn "contract" with the "Union's defenders." This system was forged not in the period after the war, when claims for war-related injuries were at their peak, but between 1880 and 1910, when the parties were engaged in armed combat and the new Republican era was being established. One in ten voters was a Union veteran, a group overwhelmingly made up of farmers and townspeople in the Northeast and Midwest. In this period, *over a quarter of all federal spending* was devoted to Civil War pensions.[11]

With the rising protests against the new capitalist arrangements and with populist forces at the doors of both parties, the Republicans passed the Dependent Pension Act in 1887, which was promptly vetoed by President Cleveland—a factor in his narrow defeat the next year. The act would have extended pensions to anybody who had served ninety days in the Union army, without regard to disability; it offered pensions to any Union veteran who claimed he was incapable of performing physical labor.

The Republicans were clear about their reach from the top downward. In 1888, a Republican campaign poem proclaimed:

Let Grover Cleveland talk about the tariff tariff tariff
    And pensions too.
We'll give the workingman his due
    And pension the boys who wore the blue.

Thus the Grand Army of the Republic, with its more than 400,000 members, backed the Republicans, who expanded a social welfare system for native-born white and pre–Civil War immigrant workers outside the South. In 1890 the Republicans passed the Dependent and Disability Pension Act. This largesse was financed primarily by huge federal surpluses made possible by high tariffs, which industrial workers also supported as such tariffs seemed to promote industrial employment.

The Republicans were about to join common people and business under the umbrella of their party. This was the essence of top-down politics that would give us the Great Republican Era of 1896–1928.

Fusing Democrats and the Common Man

William Jennings Bryan, leading a populist rebellion that sawed off the eastern pro-business wing of the party, was the true father of the modern bottom-up Democratic party. He incorporated the ragtag third-party movements that were protesting the emerging indignities and inequalities of industrial society. And amidst a crushing Democratic depression, he became the leader of a new Democratic party. He was its standard-bearer three times during the formative period of American industrialism and each time affirmed the party's identity: opposed to corporate power and ready to stand up for the common man.

Bryan explicitly linked this bottom-up party to Jefferson and Jackson. It was Jefferson, Bryan believed, who "dared to defy the wealth and power of his day and plead the cause of the common people"; and the times demanded, he believed, an "Andrew Jackson to stand, as Jackson stood, against the encroachment of organized wealth." That is the modern vision of the Democratic party. It stands with "the man who wears a colored shirt as well as the man who wears a linen collar." It offers a vision of prosperity that begins with the common man: "The Democratic idea, however, has been that if you legislate to make the masses prosperous, their prosperity will find its way up through every class which rests upon them."[12]

Bryan moved first to purify a Democratic party that had aligned itself with the creditors and eastern business interests, that had sought "sound currency" at the expense of debt-ridden farmers and industrial peace at the expense of striking workers. As a congressman, Bryan challenged what he considered the upside-down vision of the Democratic president to whom any loyalty would have been misplaced. He rejected the conventional establishment view of the angry world emerging outside: "The poor man is called a socialist if he believes that the wealth of the rich should be divided among the poor, but the rich man is called a financier if he devises a plan by which the pittance of the poor can be converted to his use." He warned Cleveland that "free government cannot long survive when the thousands enjoy the wealth of the country and the million share its poverty in common." He warned the president to step back and listen to different voices:

> Whence comes the demand? Not from the workshop and farm, not from the workingmen of this country, who create its wealth in time of peace and protect its flag in time of war, but from the middle-men, from what are termed the "business interests." . . . The President has been deceived. He can no more judge the wishes of the great mass of our people by the expressions of those men than he can measure the ocean's silent depths by the foam upon its waves.[13]

Bryan sought to make the Democratic party a protest party, a party able to co-opt all the emerging factions organizing against the new industrial order. Most of the protests, which began around 1880, had originated with the farmers. Laden with debt, facing rising costs and declining prices, they struck out at the railroads and the monopolies through the Greenback party and the anti-monopolist leagues. By 1890, the Farmers' Alliance (an outgrowth of the National Grange) was a major independent political force, particularly in the West; in the South, it merged with the Democratic party in many states. Even so, the national Democratic party was studiously indifferent to this tumult. Its post–Civil War presidential nominees prior to 1896 were almost always from New York and determined to show that they were worthy of business confidence.[14]

Opposed to the Republicans yet scorned by the Democrats, a million voters (8 percent of the total) turned to the People's party in 1892. Bryan tried to alert his fellow Democrats: "This army, vast and daily vaster growing, begs the party to be its champion in the present conflict."[15] When Bryan ran for president in 1896, he successfully joined this vast army to the Democratic party, fusing populists and Democrats and creating an identity that would live long past this failed rebellion. He forged a platform that would create a new Democratic agenda, including railroad regulation, anti-trust measures, the income tax, and most famously, bimetalism—easy money, backed by silver, to offset the deflation faced by indebted farmers. Bryan's final address to the Democratic convention in Chicago affirmed the party's new bottom-up identity:

> Having behind us the producing masses of this nation and the world, supported by the commercial interests, the laboring interests, and the toilers everywhere, we will answer their demand for a gold standard by saying to them: You shall not press down upon the brow of labor this crown of thorns, you shall not crucify mankind upon a cross of gold.[16]

Fusing Republicans and Prosperity

William McKinley, the Republican nominee in 1896, was calm and reserved, dignified; at some point along the way, William Allen White suggested, he "buttoned himself up." McKinley was an appropriate leader to join big business, the Republican party, and the nation under the banner of prosperity. The Democratic depression and the Democrats' anti-industrial protests eased the task. But McKinley was uniquely prepared to create a top-down Republican party. His entire political career had been predicated on selling the virtues of industrialism to the emerging working class in Canton, Ohio.[17]

Ohio was the crossroads of a modernizing America in the late nineteenth century and the key to a national electoral majority. It was divided by Civil War loyalties, industrial growth and farmer discontent, large-scale immigration and nativism. It gave us presidents in 1876 and 1880. Its electoral-college vote—almost always decided by fewer than a thousand votes—had provided the margin of victory in nearly every national election since the Civil War. Ohio also gave us William McKinley.

From the beginning of his political life, McKinley always had to persuade Democratically inclined working-class voters that he was on their side. He twice lost elections for prosecuting attorney in Canton before taking up the cause of striking mine workers and winning election to Congress in 1876. He struggled to hold on to that seat as historic waves shifted control back and forth between the parties. He once won reelection by only eight votes. He survived, however, by advancing issues that would capture the attention of the discontented at the bottom of the ladder. He supported severe limits on Chinese immigration and even favored silver-backed currency until his national aspirations clashed with the views of eastern financial interests.

The centerpieces of McKinley's congressional standing and his appeal to working America, however, were the tariff and economic nationalism. More forcefully than any other leader, he argued for the common interest of labor and business in promoting and protecting American industry. At the beginning, the issue was little more than bread-and-butter politics, an appeal to workers in his district to vote to protect their jobs. But ultimately he used the issue to challenge the Democrats and western farmers, who favored lower tariffs and lower consumer prices. In 1883, he made his first major statement to Congress on the issue: "Reduce the tariff and labor is the first to suffer. He who would break down the manufactures of this country strikes a fatal blow at labor. It is labor I would protect." He rooted this issue and his appeal in the common sense of working people. Protection might be frowned on in academic circles, but "it is taught in the school of experience, in the work shop, where honest men perform an honest day's labor, and where capital seeks the development of national wealth."[18]

The McKinley tariff rivaled silver as a defining issue of the day. To be for high tariffs was, in effect, to support an industrial future for America at the expense of those who worked the land. During the congressional battle of 1890, McKinley had the opportunity to elevate his vision, showing how all of America could share in an industrially led growth:

> I believe in it and thus warmly advocate it because enveloped in it are my country's highest development and greatest prosperity; out of it come the greatest gains to the people, the greatest comforts to the masses, the widest encouragement for many aspirations, with the largest rewards, dignifying and elevating our citizenship, upon which the safety and purity and permanency of our political system depend.[19]

In 1896, McKinley's vision of prosperity crashed against Bryan's vision of a country of toilers. President Cleveland's impotence before the depression made this a pretty simple choice for many working people, even though McKinley was unabashedly the candidate of big business and finance. His campaign manager, Mark Hanna, was a wealthy businessman who organized America's industrial magnates to save the country's capitalist future. Major corporations were assessed one fourth of 1 percent of capital; banks and insurance companies, a percentage of their assets; and commercial houses, according to their business volume. The railroad companies provided special fares to transport almost a million people to hear McKinley on his porch in Canton. The Republicans acknowledged spending $3.5 million on the campaign—all but a half a million raised in New York.[20]

Wrapped in the flag of economic nationalism and prosperity, McKinley took his message down to the toilers, at least to those in the industrializing states of the East and Midwest. He attacked Bryan for being backward looking and divisive, "seeking to array labor against capital. . . . It is most unpatriotic." And he spoke of a broader American prosperity, an emboldened trickle-down economics before its time. "We are all political equals here—equal in privilege and opportunity, dependent upon each other, and the prosperity of the one is the prosperity of the other." It was appropriate that McKinley ended his campaign with a national "flag day" to capture the fusion of his economic vision and the nation. Canton was draped with American flags, and McKinley did the honors: "It represents liberty, it represents equality, it represents opportunity, it represents the possibilities for American manhood obtainable in no other land beneath the sun."[21]

By comparison with McKinley's vision, William Jennings Bryan's was narrow and ultimately archaic. Silver in 1896 was supposed to represent the interests of common people across regions, yet it had less to do with interests than with a rural way of life that was under siege by the new order. Bryan Democrats were offering an affirmation that the farm was as important to America as the factory and the city—indeed, that the farmer was as central to America's identity as the worker and the businessman. Bryan honored rural and religious values, the moral content in public life against the materialism that pervaded industrial life. He was offering a Democratic party of the periphery in opposition to the gathering power of the metropole.

Bryan's bottom-up vision of the Democratic party was not particularly persuasive in the growing cities of the East and Midwest or for America's growing population of factory workers. The promised devalued currency may have offered farmers the hope of a reprieve from debt, but for the workers it represented a paycheck that would buy less. Having faced a depression, workers were looking for a vision that promised better jobs and greater prosperity. Identification with the laboring classes was not enough, particularly in contrast to the Republican commitment to protect and build up American industry. There was a labor plank in the Democratic platform, but Bryan showed little interest in it, and labor leaders like Samuel Gompers were uncomfortable with a populist alliance.[22]

The urban areas of the country marched into the Republican camp in 1896. The Democratic vote in Boston dropped from 54 to 35 percent; in New York City, from 59 to 42 percent; in Philadelphia, from 42 to 26 percent; and in Chicago, from 55 to 40 percent. In states like Pennsylvania, the rural native-stock populations became more Democratic, but in the two major cities, Pittsburgh and Philadelphia, the populace moved decisively toward the Republicans and fell under the control of Republican machines. Catholic and German immigrant voters gave up on this nostalgic Democratic party that failed to identify with their life and values and failed to offer a vision of capitalist growth.[23]

Nationwide there was an historic and enduring transformation. Eight states—mainly in New England but also New Jersey and Wisconsin—moved toward the Republicans by more than 12 percentage points. The Republicans lost ground in Colorado, Idaho, Montana, and Nevada, but they were trading the future for the past. Between 1896 and 1928, previously competitive states like Connecticut, New York, New Jersey, Indiana, California, Delaware, and West Virginia shifted sharply to the Republicans. Other states—Pennsylvania, Michigan, Illinois, Wisconsin, and Iowa—fell under one-party rule.[24]

McKinley solidified his party's ascendance in 1900 in a rematch against Bryan. His economic nationalism had now reached a larger stage, with Cuba and the Philippines in the American orbit as a result of the Spanish-American War and Hawaii established as a U.S. territory. The country had pulled slowly out of the depression and was now achieving a new self-confidence about its future, particularly with expanding markets abroad. McKinley deplored Bryan's anti-imperialism and his penchant for supporting "economic contraction." This was, as many came to call it, an age of confidence, during which commercial prosperity lifted up the nation. Millionaires like Vanderbilt and Morgan could throw grand balls and build grand homes, unapologetic about their good fortune. And this was also a golden age for Republicanism. There were so many Republicans in the House and Senate that the chambers had to be refitted to seat the swollen majorities. McKinley's triumph over Bryanism in 1900 gave the president the biggest national electoral victory since 1824, even pushing the GOP to dominance in Great Plains and Mountain states like Kansas, Nebraska, South Dakota, Utah, and Wyoming.[25]

After McKinley's death, in 1901, Theodore Roosevelt harmonized the union of common people and business, showing that Republicans understood the abuses that capitalism could wreak and highlighting the essential compatibility of business and the citizenry under top-down governance. The ascendance of top-down politics was complete. Only the bitter rift between William Howard Taft and Theodore Roosevelt in 1912 would allow the Democrats into the White House and interrupt the thirty-two years of good feeling about the Republicans and America.

Calvin Coolidge: Corporate America and the White House

Calvin Coolidge made his first foray into politics in Northampton, Massachusetts' Second Ward, where he worked to elect William McKinley in 1896. It was reported that he attended every party meeting without fail and became the Republican precinct committeeman. Thus were set in place the bookends of the Great Republican Era, McKinley (1897–1901) and Coolidge (1925–29), two presidents who comfortably joined together organized industry and America's people to create a modern America characterized by its wealth and prosperity.

Coolidge presided over a period of record prosperity, assuring people that this top-down bargain produces broad benefits at all rungs on the social ladder. During the 1920s, per capita income grew by almost 20 percent; between 1921 and 1929, the use of refrigeration grew 150 times, and automobile registrations soared from 9.3 million to 23.1 million. By the end of the decade, there was almost one car for every family and a telephone for almost every other residence. America was now discovering traffic lights, concrete roads, and roadside diners. Union membership began to fall, and strikes, seeming out of place, declined sharply. "Good times" left little room for Democrats, and voters showed them the door. In 1920, the Democrats lost the presidency in a landslide; and throughout the decade, they barely got more than 35 percent of the vote.[26]

But underneath the good times was a lot of rot. For all the new consumerism, 60 percent of Americans were still living in poverty, and income inequality was on the rise. The age was characterized by speculative boom after speculative boom, foreign loans, cheap money, inflated land prices, rising business debt, and high times on Wall Street. This was an age that rewarded excess—"through skullduggery and abuse," to be sure, wrote William Allen White; "but much more from loss of perspective and from trusting the insecure foundation of excess reserves and easy money . . . the situation grew more and more unsound and a greater and greater flood of securities, unsound securities, were placed in the hands of the American public." This was "the Coolidge bull market."[27]

But Coolidge sat satisfied and quietly atop this explosive reality. By all accounts, he was personally a model of prudence, thrift, and straightforward honesty. What better leader to join the ethic of business and government? This was a White House that honored business and the captains of industry. Andrew Mellon, arguably the wealthiest man in America, served as secretary of the treasury and as the principal architect of financial and economic policy.

Secretary Mellon offered an economic policy centered on successive income tax reductions for the wealthy. The Mellon plan, signed by Coolidge in 1926, cut the inheritance tax in half, abolished the gift tax, and reduced the basic income tax to 5 percent. Mellon elaborated a philosophy and economic theory that is by now quite familiar to Americans: "High rates tend to destroy individual initiative and enterprise and seriously impede the development of productive business. Taxpayers subject to the higher rates cannot afford for example to invest in American railroads or industries or embark on new enterprise in the face of taxes taking away 50 percent or more of any return that may be realized. . . ." *The New York Times* editorialized on the general benefit of such tax-cutting policies:

> It would lower the cost of living. It would release capital for productive industry and enterprise of all kinds. This would result in fuller employment of all kinds. This would result in fuller employment of labor, multiplication of goods and common consumption, and probably bring about a period of great and legitimate expansion of industry and commerce never surpassed in the United States.

Mellon had little patience with the progressives, like Senator Robert M. La Follette of Wisconsin, who attacked a policy that would allow the wealthy to escape its "full share of taxation." Like McKinley, Mellon deplored "the man who seeks to perpetuate prejudice and class hatred" and pit "one class of taxpayers against another." The Coolidge-Mellon vision was classless, built on faith in a business-led prosperity whose benefits would be generalized to the people as a whole. With the 1928 Hoover campaign ahead, after four tax cuts in seven years, Mellon pronounced, "In no other nation and at no other time in the history of the world have so many people enjoyed such a high degree of prosperity."[28]

Coolidge communicated contentment with the dispensation that had brought the country to such a state. He had little interest in doing anything that would disturb the direction of things or address any problem. Walter Lippmann described him as having a "genius for inactivity. . . . Mr. Coolidge's inactivity is not merely the absence of activity. It is on the contrary a steady application to the task of neutralizing and thwarting political activity wherever there are signs of life."[29] Little wonder Ronald Reagan would bring Coolidge's picture down from the attic and look back on these as idyllic times, as a model for his own top-down vision of the world.

THE GREAT DEMOCRATIC ERA

1929. It was a financial and economic collapse that would for generations destroy America's confidence in business-led prosperity. Between 1929 and 1933, under President Herbert Hoover, the nation's economic productivity declined by a third, per capita income by almost a half, wages by 60 percent. One person in four was out of a job. In some cities, like Cleveland, half the people were unemployed; in Toledo, Ohio, the figure was 80 percent. Farm income dropped by a third, and the farmers of the Southwest, northern Great Lakes, and Great Plains fell back on conditions worse than those of the 1890s. Some 5,000 banks failed. The leading index of common stock dropped 80 percent; U.S. Steel, which had climbed to 261¾ a share in good times, fell to 21¼.[30]

And Herbert Hoover's name was forever seared in the brains of Americans. He stood philosophically opposed to government action and seemingly indifferent to the people's desperate cries for help. "Economic depression cannot be cured by legislative action or executive pronouncement," Hoover told Congress in

1930. "Economic wounds must be healed by the action of the
cells of the economic body." He thus convened conferences
with economic leaders and appointed committees to document
the condition of the unemployed. But he opposed government
relief in the form of food because he thought such welfare programs should be undertaken by private organizations, like the
Red Cross; federal relief would undermine "something infi-
nitely valuable in the life of the American people." Unemployment insurance would likewise "endow the slacker." When
Congress passed legislation to create national employment
exchanges, the Republicans in the Senate voted two to one
against it, and Hoover vetoed the bill, declaring it "the most
vicious tyranny ever set up in the United States." While Hoover
took some halting steps late in his term, he is remembered more
for inaction and insensitivity before a desperate America. His
idea of government action was to ask Rudy Vallee to write a
song to help people "forget their troubles" or to implore Will
Rogers for jokes that would discourage hoarding.[31]

With Hoover and the Republicans fell the prestige and the
confidence in American business. Wall Street, the banking system, and big industry had all collapsed, failing their investors and
workers, to be sure, but also failing Main Street and the farms.
All the lavish prosperity now seemed to bespeak greed and corruption, and the country turned to Washington and a new president, Franklin Delano Roosevelt, to face the new economic
realities.

Franklin Roosevelt: "The Forgotten Man"

Roosevelt kept his party's platform deliberately vague in 1932,
and he offered an uncertain course by which to take the country out of the Depression. There was talk of "relief" and public
works, of aiding farmers to avoid foreclosure, and of lower tar-

iffs, but these were disparate pieces of an eclectic and pragmatic approach to economic policy. People did not vote for Roosevelt because of the Democratic recovery program but out of scorn for Hoover, who had mismanaged the economy, aligned himself with corporate excess, and refused to reach out a hand to the needy. They turned to Roosevelt, who intuitively and philosophically associated governance with people. He embodied a bottom-up view of the world that would soon be associated with his party.

In the spring of 1932, during his campaign for the presidency, Roosevelt aligned himself with the "forgotten man": "These unhappy times call for the building of plans that rest upon the forgotten, the unorganized but the indispensable units of economic power, for plans . . . that build from the bottom up and not from the top down, that put their faith, once more in the forgotten man at the bottom of the economic pyramid." He scorned a Hoover administration that "has sought temporary relief from the top down rather than permanent relief from the bottom up."[32] Roosevelt's forgotten man created a new center of gravity for government and society. For this moment, people, not business, had prestige and standing.

The older powers in the Democratic party, still trapped in the conventional wisdom of the Great Republican Era, were uncomfortable with this return to Bryanism, though Roosevelt himself thought of it more as a return to the spirit of Andrew Jackson. Alfred E. Smith, the party's 1928 presidential nominee, said, "We should stop talking about the Forgotten Man and about class distinctions." He vowed to fight this shift to the bottom: "I will take off my coat and vest and fight to the end any candidate who persists in any demagogic appeal to the masses of the working people of this country to destroy themselves by setting class against class and rich against poor."[33] But the conventional wisdom and Republicanism gave way in 1932, when

Roosevelt overturned Hoover's 1928 win. Then Hoover had taken 58 percent of the vote and every state outside the Deep South except Massachusetts and Rhode Island; Roosevelt in 1932 won 57 percent of the vote and every state in the West, the Midwest, and the South.

The New Deal represented a turn to government to provide relief and lead America out of the Depression. It had less to do with ideology and a formal philosophy of government than with a desire, as Roosevelt put it, for "bold, persistent experimentation."[34] But make no mistake, government moved on a broad front: market controls in agriculture, bank regulation, standards in the workplace, labor-management relations, minimum wage, unemployment insurance, Social Security, relief and public works, electrification and expanded credit and investment.

In almost every sphere, the New Deal proved impatient with market outcomes. On his first day in office, Roosevelt declared a bank holiday, later reopening the banks under a new regime of regulation. In agriculture, the administration abrogated the market in favor of acreage allotments and production controls, marketing agreements and regulation of processors. For industry, it created the National Recovery Administration to bring labor and management together to write their own "codes of fair competition." These codes eventually covered 95 percent of the industrial workforce; through them the NRA attempted to set minimum wage levels, maximum hours, and proper working conditions and to create a right to organize and bargain. More enduring than the codes was the alphabet of national credit and financing institutions—REA, FNMA, and RFC—that brought electric power to the South and West and rural America, revolutionized home mortgages, and made possible a boom in home ownership. Finally, the Social Security Act set up a contributory "insurance" plan to help all Americans cope with periods of dire

economic need, such as old age and retirement, disability, or loss
of a parent.[35]

The concept of Social Security was embedded in a deep
commitment to employment. The retirement benefits were
themselves constructed as a reward for a lifetime of work. And
providing relief was always secondary to stimulating or providing public employment. Between 1933 and 1940, government
spending to create jobs for the unemployed exceeded all spending on public assistance. This policy followed a Roosevelt
maxim: "Provide work and economic security to the mass of the
people in order that they may be free to live and develop their
individual lives and seek happiness and recognition."[36] The common sense of this era no longer accepted jobs and prosperity as
providential. It now took for granted the responsibility of government to honor work and create employment.

With the 1936 election in front of him, Roosevelt began to
elaborate his bottom-up vision, forming it into an assault on the
prestige of corporate America. He prefaced the year and his
reelection campaign with an annual message, for the first time
delivered during an evening joint session of Congress. He
alerted the American people to the hatred that he had earned
from "entrenched greed." This "resplendent economic autoc-
racy" seeks to take the government "for themselves" and offer
"enslavement for the public." On accepting his renomination at
the Democratic convention, Roosevelt pointed out that the
equality of the individual was threatened by the concentrated
power of the "economic royalists." In the face of such power and
selfishness, "the American citizen could appeal only to the organized power of Government." At the close of the campaign,
Roosevelt made the association complete: "There was no power
under Heaven that could protect the people against that sort of
thing except a people's Government in Washington." Free enterprise was right for America, but concentrated power in the cor-

poration had become a "kind of private government, a power unto itself—a regimentation of other people's lives."[37]

Roosevelt was booed on Wall Street but not at the polls. The voters in all but two states confirmed the new center of gravity.

The Democrats were now broadly associated with a popular prosperity, even if a slowdown threatened the recovery late in the decade and even if the country did not fully regain its economic footing until the start of the Second World War. The period from 1933 to 1937 produced an extraordinary growth in production, up 12 percent each year. At the same time, the government became the employer of last resort. In 1939, before the wartime boom, three million of the ten million unemployed were put to work in public-employment projects, under the Works Progress Administration, the Civilian Conservation Corps, and the National Youth Administration.[38] The Democrats were focused on growth and jobs, beginning with the forgotten man.

Truman to Kennedy: From People to Growth

Harry Truman, as a teenager of sixteen, traveled with his father to Kansas City to hear William Jennings Bryan accept his second Democratic nomination for the presidency. Father and son were now "Bryan men," and as Truman's biographer David McCullough observed, "Bryan remained an idol for Harry, as the voice of the common man."[39] The connection to Bryan was evident when Truman took to the floor of the Senate in 1937 to assail the "wild greed" of big business and to warn of the people's desire to even things up:

> We worship money instead of honor. A billionaire, in our estimation, is much greater in these days in the eyes of the people than the public servant who works for public interest. It makes no difference if the billionaire rode to wealth

on the sweat of little children and the blood of underpaid labor. . . .

It is a pity that Wall Street, with its ability to control all the wealth of the nation and to hire the best law brains in the country, has not produced some statesmen, some men who could see the dangers of bigness and of the concentration of the control of wealth. Instead of working to meet the situation, they are still employing the best law brains to serve greed and self interest. People can stand so much, and one of these days there will be a settlement.[40]

Truman faced a daunting challenge in 1948 if he was to demonstrate that the Democratic Era was more than a personalized achievement of Franklin Roosevelt. Faced with the defections of southern Democrats to the Dixiecrat splinter candidate, Governor Strom Thurmond of South Carolina, and of the old left to former vice president Henry Wallace, Truman had to reach deep into the Bryan-Roosevelt bottom-up well—and he did. Down 44 to 31 percent in the polls to New York's Governor Thomas E. Dewey on September 9, Truman headed west by train. In Dexter, Iowa, before a crowd of farmers, Truman recalled Republican indifference to the economic plight of the people: "You remember the big boom and the great crash of 1929. You remember that in 1932 the position of the farmer had become so desperate that there was actual violence in many farming communities. You remember that insurance companies and banks took over much of the land of small independent farmers." And then he puzzled, "I wonder how many times you have to be hit on the head before you find out who's hitting you?" The answer for farmers and the common people was in the defining difference between the parties: "The Democratic Party represents the people. . . . The Democratic Party puts human rights and human welfare first. . . . These Republican gluttons of privilege are cold men. They are cunning men. . . . They want a return of the Wall Street economic dictatorship."[41]

Dewey rejected this appeal to class, as McKinley and Hoover had, calling on Americans to "rediscover the essential unity of our people." But voters were more comfortable with leaders thinking from the bottom up and more confident of the Democratic claim on prosperity. The economy was booming, farm prices were up, and unemployment fell below 4 percent—despite fears of a post-war downturn. After the war, the Employment Act of 1946 affirmed in law that maximizing employment was now a central function of government. Escaping the Depression-era psychology and assumptions about scarcity and distribution, the Truman administration began to formalize America's commitment to economic growth and opportunity. Growth financed America's commitment to building its sturdy middle class— financial incentives set off a private construction boom, including five million new homes built before 1950, and paid GI benefits, including the reimbursement of college tuition and the underwriting of low-cost mortgages. Truman delivered for the common person, and they remembered.[42]

The Eisenhower interlude did little to challenge the Democratic ascendancy. Dwight Eisenhower explicitly accepted the New Deal and Social Security and governed more as a national hero than as a partisan figure. He offered no Republican vision of top-down prosperity. Indeed, he presided over recessions in 1953, 1958, and 1960, and in his second term unemployment averaged 6 to 7 percent, allowing John Kennedy to run under the banner of getting "the country moving again."

Kennedy put the Democratic stamp on growth economics—based on a now legitimate Keynesianism and on a confident American internationalism. Democrats now believed, as science, not just as an ideology, that the economy could be managed—in particular, when things turn bad, government could "stimulate" the economy to sustain growth and employment. In 1962, Kennedy proposed an investment tax credit to encourage business to create jobs, followed in 1963 by a major tax cut to stimulate consumer demand. The bottom-up vision no longer revolved around public works or public employment but around a federal commitment to producing economic growth. Though conservative Democrats in Congress hesitated because of continuing worries about balancing the budget and avoiding inflation, the Keynesian view won out when Lyndon Johnson put his stamp on it.[43]

The Democratic commitment to growth was buttressed by an expansive view of America's role in the world. Republicans traditionally had sought to protect U.S. industry and limit the country's dependence on world trade. McKinley was the author of the McKinley tariff, and Hoover gave us the highest barriers ever, Hawley-Smoot, which helped bring world trade to a near standstill. From Bryan to Roosevelt to Truman, Democrats had sought lower tariffs. Kennedy's Trade Expansion Act of 1962 represented an historic step toward free trade. Both Truman and Kennedy had earned their anti-Communist stripes, building alliances abroad and pushing the United States to a worldwide leadership position. Their confidence in America's ability to lead and grow allowed Americans an innocent faith in permanent growth—the apparent legacy of three decades of Democratic leadership.

Democratic Decay: Catholic America

Immigrant and Catholic America is at the center of this story, especially in regard to the Democratic party. Refugees from Ireland, Italy, Germany, and eastern Europe became middle America, torn between the values and interests of the major contending forces in America. They came to build America, to work in the factories and mines; they struggled to organize unions and to bring security to their work. They took over the big cities as their own, created their own neighborhoods, fraternal orders, and societies; they built communities around their churches and schools. And then they moved out to suburban places with backyards, like those in Macomb County. Others also figure in this story—from Scandinavia and Russia, some Protestant and some Jewish. Together they lived this American experience and helped form the middle ground that would arbitrate between the historic parties. But it is among Catholics that the struggle over ideas and ideologies has been most dramatic.

When Catholic America was won over to the New Deal formula for people and prosperity, the Democrats gained the national majority that would allow them to preside over the Great Democratic Era. It could not have happened without the Democrats' solid support in the South as well, but that was more about history and old wounds and the New Deal's spending for electrification, public works, and economic development.[44] It had little to do with the New Deal's vision or compact with working America. The battle of ideas was waged and won among Catholic voters. And later, when Catholics began to wonder about their place in this Democratic world, the Democratic ascendance would come undone and ultimately collapse.

That Catholics would come to play this role was first evident in the schools of Chelsea and New Bedford, Massachusetts, and Chicago. A report to Congress in 1910 showed that two out of every three pupils in these schools were the children of immigrants. At the same time, immigrants and their families constituted three quarters of the population of Milwaukee, Chicago, Cleveland, and Detroit. These immigrant children would soon dominate the cities as adults and form the core of New Deal

America. But they carried with them, even before the Depression, all the pain of urban poverty and impoverished working conditions.

It was Al Smith, the Democratic candidate for president in 1928, who first gave their Catholicism political expression. Al Smith was unapologetically Catholic and ran a campaign for urban and Catholic America. He drank openly, despite Prohibition, and spoke with an undisguised Irish brogue. This was no longer the party of Bryan, rural Protestantism, agrarian radicalism, and Prohibition, but it was just as much a common man's party as any Bryan had envisioned. Catholic states, like Massachusetts and Rhode Island, went Democratic for the first time, and immigrant cities began to take on a Democratic character: Boston voted 67 percent for Smith; New York, 60 percent; Milwaukee, 53 percent; and Cleveland, 52 percent. Wayne County, including Detroit, had been a Republican bastion in 1924, voting 75 to 80 percent for Republican candidates, but dropped to 62 percent in 1928 and then utterly collapsed, voting 39 percent Republican in 1932.

With the Depression and Franklin Roosevelt, the rest of urban and downscale America joined the Catholics to establish the ascendant New Deal coalition. By 1936, the Democrats were winning at least two thirds of the Catholic vote in nearly every city in the country. Roosevelt and the Democrats had become the primary instrument for championing ordinary people and protecting them from the adversities of modernization and for advancing a general prosperity. In 1946, 62 percent of Catholics still identified themselves as Democrats—double the number identifying themselves as Republicans. In 1948, Truman ran a campaign that affirmed the class polarization and party images. There was an affinity among Catholic voters for this "give 'em hell, Harry," who had little patience with the Communists and the economic and cultural elites.[45]

And yet the Democratic ascendancy began to erode almost at the moment of its creation, beginning with the Catholics who grew uncertain about their place in the coalition. Some of the discomfort was just a matter of turf wars. The Irish had been first on board and had corralled many of the county and party positions at the local level, but this coalition soon had to accommodate Italians, who clashed with Tammany Hall in New York, not to mention the intellectuals and others who had bigger ideas than patronage. Irish, Italian, and German voters also grew uncomfortable with Roosevelt's pro-British and anti-Axis (read, anti-German and Italian) views.

Catholic voters were looking for political alignments that respected their working-class way of life. They respected leaders who respected them—dirty hands and immigrant habits and all. Their bottom-up politics was not mere economic policy; it was cultural. The establishment had snubbed them, but they refused to blend in.

Defection from the Democrats began in 1940, though Roosevelt probably still took 60 percent of the Catholic vote in New York and 70 percent across New England. But there were important signs of defection in the New York City area: German and Irish voters in Queens, Irish and Italians on Staten Island, and Italians in Passaic and Jersey City, New Jersey.[46] Truman retook important ground in 1948, but the Republicans had regained control of the Congress in 1946 and 1950 with evident headway among Catholics.

While 1948 was consolidating for Catholics, it proved traumatic for the white South. Roosevelt left white dominance there largely undisturbed, but southern conservative leaders were right to believe that a Democratic party, serious about helping people and building from the bottom up, would eventually clash with the traditional prerogatives. While Democratic leaders in the South welcomed electricity and large-scale public works projects, they generally opposed legislation to set a minimum wage and recognize labor unions; they successfully excluded rural and domestic workers from the ambit of Social Security. And they also worried, rightly, that blacks might presume to think that they too were part of Roosevelt's social contract. Despite Roosevelt's extraordinary caution about race, the national Democratic party was becoming a threat to, rather than a prop for, white supremacy. The adoption of a strong civil rights plank at the Democratic convention in 1948 was a turning point, and the splinter candidacy of Strom Thurmond that year an ominous sign.

The losses in the South were real enough, but in an important sense they were artificial to the Roosevelt bottom-up vision. The South's support for national Democrats had little to do with the dominant images or ideology of this Democratic era; it was about white supremacy, not jobs programs. Democrats were supposed to suppress race as a national issue, thus allowing southern whites the space to develop economically while retaining their racial privileges.

But when the national Democrats took actions that undermined this historic bargain, many in the South felt free to move toward more natural positions on economic and other issues. That is why Eisenhower's biggest gains in 1952 came in metropolitan areas in the border South—Dallas and Houston, Texas; Richmond, Virginia; St. Petersburg, Florida—where the economic conservative vote was to be found. In this sense, the cracks in the Old South were drawing away votes from the dominant Democrats but also weakening some of the forces inside the party that opposed bottom-up policies.

But in the Deep South, in the Dixiecrat states, the Democrats began to lose ground among poorer whites—thus seeing the downscale Democratic base being cut away. These states came close to voting for Eisenhower in 1952, and all supported

him over Illinois's Governor Adlai Stevenson in 1956, as did
Florida, Tennessee, Texas, and Virginia in the border South. The
swing to Eisenhower in the Deep South brought along upper-
and lower-class whites—both of whom were looking for a new
home that would protect white privilege.[47]

But the defection of southern states on the race issue only
exaggerated the importance of immigrant Catholic voters on the
ideological and cultural issues. Catholics emerged from the Second World War as the swing vote without which it was impossible to imagine a bottom-up majority. They were the heart of
industrialized and metropolitan America outside the South.
Senator Joe McCarthy exposed the tension in the Democratic
camp: he did not offer Catholic communities any notion of
Republican prosperity, but he reached working- and lower-
middle-class voters by attacking what the historian Kevin Phillips
described as the "conspiracy, subversion and betrayal of the establishment." He sought to unmask the alleged Communists in government and warred with the cultural elites in Hollywood. The
Irish liked this tough anti-Communist and anti-establishment
figure who was openly supported by the hierarchy of the
Church. He tarred Democrats as cultural elitists soft on communism, thus appealing to many of the anti-Soviet immigrants from
eastern Europe.

Rather than return to populism or to a direct appeal to
downscale voters, the Democrats in 1952 muted the party's class
appeal and identification. Adlai Stevenson was uncomfortable
with the rhetoric of Roosevelt and Truman. In his elegant
speeches, there was no class war, no "economic royalists"—and
no cultural affinity with immigrant America. He dropped Truman's call for universal health insurance, distanced himself from
most of the Fair Deal and big labor. Stevenson was urbane and
witty, and the Democrats made significant gains among those
with above-average incomes, particularly the college educated

and professionals. Indeed, upscale identification with the Democrats rose between 1956 and 1964, at which point Democrats
outnumbered Republicans among college-educated voters and
professionals. That landmark, however, represented a fundamental blurring of this Democratic era: it was less and less centered
on the working culture of the country.

Kevin Phillips makes much of the switch. In the 1950s and
early 1960s, silk-stocking areas, along with Jewish and black
neighborhoods, were becoming Democratic. There is something
odd and revealing about a so-called bottom-up party when it is
doing so well in Scarsdale and Beacon Hill and along Park and
Fifth Avenues.

General Eisenhower made the swing away from the
Democrats easy for Catholic immigrant voters and, as we saw
earlier, southern whites. The Republicans gave up the challenge
to the New Deal and offered no economic vision of their own.
But they offered a strong, patriotic, nonpolitical, and unifying
figure open to Americans of all stripes, thus furthering the
Democratic decay.

Eisenhower benefited from the declining association of
Catholics with the Democratic party: a 31-point Democratic
advantage in 1940 declined to 23 points in 1948 and to 20
points in 1956. That decay was transforming Catholics into a
swing bloc, accounting for most of the tide toward Eisenhower, in both 1952 and 1956. Eisenhower carried 44 percent
of the Catholic vote in 1952 and 49 percent in 1956. He ran up
big numbers in Catholic and immigrant centers in the Northeast, like Staten Island (77 percent); Jersey City (62 percent)
and Perth Amboy (61 percent), New Jersey; Fall River (58 percent), Massachusetts; and Providence (56 percent); and in low-
income Irish, Italian, and Polish areas in Chicago. In 1952,
Eisenhower confounded any top-down or bottom-up view
of the world when he won a majority of the high-school-

educated voters and, astonishingly, broke even among those with even less education.

A Catholic John Kennedy's candidacy halted the decay. Catholics cast 70 percent of their votes for this Democrat who embodied the immigrant dream. Kennedy ran well in Irish, Italian, and Polish precincts in the Midwest and brought Catholic Democrats back to the fold in Jersey City, Perth Amboy, and Scranton. Indeed, all across New England, Democratic support in the Catholic areas returned to the 1948 Truman levels. In the new suburban areas where immigrants were redefining the American dream, Kennedy touched Catholic voters. He took 63 percent in suburban Macomb County. In his own special way, he retold the immigrant story and tried to reassociate it with the Democratic leadership of the country. This was a Democrat who lived and idealized his ethnicity, honored family, disliked Communists, and attacked the Republican recessions that had left America stagnant. Kennedy was no populist in a Truman mold, but he reopened the Democratic door to the values of the lower middle class.[48]

In 1964, however, even as Lyndon Johnson piled up Democratic majorities across the country, there were signs of change and decay. The Deep South became the geographic center of the Republican party as Goldwater carried the Dixiecrat states of South Carolina, Mississippi, Alabama, Louisiana and Georgia. Goldwater, who opposed the Civil Rights Act, demonstrated that a conservative Republican could appeal successfully to poor whites, at least in the Black Belt, where racial sensibilities were aroused. In the North, George Wallace took almost a third of the Democratic primary vote in Indiana and Wisconsin. He carried white working-class areas in Gary, Hammond, and East Chicago, Indiana, and the Polish areas of Milwaukee. The Great Democratic Era was losing its historic force from the bottom up.[49]

Neither Kennedy's triumphant years nor Lyndon Johnson's landslide win over Goldwater stopped the decay that threatened the Democratic ascendancy. The bottom-up vision needed to be renewed if it were to capture the imagination of these ethnic voters reborn in suburban America. It needed to find new ways to rebuild identification with the Democratic party, new ways to protect people and ensure prosperity.

4. FAILED RENEWAL: THE GREAT SOCIETY

POLITICAL life in the aftermath of the two great-party dramas was muddled but also benign. Ordinary Americans had survived a great war and the Depression. They were busy tending to their dreams, which now included cars and yards and college. For millions of black sharecroppers, the burgeoning cities offered their own version of the American dream. Rock and roll was ascendant, and so was the new confidence in growth and American strength. *Sputnik* was a party wrecker, to be sure, but few doubted that the United States would lead, maybe even to the moon.

And politics? It was settled and boring, and even if electorally inconclusive, for most Americans it was okay. The New Deal and the Cold War were off the political bargaining table, protected by a bipartisan consensus that suppressed debate about anything really interesting. There was no sign of an aggressive, self-confident pro-business Republicanism. Andrew Mellon and Calvin Coolidge were still in the closet. President Dwight Eisenhower represented the country's comfort with its postwar and post-Depression identity. Stevenson and Kennedy did little to disturb things and left the common man in the Democratic closet. Top-down and bottom-up politics had just become a blur in the middle.

Presidents were generally popular and were trusted as a matter of course. Two thirds said they "approved" of Eisenhower's performance as soon as he was inaugurated; just 7 percent were disgruntled and disapproving. Public approval remained in that range or higher—one month reaching 79 percent—until the recession of 1958, when it dipped just below 50 percent. At that low point, 36 percent, about a third of the population, expressed negative views of the president. John Kennedy assumed office in this era of good feeling: 72 percent expressed immediate approval for this glittering and young presidency, and 78 percent stood by his successor, Lyndon Johnson, in the aftermath of the assassination. The disgruntled and alienated could barely be found by pollsters: 6 percent as Kennedy assumed the presidency and 2 percent for Johnson.[1]

In contrast to the simmering anger today, three quarters of Americans believed you could always or usually trust the government in Washington to do "the right thing": 73 percent in 1958, rising to 76 percent in 1964. Nearly two thirds (64 percent) thought the government was run for the benefit of all, not for the special interests. In 1960, three quarters (73 percent) rejected the idea that public officials were indifferent to ordinary people like themselves.[2]

But the country's mood, for all its serenity, was disquieting. America got its first taste of gridlock. Divided government at the outset of the 1950s and a congressional impasse right up to Kennedy's death left domestic political life inconclusive. Nixon and Kennedy debated the fate of some obscure islands, Quemoy and Matsu, and Kennedy offered a vague commitment to get the country "moving." He won in 1960, but not easily and only after the Republicans, once again, stood stubbornly silent before a deepening recession. In the end, Kennedy managed only 50.1 percent of the vote, and growth states like Florida and California were lost to the Republicans. The Democrats won Texas and

Illinois by a hair, but only by putting a Texan on the ticket and pushing Chicago's Daley machine to some of its most creative moments. In the midterm elections of 1962, the Democrats garnered only 52.7 percent of the congressional vote. At the time of Kennedy's death, the president's domestic program—including Medicare, aid to education, and mass transit—was bottled up in Congress and his popularity falling. In this benign and muddled political world, neither party could establish a firm or governing majority. The two great-party eras and great partisan ideas that had shaped modern America now seemed muted and without much force.

The still was shattered by the Great Society—Lyndon Johnson's bold and ultimately failed attempt to master the racial upheavals and changing world of the 1960s. In the process, he sought to remake and renew the Democratic party's vision and constitute a new governing majority. While John Kennedy had sought to contain and put off the consequences of the emerging race issue, Johnson accepted the historic challenge and gambled on his ability to overturn the political order and create something new based on moral and enduring principles.

America was forever changed by the fury of the political debate between 1964 and 1968. In that short period, the country struggled with historic challenges at home and abroad that redefined America and the American dream. Old assumptions came under siege—in the family and the neighborhoods, in the U.S. capital, and on the world stage. And the backlash in defense of convention contained its own fury that reshuffled forever the identity of the political parties. The Democratic association with the people emerged narrow and racial, even elitist, stripped of pretensions about growth and prosperity and weighed down by taxes and big government. Republicans, now under the banner of law and order, suddenly found themselves able to reach down and carry on a conversation with working America.

It was a period that began with idealism and a sense of certainty. Lyndon Johnson had vanquished the extremist Barry Goldwater, who might have tampered with Social Security and the bomb. A momentous civil rights struggle captured the moral high ground in the battle against a brutish racism in the South. The bipartisan consensus, reflecting America's expanded conscience, now stretched to include civil rights and equal justice. Democrats and Republicans joined together to break the white southern stranglehold on the Constitution. Upon signing the Civil Rights Act of 1964, Lyndon Johnson told a national TV audience about America's new view of racial discrimination: "Our Constitution, the foundation of our republic, forbids it. The principles of our freedom forbid it. Morality forbids it. And the law I will sign tonight forbids it." The Civil Rights Act of 1964 and the Voting Rights Act of 1965 had passed with overwhelming Republican support in both houses.[3] Official America was now opposed to racism and supportive of broad initiatives to achieve racial justice—to overcome the legacy of slavery and America's century-long indifference to white supremacy. Unofficial America was less enthusiastic about the new principles, though even it became part of a new national consensus opposed to discrimination and racism. That is Lyndon Johnson's legacy to the country.

In crushing the conservative challenge in 1964, Johnson offered his new vision of a Great Society. It included civil rights and a War on Poverty but much more as well—a social compact that addressed human needs in a broad range of areas: medical care for seniors and the poor, federal aid to the public schools and to college students, assistance for Appalachia, a higher minimum wage, targeted assistance to the cities, housing for low-income families, and a new federal department for housing and the cities. It also included new initiatives in the arts, environmental regulation, and consumer protection.[4] Lyndon Johnson became the voice of America's moral obligation to achieve social change, and at the outset the American people stood with the president; they supported his first major civil rights initiatives, Medicare, aid to education, and even the War on Poverty—the latter, by 73 to 27 percent. More than 60 percent approved of his performance in office right to the end of 1965.

But the images of peaceful ministers and college students being beaten by southern rednecks soon gave way to more ambiguous pictures and a bolder challenge to the established order. The rioting that swept Watts in 1965 spread in 1966 to Chicago, Cleveland, and 41 other cities; in 1967, it spread to 164 cities and included especially violent upheavals in Newark and Detroit; and after the assassination of Martin Luther King in April 1968, it spread to almost every city in America. King, even before his death, was competing for space with black-power leaders like Stokely Carmichael, H. Rap Brown, Huey Newton and Bobby Seale, all defiantly trampling on white sensibilities. At the same time, America faced growing protests against the country's involvement in Vietnam. The cameras shifted from the growing popular opposition to flag burning, Yippies, drugs, and counterculture. In communities across the country, people believed that social order was breaking down, and crime statistics demonstrated a growing assault on the lawful. By the end of 1968, the concern with civil rights was overtaken by the concern with crime and racial strife.[5]

The Democrats pretended through it all that the focus on the rights and the needs of black and urban America was simply an extension of bottom-up principles—just the next generation of the common person championed by the party of the people. The 1964 landslide, after passage of the Civil Rights Act and affirmation of the War on Poverty, only confirmed the Democrats' renewed sense of purpose. There was no necessary contradiction between their identification with blue-collar and middle

America and their commitment to civil rights. The UAW, after all, had moved to the front ranks of the 1963 March on Washington for Jobs and Freedom. In a 1967 address to the nation, Johnson declared that "conscience" required that the country relieve the conditions of poverty:

> The only genuine, long-range solution for what has happened lies in an attack—mounted at every level—upon the conditions that breed despair and violence. All of us know what those conditions are: ignorance, discrimination, slums, poverty, disease, not enough jobs. We should attack these conditions—not because we are frightened by conflict, but because we are fired by conscience.[6]

For Johnson, that conscience was a drive to uplift the downtrodden and make equality a reality, thus redeeming the unrealized promises of the New Deal bottom-up compact. Tackling civil rights was taking up the reforms that Roosevelt had left incomplete or unaddressed.[7]

Johnson's interpretation of the contract with downscale America required jettisoning the Bull Connorses and George Wallaces of the Deep South, but the Democrats did not dare walk away from the old ethnic neighborhoods in the cities or the new middle-class neighborhoods in the suburbs. Despite the bitter clashes in 1968 on the streets of Chicago, they did not dare disown Mayor Daley. For all the bravado at the 1972 Democratic convention, including the expulsion of Daley and his Chicago delegates, McGovern sued for peace. Yet Johnson's redemption of the New Deal contract offered anything but enduring tranquility.

With the advent of school busing, it was no longer possible to avoid the clash of interests and the clash over the meaning of *bottom up*. The different dreams of the Democratic base were about to clash in the school yards of suburban America. Before the end of Johnson's term, it was apparent that the battle for racial equality would not be confined to small towns in the South. The courts were confronting the problems of metropolitan segregation, both North and South, and proposing radical new vehicles for effecting change. The Supreme Court rejected volunteerism and "freedom of choice," and the Johnson Justice Department began bringing suits against northern suburbs, such as those of Chicago, Indianapolis, Tulsa, and St. Louis. In the early Nixon administration, the battle for civil rights became a battle over court-ordered busing, which produced a firestorm in cities like Detroit. It also brought home the debilitating contradiction at the heart of this attempt to remake the Democratic party. Thomas and Mary Edsall rightly observe that "busing transformed the politics of city after city. . . . it drove home with most clarity the realization that the new liberal agenda would demand some of the largest changes in habit and custom from the working-class residents of low and moderate-income enclaves within the big cities—enclaves with often heavily Irish, Polish, Italian, or Slavic populations."[8]

RACE AND THE END OF DEMOCRATIC POPULISM

Democrats had labored for perhaps a century to keep race off the national agenda—at no little cost to black Americans. The Democrats had fashioned a party of the people, a bottom-up party, but one created within a national political space that was largely and artificially white. As long as they could suppress the race issue, they could pretend that this fiction did not matter. So the national Democrats under William Jennings Bryan, even as they were reaching out to the common person, stayed silent as white supremacist Democrats in the South drove blacks off the voter rolls and into segregated Jim Crow schools, trains, and public accommodations. Some populist factions in the South broke with convention and allied with the blacks, but the Democrats' common person only occasionally came to encompass black sharecroppers. In the South, the Democratic party romanticized its white-supremacist history—having overthrown the Reconstructionist regimes and protected the white South against federal intervention. Woodrow Wilson (a native Virginian) paid respect to southern white sensibilities by segregating the civil service and the nation's capital to the extent possible. The growing urbanization of blacks in the North brought some patronage, some seats at the national convention, and even some representation—in 1934, a black congressman from Chicago—but the Democrats still preferred silence on the question of racial equality. That silence allowed the party to build a majority atop white immigrants in the North, farmers in the West, and poor whites in the South with the assent of the southern oligarchy.[9]

In the Depression, blacks gravitated to the New Deal despite the silence because there were genuine benefits; broad gains were made by all workers and farm laborers. But the social insurance at the heart of the New Deal—old-age and unemployment insurance—barely touched blacks. States were given great latitude in setting benefit levels, and farm and low-wage service occupations were excluded from coverage, leaving the black South largely outside the New Deal social contract. Roosevelt appointed more blacks to federal positions, but he steadfastly refused to back any civil rights legislation, fearing that southern opposition would jeopardize his overall economic program. Between 1937 and 1946, over 150 bills on the poll tax, lynching, and fair employment were introduced into the Democratic Congress, but none got Roosevelt's support and none passed. Roosevelt's wartime executive order barring racial discrimination was limited in scope and was repealed after the war.[10]

Harry Truman was the first national leader to breach this silence as northern Democrats, like Hubert Humphrey from Minnesota, began to demand a more inclusive race-neutral bottom-up vision. But those brave moments were the exception; and Democrats continued to suppress racial issues throughout the 1940s and 1950s. Adlai Stevenson went out of his way in 1952 and 1956 to reassure the white South and to invite southern voters back into the Democratic camp—seeking to avoid another Dixiecrat rebellion. He warned against moving too fast on racial equality, recognizing that southern leaders were dealing in good faith with "their local difficulties" and pledging his belief that "further government interference with free men, free markets, free ideas, is distasteful to many people of good will."

The truth is that before 1960 the Republicans were more in the vanguard on civil rights—in their party platforms and in congressional voting. Dwight Eisenhower had ordered federal troops into Little Rock in 1957 to enforce the integration of public schools, and he also introduced civil rights legislation that year. As late as 1960, voters found the parties indistinguishable on the race issue.[11]

The Democrats were the party of liberalism in 1960, but in those times liberalism lacked a racial character. The Democrats were associated with the advancement of social welfare policies, but in the public mind that had little to do with achieving racial equality.[12]

John Kennedy's now famous inaugural address that challenged the nation and a generation to take up the torch and demonstrate vigilance in the defense of freedom did not mention civil rights. In the final draft, Kennedy had reluctantly extended America's commitment to "human rights . . . around the world" to include people "at home." He urged patience on the civil rights leaders and the freedom riders in the South and urged his own officials to keep him out of "this Goddamned civil rights mess." With the concerns of the Michigan congressional delegation in mind, he delayed introduction of an executive order on housing until after the 1962 midterm elections. Congresswoman Martha Griffiths had warned the president:

> Most of the white people have resigned themselves to the fact of integration, but the suburbs of Detroit believe it will be years before it applies to their exact areas. . . . No Democratic Congressman, from suburbia, to whom I have talked, believes he is in any danger of losing colored votes; but he does feel such an order could cost white votes.
>
> In case the counsel of those seated less close to the fire than I am prevails, however, and I lose this election. . . . Can I have the next Supreme Court vacancy, where I can legislate in safety far from the prejudices of the precincts?

But the rising tide of civil rights protests and the recalcitrance of southern leaders finally forced Kennedy to act. Almost two and a half years into his term, Kennedy introduced comprehensive civil rights legislation.[13]

By 1964, the civil rights rebellion in the South and the massive black immigration to northern cities exposed the contradictions in the Democrats' strategy. Their bottom-up vision could no longer be forged in a white political space, and the party responded to this historic challenge by becoming the champions of racial equality. Yet even as they advanced justice, they produced a profound trauma for the party and the country. There was a political explosion in the white rural South and the white urban North as old alignments were shattered and, perhaps more important, *bottom up* was redefined in racial terms. For a brief moment, it looked as if Johnson's renewed commitment to equality would offer a new social agenda and forge a new majority. But in the process, the president fused liberalism and racial liberalism, the Democratic party and racial equality. Social welfare lost its broader meaning. The Republicans, by opposing this new agenda, reached down into the Democrats' old downscale base and challenged their claim to speak for working America.

The redefinition was formalized when Lyndon Johnson looked into the TV cameras and proclaimed, "We shall overcome." He placed the nation irretrievably and without reservation behind the principle of racial equality, but he also shattered the Democratic party's silence on race and, indeed, took ownership of the issue. Johnson elaborated Kennedy's civil rights proposals and advanced a sweeping federal takeover of the electoral process in seven southern states. Black registration in Mississippi, as a consequence, increased from a half a percent in 1960 to two thirds by 1970. In 1965, on the eve of the passage of the Voting Rights Act, Johnson told a Howard University audience that for all the progress, this was just the "end of the beginning." America was entering "the more profound stage of the battle for civil rights": "We seek not just legal equity, but human ability, not just equality as a right and a theory but equality as a fact and equality as a result."[14]

As political scientists Edward G. Carmines and James A. Stimson observe, the Democrats were becoming "the home of racial liberalism." The party platforms built to a crescendo of racial affirmation: from 1968's hailing of landmark civil rights legislation to 1972's call for "enacting new legal rights" to accomplish "a more equal distribution of power, income, and wealth" and its support of busing to eliminate school segregation. The Democratic nominees who followed Johnson—Hubert Humphrey and George McGovern—proudly associated the party with this new vision of equality.[15]

The Republicans responded with an affirmation of a different kind. In 1964, the national Republican party broke with the national and official consensus on civil rights—and with the party's own history since the Civil War. At the time, the northeastern liberal wing of the party thought it an aberration. But

Barry Goldwater, who voted against the Civil Rights Act of 1964, sent a message heard loudly in the Deep South, where the overwhelming majority of lower-income whites voted Republican; even in defeat, he sent a message to the nation that conservatism and racial conservatism were being joined. Four years later Richard Nixon backtracked slightly on the issue, accepting the Civil Rights Acts as settled law but declaring during the campaign that no further laws were needed. He ran under the banner of law and order and set the party against "federal intervention." Though the Nixon administration sent some mixed signals on civil rights at the outset, the Justice Department intervened, for the first time in a generation, to slow desegregation and to oppose busing. Nixon nominated a series of high-profile southern white conservatives to the Supreme Court (though two were rejected by the Senate) and before the 1972 election advanced his own anti-busing legislation that would put a moratorium on further court-ordered busing.[16]

Nixon could be more polite and indirect because George Wallace was not. Nixon mounted the main assault on the Great Society and racial liberalism, whereas Wallace led a protest of the common man—largely white and downscale voters who historically had found their home within the Democratic party. In 1964, the Alabama governor took his rebellion to the northern Democratic primaries, where he captured a very large proportion of the white Democratic base: 33.9 percent in Wisconsin, 29.9 percent in Indiana, and 42.7 percent in Maryland. In 1968, he took his cause to the Democratic primaries and then, in an independent candidacy, to the suburban white ethnic neighborhoods and the bastions of organized labor. He attacked the "liberals and intellectuals—intellectual morons" who had "destroyed the federal government." He attacked the federal government for "trifling" with children and for invading people's property and homes. Above all, Wallace made his appeal to the common person, who was no longer represented by the disfigured Democratic party:

> I think that if the politicians get in the way in 1968, a lot of
> them are going to get run over by the average man in the
> street, this man in the textile mill, this man in the steel mill,
> this barber, the beautician, the policeman on the beat. They
> are the ones—and the little businessman—I think those are
> the mass of people that are going to support a change on
> the domestic scene.

Wallace marched into Cicero, Illinois, and offered this immigrant suburb a populist window on the world. He attacked "these newspaper editors, that look down their nose at every workingman in Cicero, on every workingman in the United States and calls them a group of red-necks or a group of punks." By rejecting the racial agenda of the intellectuals and bureaucrats, his movement would offer a real domestic agenda for the common person, which means "we're talking about schools, we're talking about hospitals, we're talking about the seniority of a workingman in his labor union, we're talking about ownership of property." That 21 percent stood ready to support Wallace, at least in the opinion polls in mid-September, and that 14 percent voted for him in November, represented a white populist critique of the Democratic party's attempt to redefine itself.[17]

Kevin Phillips, as strategist for the 1968 Nixon campaign and conservative interpreter of the 1968 upheaval, was explicit about the politicization of the race issue and the Republicans' goal of making the Democratic party a "Negro party." This was not idle theorizing. The Republican campaign understood that the Democratic coalition was in trouble because the ascendant liberalism of the Great Society "aligned that party with Negro demands" but proved incapable of coping with the civil rights revolution or diffusing the racial tensions in the country. The demands, instead, became primary Democratic principles—

seemingly displacing the Democrats' broad interest in economic populism. Now the poorer whites in both the North and the South were open to Republican candidates and social conservatism, which could respond to this "populist revolt of the American masses." Indeed, in 1968, four out of five white southerners voted for either Wallace or Nixon. Phillips cynically urged Nixon to continue civil rights enforcement to further the transformation: blacks would gravitate to the Democratic party, and southern racial conservatives would be further "pressured into switching to the Republican Party." In Phillips's view of the world, there was now a new primary divide in American politics formed by the "Negro socioeconomic revolution" and the Democrats' association with black demands.[18]

Some of the execution was clumsy and even unsuccessful in the short term, but the Nixon administration reinforced these racial and elitist associations. Spiro Agnew described the project as a "positive polarization of the electorate." He associated Nixon with "the silent majority" counterposed to the "radical liberals," who ran under the cloak of the Democratic party. The elites poured abuse on him, but Agnew was unapologetic about his purpose. "Dividing the American people has been my main contribution to the national political scene since assuming the office of vice president," he declared. "I not only plead guilty to this charge, but I am somewhat flattered by it."[19]

The civil rights revolution and the hard work on both the Democratic and Republican sides produced a radical transformation of America's ideological world. The liberal-conservative division, which was full of internal contradictions and lacked a racial character in 1960, had been transformed into two coherent worldviews that by 1972 were predominantly racial in character. It is hard to underestimate the importance of this change. Carmines and Stimson, in their groundbreaking study using national surveys from 1972, demonstrated that liberal-conservative ideology was now explained primarily by beliefs about integration and black protests (and to a lesser extent by views on individual rights, marijuana, and Vietnam).

But perhaps just as important, Carmines and Stimson found that the liberal-conservative dimension had lost its class character: liberalism was no longer correlated with populist beliefs, such as taxing the wealthy. The great struggle to renew the Democratic party had offered a new mission for the disadvantaged but in the process had allowed the old bottom-up view of the world to pass from the Democratic orbit. It is doubtful that Democratic leaders could have affirmed their support for racial equality and escaped the ire of working- and lower-middle-class white voters. These historic and necessary changes simply put too much of the old order at risk. But the consequences were real enough: this party of the disadvantaged was no longer a bottom-up party.[20]

THE END OF UNIVERSALITY

The New Deal had offered people a form of social insurance against the uncertainties of modern industrial America. In practice, the policies were incomplete—for example, excluding farm and low-wage service workers—but over time, Democrats and Republicans competed to fill in the holes. Unemployment benefits were extended, as were retirement benefits, and Medicare was introduced. The social insurance was universal—available to all who contributed without means testing in times of adversity (illness and unemployment), in old age, and at retirement. The system was hostile to "welfare" and dependency and partial to employment and growth. As Ted Marmor and other social scientists define it, "Social insurance is designed to help families maintain the security they have achieved through productive

work." Nearly everybody within the purview of Roosevelt's
vision had a vested interest in preserving this social insurance
network that they had helped fund.[21]

While Kennedy introduced some programs targeted at the
poor, particularly in Appalachia, he highlighted those that would
expand the universal contract. In his run for president in 1960,
Kennedy mentioned health insurance for the elderly in almost
every speech and, indeed, introduced Medicare legislation in the
Senate to elevate the issue in the campaign's last months. In the
first two years of his presidency, Kennedy only rarely devoted his
energies to any domestic initiative. Cuba, Berlin, Khrushchev,
and Vietnam were consuming. Yet in May 1962 the administration organized a campaign of thirty rallies to support the enact-
ment of Medicare, topped by a rally at Madison Square Garden
that was carried by the three television networks.[22]

But faced with the civil rights rebellion, Lyndon Johnson
changed the character of this social contract. The problems of
black America, Johnson declared at Howard University, are distinct and entrenched: "Negro poverty is not white poverty." The
widening gulf between the races suggests "another nation" and
a unique "American failure." He promised to "dedicate the
expanding efforts of the Johnson administration" on all "fronts"
and on "a dozen more." Over 70 percent of Johnson's legislative
Great Society initiatives were targeted at the poor, particularly
black poverty. Thirty-nine new program initiatives had doubled
the amount of federal spending on the poor by the end of the
1960s. The War on Poverty established community-action projects in cities and communities all across America—in effect,
creating for the poor separate social welfare institutions whose
client base was half minority. And Johnson attached means-
tested programs like food stamps, Medicaid, and subsidized
housing to the existing, previously universal social-insurance
institutions.[23]

But this shift of America's social welfare policies to disadvantaged populations was a trap that threatened to undermine the political foundations of social insurance. Johnson advanced a moral and national purpose that carried the people with him for only a few short years. By 1967, 60 to 70 percent of the public thought the administration had gone "too far"; only 17 percent of whites in 1968 thought the War on Poverty was doing a good job. In the end, the identification of the Great Society with the poor alone marginalized the beneficiaries, dissipated public support, and blocked any broad, enduring alignment of black and white support for dependable social insurance.[24] Even broad programs, like Medicare, were obscured by the dominant focus on the disadvantaged. These were angry times that left little room for tolerance and broad social purpose. Idealism and racism clashed, and the Democrats placed their hopes for renewal with the former. But for middle America, that idealism represented a kind of betrayal, turning the social insurance of Franklin Roosevelt into the welfare of Lyndon Johnson. Kevin Phillips immediately recognized the consequences of this shift for the old bottom-up party: "As liberalism metamorphosed from an economic populist stance—supporting farm, highway, health, education and pension expenditures against conservative budget-cutting—into a credo of social engineering, it lost the support of poor whites."[25]

Some twenty years later, after years of defensiveness and defeat, New York's Governor Mario Cuomo tried to elevate and broaden the Democratic vision contained in the Great Society. At the 1984 Democratic convention, he advanced "the idea of family, mutuality, the sharing of benefits and burdens for the good of all: feeling one another's pain; sharing one another's blessings reasonably, honestly, fairly—without respect to race or sex or geography or political affiliation." The party, he said, is driven by a mission to feel and "avoid pain," while to do otherwise would be "our failure."[26] The delegates cheered this unapologetic assertion of a Democratic mission, but this was a mission of compassion and sharing, a mission to address the needs of those hurting the most. It left middle America wondering about its own pain and when that would motivate the passions of the Democratic party.

THE END OF GROWTH AND THE DEMOCRATIC EMPIRE

The Democratic vision once told a story whose last chapter was optimism and growth. Against the backdrop of the Depression and in the face of a hostile world, the party gave life to public and collective effort; it honored work and stood with working people against corporate power; it sold social insurance against the prospect of adversity; it won acceptance for an economic model that encouraged government spending and rising personal incomes as positive social principles; and it sought to secure the future by promoting an American hegemony on a world scale.

But the New Deal vision sank in the mire of Vietnam. The assurance of economic security for America's workers was an optimism born of national greatness, embedded in an expansive view of America's interests and role in the world. The rapid growth of productivity, employment, real wages, and exports in the years following the Second World War seemed to confirm the link between America's economic promise and its world role. John Kennedy was the last Democratic president to articulate this expansive vision. He advanced a vision of America that was central to New Deal liberalism, a vision of America as a leader among nations, as a model, as rich but generous, respected and envied. He understood the unique identity that allows Americans to feel special and secure.[27]

The humiliations in Vietnam challenged that vision and, consequently, the hold of Democratic ideas on America's workers. The Johnson administration reduced Kennedy's expansive vision to a crude struggle with communism and to an international game of dominoes that the United States seemed on the verge of losing. Worn down by the bitter party battles over America's overextended Vietnam-era military posture, the Democrats began to pull back from the country's world role. This retreat would bear its bitter fruit during the protracted Iran hostage crisis of 1979–81 and, when accompanied by Soviet adventurism in Afghanistan, would leave the Democrats without any credible posture on national security.

The economic theories of John Maynard Keynes had been a wonder for Democrats. Armed with his model and his assumptions, they could advocate income growth for the working population, increased consumer demand, and government spending. Such policies served both the particular interests of their electoral base and the universal interest in stable economic growth, allowing them to preach both class politics and economic expansion. There was a unity in their economic thinking that inspired confidence that the Democrats knew where they were taking the country. Indeed, when Kennedy won the presidency in 1960, the Democrats enjoyed a fifteen-point advantage in the polls on the issue of their ability to "keep the country prosperous" (46 to 31 percent), which grew to thirty-two points for Lyndon Johnson in 1964 (53 to 21 percent).[28]

Kennedy's tax cuts and increased defense spending moved the country forward economically—unemployment dropped from 5.7 percent in 1963 to 4.5 percent in 1965—and enhanced the authority of the Democrats' Keynesian model. But the Great Society and the Vietnam War soon brought massive increases in government spending—up 8 percent a year (in real dollars), more than double the rate for the Kennedy presidency.

With the growing inflation, Johnson was forced to impose a 10 percent income tax surcharge in 1968. The Democrats suddenly no longer enjoyed any real advantage on the issue of the economy in the public mind—just three points in 1968 (37 to 34 percent).[29]

The high inflation, slow growth, and rising tax rates of the 1970s—and the high budget deficits of the 1980s—broke voter confidence in the Keynesian model and its assumptions. Stimulating demand through government spending looked profligate, seeming to favor recipients over the needs of society as a whole. Government largesse began to look like an extravagance that society could not afford, and middle-class voters, now ravaged by taxes and inflation, wondered how their interests were being served.[30]

The Democrats' shrinking world vision had stark and deflating consequences at home as the party failed to appreciate the connection between America's special place in the world and the vitality of its economic message.

FLIGHT FROM THE GREAT SOCIETY

In the 1968 presidential election, the American people rejected not only Lyndon Johnson and Hubert Humphrey but also a social contract premised on the needs of the most disadvantaged rather than on the needs of the people generally. The Democrats had responded to a changing America with courage and moral purpose, but the American people rejected their approach— much as it had spurned William Jennings Bryan's attempt some seventy years earlier to shape a changing industrial America to accommodate the needs of ordinary people.

The extent of the Democratic collapse was quite breathtaking. Humphrey took less than 43 percent of the vote, a collapse of 18 points from Johnson's high-water mark in 1964. The great majority of Americans voted for candidates who opposed the Great Society: 43 percent for Nixon and 14 percent for Wallace.

The Democratic collapse was most pronounced among downscale, lower-middle-class voters: manual workers (down 21 points), farmers (down 24 points), and high school graduates (down 20 points). In Delaware County, a white suburb of Philadelphia, Wallace support was strongest in skilled and unskilled blue-collar areas, the areas, in fact, where John Kennedy had run the strongest. Catholic immigrant voters, diverted by the Kennedy presidency, reacted sharply to the upheavals that were now taking place in their school yards. Only 27 percent of Catholics had voted for Goldwater in 1964, but by 1968, 37 percent crossed the line. In 1972, Catholic America would offer its verdict on the new Democratic party: two thirds voted Republican. Below the Mason-Dixon line, Kevin Phillips points out, "Hubert Humphrey was annihilated," taking less than 20 percent of the white vote, and so was the national Democratic party. In 1972, Nixon would take 78 percent of the white southern vote.[31]

That the Great Society vision was in trouble was already apparent in 1966. By September, a majority of the public for the first time concluded that the federal government was pushing civil rights too far. The Democrats splintered in Maryland to nominate a "home is your castle" Democrat; Republicans nationally gained eight statehouses, including the governorships of Arkansas and Florida, with Ronald Reagan winning election in California; Republicans doubled their numbers in state legislatures in the South, gained a net forty-seven seats in the U.S. House, and picked up U.S. senators in Tennessee, Texas, South Carolina, and Illinois, where white Chicago-area voters abandoned the liberal Paul Douglas.[32]

George Wallace's populist and racist campaign gave many of these defecting lower-middle-class white voters a vehicle for expressing their disaffection with the new Democratic direction without having to vote for a pro-business Republican. Wallace obviously ran strong in the South, carrying five Deep South states that had been looking elsewhere for some bulwark against integration and doing particularly well among poorer whites. But nationwide Wallace took his campaign into the working-class base of the Democrats, carrying 15 percent of those without a college degree and 15 percent of manual workers.

The Wallace populist campaign set off a national struggle on the shop floors, where unions had historically aligned their members with the Democrats. But race riots, federal support for busing, and targeted social welfare policies left these bastions unguarded before Wallace's fiery call to arms.

After Labor Day in the 1968 campaign, the Wallace presence began to be felt in the heart of the industrial Midwest. In Monroe, Michigan, a city dominated by Ford and paper manufacture, Wallace polled 27 percent. In Flint, site of the sit-down strikes, the workers at the GM Tenstedt plant, UAW Local 326, endorsed Wallace; at Local 599, the Buick plant, 49 percent voted for Wallace; at Local 659, the Chevrolet plant, the 20,000 UAW members decided to make no endorsement. The AFL-CIO polled its own members and found Wallace taking 25 percent of the vote in Pennsylvania and 32 percent in Connecticut.

The unions leaders organized a desperate campaign to win their members back to Hubert Humphrey. The Machinists, UAW, Steelworkers, and AFL-CIO attacked Wallace's labor record in Alabama—a low-wage right-to-work state with primitive child-labor laws and a union-busting highway patrol. They won some voters over but not enough to turn the election or to restore the party's working-class base. Law and order, not solidarity forever, would govern the immediate future. Among white union households, Nixon took 42 percent of the vote and Wallace won 15 percent in the end (including 22 percent of white union members themselves), leaving Humphrey with an embarrassing 43 percent in the core of the organized downscale electorate. In 1972, Nixon's union vote would climb to 60 percent, leaving the Democrats' proud labor history in tatters.[33]

Blacks joined this renewed Democratic party in 1964 and have proved loyal supporters ever since, almost always giving Democrats over 90 percent of their votes. The massive black shift to the Democrats has kept the party competitive, particularly in the South, but it could not compensate nationally for the massive defection of southern whites, northern Catholics, and union members. This new social contract bound minority and many professional and better-educated liberal voters together in their own project of national and party renewal. It was a marriage, to paraphrase David Apter, of the functional elites and the marginal to create new social meaning—probably at the expense of a middle class that was losing standing.[34] But the middle class was in revolt.

EXPLOSION OF ALIENATION

The failure of Democratic renewal between 1964 and 1972 brought an explosion of distrust and alienation. This period was characterized by events of extraordinary scale—from the civil rights marches and urban riots to the Vietnam War and anti-war protests, framed on either end by assassinations. It brought what E. J. Dionne describes as a "cultural civil war" that trapped and distorted our political debate; it produced a "flight from public life." Kevin Phillips goes even further, writing that "the 1960s and 1970s were second only to the Civil War and the decade preceding it as a time of national breakdown."[35]

We now understand that this was the biggest explosion in disaffection before the present time. Belief that the government could be trusted to do "what is right" dropped 22 points between 1964 and 1970; belief that government is run "for the benefit of all people," not for the "few big interests," dropped 26 points between 1964 and 1972. Before all this upheaval, 64 percent of Americans believed that government worked for the people, and by the end just 38 percent believed so. In 1960, three quarters rejected the idea that politicians did not care "what people like me think," but by 1972 less than half held on to this faith. (See Appendix, Figure A.1.) In this period, voters discovered government waste: the belief that there is "a lot" of it jumped from 49 percent to 69 percent—where it remains to this day. At the end of the period, confidence in Congress collapsed to just 21 percent—half of the confidence level of 1966. Confidence in the executive branch of the federal government was only slightly higher, at 27 percent.[36] (See Appendix, Figure A.2.)

People expressed their disaffection by staying away from the polls: turnout dropped 5.2 percentage points (from 62.3 to 57.1 percent) between the elections of 1968 and 1972—the biggest drop in voter turnout for a presidential election since 1944 and 1920, when world wars took millions of people away from the polls.[37]

There is a temptation to associate this upheaval with the Vietnam War because for so many today that war was the defining event of that time. Indeed, many voters look back at Vietnam and focus less on the war than on the "deceit," as reflected in these 1990 comments: "Aside from my friends being killed, was that . . . it finally hit me how rotten our government really can be." "My own personal anger. Where does it come from? It comes from being deceived." "I think the Vietnam War did more to destroy American people's faith in government than anything else. . . . No question. . . . They just lied to us." "My country was leading a path of deceit."[38]

Although the war clearly exacerbated public alienation from government and political leaders, it alone cannot account for the scale of this upheaval. As Arthur H. Miller found in his early work on alienation during the 1960s, political trust among white voters plummeted before discontent with the war became pervasive. Indeed, a majority of Americans did not clearly turn against the war until mid-1968.[39] The failed Vietnam War and the "deceit" no doubt contributed mightily to the rising alienation in America, but the explosion of the mid-1960s was mainly rooted in civil rights, riots, and the Great Society. They produced, Miller writes, a decisive block of "alienated individuals who are fearful of change."[40]

The Democratic party under Lyndon Johnson faced a historic challenge and sought to revitalize itself as a people party by enfranchising and incorporating millions of black Americans and by championing the needs of the disadvantaged. It produced an historic tumult. By politicizing and nationalizing the race issue, both parties effected a wholesale upheaval in party politics. For white middle-class America, this tumult represented a broken contract that alienated the citizenry from politics.

◆　◆　◆　◆

After losing the 1980 presidential nomination to Jimmy Carter, Ted Kennedy spoke to the Democratic convention at Madison Square Garden. He returned at this late date to the image of a Democratic party that had been crushed by the wreckage of failed renewal and middle-class revolt. He reconnected the party with Thomas Jefferson and Andrew Jackson and reminded his audience that its purpose began with the "humble"—the "cause of the common man and the common woman," "those who have no voice," "those who are forgotten." Rather than calling for narrow welfare policies, Kennedy demanded an economic policy in which "employment will be the first priority." "The party of the people," he said, "must always be the party of full employment." He called for "better," not "bigger," government and reminded listeners of the party's support for deregulation. And he spoke to the alienated middle, to remind them of a broader vision: "The middle class may be angry, but they have not lost the dream that all Americans can advance together."[41]

But the content and the imagery went unnoticed. The failure of Democratic renewal was so complete that rhetoric could not break clear of the rubble. Nobody was listening outside the convention hall, for Kennedy and the Democratic party were so closely associated with racial liberalism that middle America could not see through it to find its interests or dreams. There were no work values, no growth, no common person. This shattered party could not represent America from the bottom up.

After 1968, the stage was set for the Republicans to make their own attempt at renewal.

5. FAILED RENEWAL: THE REAGAN REVOLUTION

WITH the Great Society in ruins, Republicans were positioned to reclaim the leadership of the country. Almost 57 percent, after all, had voted for the anti–Great Society candidates, Richard Nixon and George Wallace. But as Theodore White observed, this was a "negative landslide" and not an affirmation of new Republican ideas. It was a new Republican majority only in a demographic sense, as Kevin Phillips himself would acknowledge in his later works.[1] This emerging majority was still awaiting an organizing idea.

Richard Nixon had found an initial formula for winning—first law and order, then opposition to busing—that destroyed any pretense about Democrats' representing working America and associated the Republicans with the "forgotten Americans." Civil rights and urban disorders opened up a conversation between the Republicans and both working-class voters in the cities and poorer whites in the South who had turned their backs on the Democrats. There was a lot of emotion and anger in that conversation, but there was not a lot of new ideas. Rebellion was not itself a new majority. Being against civil rights and seeking a cultural bond with Catholic America did not constitute renewal. Nixon kept the Democrats in turmoil, but he did not renew his party and thus could not create a new Republican era.

Ronald Reagan, however, did offer new ideas and a vision and for a few short years was poised to realign U.S. politics. Reagan reconnected the modern Republican party with Coolidge and McKinley. He sought to restore confidence in business and markets and asked ordinary people to share in a business-led prosperity. He sought to lift the burden of taxes and create a bond with middle-class America, whose values and interests had been betrayed by the "tax and spend," anti-growth Democrats. Reagan offered top-down optimism to counter the Democrats' narrow bottom-up pessimism, and it worked.

RICHARD NIXON'S FORGOTTEN AMERICANS

Richard Nixon in 1968 took over the mantle of a changed Republican party that had expanded its appeal beyond the eastern establishment. Nixon found a language and emotions that tapped into the discontent right down the socioeconomic ladder, telling the Republican convention in Miami Beach that his presidency would represent the "forgotten Americans." These were the same working people whom Franklin Roosevelt had in mind when he spoke of the "forgotten man" and whom Bryan appealed to as the "toilers everywhere." Nixon's goal, however, was not to empower such people within the industrial order, as Democratic leaders aspired to do, but to represent "Joe Six-Pack" against the liberal establishment. Nixon gave voice to the sense of betrayal and put middle America—"the non-shouters, the nondemonstrators"—back on a pedestal. "They're good people," Nixon observed. "They're decent people; they work and they save and they pay taxes and they care." His campaign media were punctuated by a reminder of the stakes for middle America:

> This time
> Vote
> Like your
> Whole world
> Depended on it
> Nixon[2]

Nixon put the Republican party on the side of law and order and thereby placed his top-down party in conversation with the lower middle class, who now said crime in the streets was issue number one. Explicit race-baiting was left to Wallace, but there was no mistake about the centrality of race to new conservatism. In his campaign media, Nixon warned of the "violence and fear which pervades this nation and its cities today," making the easy association between the deluge of programs for the unemployed, cities, and the poor and the "ugly harvest of frustration, violence and failure."

Late in the campaign, with the race skidding to an uncertain end, the Nixon TV spots interspersed stuttering and disembodied still shots of Hubert Humphrey with dramatic shots of what had become senseless in America: shouting, swarthy antiwar protesters, soldiers comforting the wounded, body bags and the porches of blue-collar America. Nixon promised "to rebuild a respect for law across this country" and "recognize the first civil right of every American"—"to be safe from domestic violence." A somber Nixon intoned, "So I pledge to you: we shall have order in the United States."

A few of the Nixon commercials warned against "pouring billions of dollars into programs that have failed," and the candidate promised to "enlist private enterprise, which will produce progress, not promises, in solving the problems of America." But the Nixon law-and-order campaign avoided the philosophical conservatism and ideological certainty of Barry Goldwater.

Nixon's crude appeal to the working class was not to be muddied by ideology. There was little talk of unleashing business or
confronting the middle class's social welfare state.[3]

In 1964, Goldwater had fashioned a conservatism that questioned the federal government's role in promoting education
and social welfare, including "free retirement"; that championed
the "natural operation of the free market" in agriculture, eschewing attempts to prop up farm incomes; that would seek to
limit the "enormous economic and political power now concentrated in the hands of union leaders"; and that would eliminate any progressive taxation that is "confiscatory" and intends
to "to bring all men to a common level." Goldwater's campaign
was more about achieving "the maximum amount of freedom
for individuals" than about achieving prosperity or uplifting
working people. He won the votes of poorer whites in the Deep
South, where opposition to the Civil Rights Act was sufficient
to establish his bona fides, but elsewhere working-class America
was deeply suspicious of this ideological assault on the state.
Poorer whites in the hill counties in the South, Kevin Phillips
points out, voted heavily against Goldwater as an "economic
conservative" opposed to the New Deal.[4]

In 1968, Nixon preferred a conversation without ideological
content. Only on race and civil rights questions did Nixon put
down his marker and speak and act with ideological consistency.
From his opposition to new civil rights laws to his later Supreme
Court appointments and resistance to school busing, Nixon
made clear his party's opposition to civil rights. Here Nixon
found his own conservative voice: he described busing as "a new
evil . . . disrupting communities and imposing hardship on children—both black and white."[5] After repudiating the moderate
civil rights wing of the administration, Nixon's Justice Department interceded with the courts to slow the enforcement of
integration plans and proposed anti-busing legislation in Con-

gress. As president, Nixon repeatedly directed his administration to adopt the most conservative line possible on civil rights, to make clear he did not believe in integration, and indeed to adopt a hard line that would risk being called "racism." His goal was to assure political gains in the South and to make the "silent majority" of "blue collar, Catholic Poles, Italians, Irish" a political reality.[6]

When Nixon stepped before the Republican convention in 1972 to accept the nomination and set the stage for his second-term agenda, he was painfully clear about the place of race and civil rights. Right up front, immediately after the pleasantries, he set out the main differences between the parties: the Republicans "unite us" and the Democrats divide "Americans into quotas" and are "totally alien to the American tradition." "Americans don't want to be part of a quota," he told the convention. "They want to be part of America. This Nation proudly calls itself the United States of America."[7]

This was racial conservatism, not business conservatism. We shall see later that this tactic was sufficient to fracture the Democratic party and win national elections, but not sufficient to renew the Republican party and create an enduring majority.

Conservatism Without Business

Richard Nixon declined to seek a mandate on conservative ideas or on a new top-down vision for America, perhaps having overlearned the lessons of the Goldwater defeat. He was content to inflame the rebellion in the country while remaining self-consciously vague on rolling back the New Deal or even the Great Society. John Ehrlichman and John Mitchell, who brought no particular conservative credentials to the 1968 campaign, and H. R. Haldeman, who described himself as "essentially a mechanic," insisted on a vacuous campaign. Nixon had no "one hundred days" because he was elected without a program of change.[8]

Some conservatives, like William Rusher of the *National Review,* viewed this contentless conservatism as a betrayal of the faith: Nixon, he said, "cynically abandoned, between 1969 and 1972, most of the conservative principles that justify participation in politics." One of Nixon's speechwriters saw the Nixon problem as more basic: "no guiding ideals."[9] In fact, after coming to office, Haldeman began a search for ideals that would situate Nixon's limited agenda. He sent a note to speechwriter William Safire: "Few seem aware of the Nixon political philosophy, of his vision of America—outside of his hope for domestic tranquility. . . . The President feels that this general subject area of what the President's philosophy is would be worth some work and effort by our PR group. Would you please follow-up?" One searches the Haldeman diaries in vain for any serious discussion of conservative ideas that might challenge the assumptions of the Great Society. About as far as he got was thinking about changing the name of the Republican party to the Conservative party because polls showed the latter winning higher support.[10]

Nixon devoted his first term to two domestic initiatives, the family-assistance plan and general revenue sharing, neither of which did anything to advance a conservative vision. Family assistance and welfare reform were pushed by a Democratic appointee and later Democratic senator from New York, Daniel Patrick Moynihan, with the support of liberal bureaucrats over the opposition of conservative economists in the administration. Revenue sharing between the national and local governments was the keystone in Nixon's aspiration for a "new federalism." While it promised a government closer to the people, it did, after all, promise government, indeed, more government and thirty billion dollars of more spending, not lower taxes. Nixon failed to recognize—and so missed the opportunity to ride—the surge of anti-tax sentiment that coincided with his first campaign and early years in office, between 1966 and 1969.[11]

Spooked by the prospect of a Ted Kennedy presidential candidacy in 1972, Nixon introduced his own family health insurance plan in February 1971. It guaranteed every American basic health insurance benefits by requiring that employers insure their workers and dependents and by subsidizing insurance for low-income families.[12]

Nixon was predisposed to freer markets, but few principles constrained his pragmatic frame of mind when it came to the economy and the federal budget. He repeatedly rejected budget cuts proposed by his own administration and accepted deficit-increasing budgets despite fear of rising inflation. He presided over a massive 20 percent increase in Social Security benefits in 1972, and with the presidential election approaching he accelerated federal spending to minimize unemployment. By 1974, when Nixon finally showed some real interest in budget cutting, his administration's proposed spending on social programs stood 58 percent above what Lyndon Johnson had advanced for the Great Society.

Though the broad regulatory initiatives came mainly from the Democratic Congress in this period, Nixon did little to stall the surge of regulation or social spending. In his role, described by David Mayhew "variously as initiator, acquiescer, foot-dragger, and outright vetoer," Nixon helped lead the country to an extraordinary outpouring of regulation—perhaps the greatest era of regulation since the early New Deal: clean air and water, consumer and workplace safety, and women's rights. Up against the pressures of growing inflation, big wage settlements in major industries, and a world monetary crisis, Richard Nixon, the Republican, opted for national wage and price controls. Nixon topped every other postwar president on the number of new statutes and new agencies created to regulate business.[13]

Nixon was content to manage America's domestic affairs and take advantage of the racial carnage that had allowed the Republicans to occupy the White House, but he did not challenge Democratic orthodoxies and, more important, did not try to advance a Republican idea about helping people and ensuring prosperity.

Upheaval Without Realignment

Backlash, as Walter Dean Burnham has written, has throughout our history provided "intensely combustible materials for electoral warfare," but it is weak material for producing something more permanent. Racial conservatism helped break the Democratic hold on middle America, but it did not renew the Republican party. It created, instead, a new rootlessness and volatility. The established party patterns, fairly stable up to 1964, shifted sharply after the upheavals that shook the country. Identification with the Democratic party dropped from 45 percent in 1968 to 41 percent in 1972, where it stayed through 1980. But the political turmoil produced no Republican gains: there were no more self-proclaimed Republicans in 1980 (23 percent) than there were in 1964 (25 percent). Some surveys showed Republican gains between 1968 and 1972, but others did not, and the long-term failure to build a base is evident in all the surveys.

The real story of the 1970s is the growth of political independents, not Republicans. The provocative Republican course, set by Nixon, fostered rootlessness but offered these alienated voters little that would invite a longer-term identification with Republicanism.

The number of voters expressing no party affiliation whatever started to rise in 1966 and quickly exceeded the number who called themselves Republicans. Prior to 1968, about a quarter of Americans, with stark consistency going back to 1952, had described themselves as independents (including those leaning toward a party); that figure jumped to 31 percent in 1968 and to 36 percent in 1972, where it has remained ever since. The growing independent bloc drew primarily on southern whites (independence up from 18 to 38 percent between 1960 and 1970) and white Catholics (independents up from 18 to 30 percent), who pulled away from the Democrats. Working-class support for the Democrats dropped sharply in 1968 and again in 1972. That was balanced, to some extent, by the growth of independents in the Northeast (24 to 34 percent) and among college-educated voters (21 to 34 percent), who pulled away from the Republicans.[14]

The Watergate scandal put on hold Republican hopes to remake the political world from the White House. After it, support for the national parties actually steadied; the surge of political disaffection and distrust eased, but continued to simmer.

Assessments of the country's economic prospects during the 1970s sunk to new lows, and amazingly, people began to look backward in time, rather than forward, for a better America. (See Appendix, Figure A.3.) The state of the economy—negative growth and double-digit inflation by 1980—threatened public confidence in the future, and Jimmy Carter offered little more than a rationalized gloom. More than a year before the 1980 election, he went before the American people and lamented "the crisis of confidence" and "the growing doubts about the meaning of our own lives and in the loss of a unity of purpose for our Nation." He regretted that so many "worship self-indulgence and consumption" and deplored Washington, where "you see paralysis and stagnation and drift." Dubbed the malaise speech, it sapped the country of optimism and left the American dream lifeless.[15]

Underneath, this growing pessimism combined with political rootlessness and disaffection to fuel a growing tax revolt in the countryside. Incomes were declining, inflation was rising, and between 1953 and 1976, taxes had nearly doubled for the average family, rising 92 percent, twice the rate of increase for those at the very top. In 1978, a popular tax revolt in California, Proposition 13, rolled back property taxes and was followed by a wave of anti-tax ballot issues across the country. Between 1980 and 1982 almost 70 percent of Americans came to believe that their taxes were too high.[16]

Ronald Reagan prepared not just to ride the tide but to do much more—to restore the ideas that had allowed people to feel confident in Republican national leadership.

THE REAGAN FAITH

Ronald Reagan projected a self-assurance and a sense of history that began with his easy association with Calvin Coolidge and the Great Republican Era. Nixon never understood the possibilities, never understood the necessity, of such a connection, but for Reagan the connection was immediate. Just minutes after he took the oath of office, the White House curator removed the portraits of Jefferson and Truman from the cabinet room across from the Oval Office and put up the portrait of Calvin Coolidge. For Reagan, Coolidge offered a confident vision about business, investment, and prosperity that had been lost to the country now for some five decades:

> If you go back, I don't know if the country has ever had a higher level of prosperity than it did under Coolidge. And he actually reduced the national debt, he cut taxes several times across the board. And maybe the criticism was . . . that [he wasn't] activist enough. Well, maybe there's a lesson in that. Maybe we've had instances of government being too active, intervening, interfering.

He failed to note that Coolidge's "across-the-board" tax cuts gave breaks to just 2 percent of the population, but he was confident that such policies would bring a general prosperity. And Reagan failed to take note of the crash and depression that had followed the speculative boom of the 1920s, leaving this top-down world in disrepute. Those historic realities were, for Reagan and many Americans, less important than the faith.[17]

Nixon had had no such faith to guide him, which is why racial conservatism was so central to his political world. Reagan certainly shared Nixon's aversion to civil rights and quotas and could recite the Republican mantra with the best of them, but he also saw that the Republicans' tough stances against civil rights, crime, and the anti-war protesters never successfully wedded downscale America to the Republican party. Reagan understood as an article of faith that Republicanism had to reclaim and renew its top-down vision of America.

Reagan reached out to ordinary people: he touched them first with his essential honesty and then with his heartfelt proposal to lift their financial burden by cutting tax rates. He sought to restore faith in the market and in entrepreneurship in order to allow people once again to believe that American business could lead America to a new age of growth and prosperity. For a moment, it all seemed quite magical; it was, as the campaign ad suggested, "morning in America."

A New Age of Business

Ronald Reagan understood better than establishment Republicanism that a top-down view of the world could win broad support in society only if business was honored and valued. Businessmen had to be seen as the creators of wealth and jobs, the engines of growth. McKinley and Coolidge understood that business and industrial prestige and leadership were the best counter to populist assaults on the market and Democratic claims to represent the people, and Reagan planned to follow their lead.

From 1954 to 1962, Reagan had been the host of *General Electric Theater,* and as such he promoted not appliances but the notions of capitalism and progress. This was not just any corporation or product. This was General Electric, a company that was selling technology, progress, and a better life for America's emerging middle class. GE had created the House of Magic in the 1930s to display how corporate invention could improve the quality of life for the average family and, twenty years later, had modernized Reagan's California home so that he and his wife, Nancy, could be filmed talking about their "electric-powered home." They unveiled the Carousel of Progress, which opened at the 1964 New York World's Fair before moving on to Disneyland and Disney World, joining the most scrubbed and progressive images in America's big-business world. Reagan threw himself into this world, visiting all 135 GE plants and offering his vision of a nation in which business would be free to create a richer life for everybody.[18]

The post-GE Reagan associated himself not with the big corporations in the East and in the industrial Midwest but with the Sun Belt entrepreneurs. This newer brand of capitalist was more individualistic and entrepreneurial, more self-confident about its new wealth and social role, and skeptical of the old capitalist world of GM and U.S. Steel, which had traded innovation for predictability. That old world had come to terms with unions and government, whereas the new one wanted to break free.[19]

As president, Ronald Reagan gave voice to a romanticized view of business long absent from the political debate. The president of the United States now fully identified wealth as a positive good for everyone in society. He passed on to all who would listen a kind of bible of the new ethic, George Gilder's *Wealth and Poverty.* Gilder scorned defenders of capitalism who apologized for its values and expressed ambivalence about its ends. The starting point for Gilder (and Reagan) was the entrepreneur: "creative" and courageous, willing to face danger and "radical perils and uncertainties" and "fight." The possibilities for investment, production, and growth lie in the liberation of the entrepreneur. The entrepreneur is the "creative center of the system."

Gilder recognized that "the belief that the good fortune of others is also finally one's own does not come easily or invariably to the human breast." But honoring the good fortune of the entrepreneur who creates wealth is in the end the "golden rule of capitalism"—it means having faith that the growth of wealth means a more prosperous country.[20]

Gilder's "golden rule" was at the core of supply-side Reaganomics, which asserted confidently that tax cuts for the wealthy and business would bring economic growth and a general prosperity. This assertion required a lot of faith. As David Stockman explained, "It's kind of hard to sell 'trickle down,' so the supply-side formula was the only way to get a tax policy that was really 'trickle down.' " Since the "means of production" are located within the entrepreneurial world, Gilder argued, freeing business and the wealthy from taxes frees money for investment and growth. In the end, "the benefits of capitalism still depend on capitalists."[21]

The ideas, for all their limitations, gained authority because they were buttressed by a raft of new and emboldened conservative think tanks and institutions that would help develop and legitimate conservative thinking about religion and politics, markets and regulation, taxes and government spending, defense and communism. Gone was the Nixon era, when a conservative president governed without a conservative ideological infrastructure. Reagan's ideas were now situated in an elaborate interlocking network of conservative institutions.

David Ricci's study of think tanks, *The Transformation of American Politics,* describes the surge in the 1970s: the congressional Republican Study Committee, and the Heritage Foundation, established in 1973; the Senate Steering Committee, the Committee for the Survival of a Free Congress (now the Free Congress Political Action Committee), the National Conservative Political Action Committee, and the Conservative Caucus, set up in 1974; the Christian Voice and the Religious Roundtable, set up in 1978; and the Moral Majority (now the Liberty Foundation), set up in 1979. The conservative American Enterprise Institute, which predates these organizations, expanded its budget, with corporate help, tenfold during this period. Corporations also contributed to a conservative organizational revival within their own ranks, beginning with the Chamber of Commerce and the National Association of Manufacturers. Many of these think tanks had been created by conservatives upset with Nixon's lack of ideological seriousness, and they were ready to help the new president reshape the Republican agenda. Thus when Ronald Reagan took office, the Heritage Foundation was able to hand over to his transition team a volume called *Mandate for Leadership,* a program for curtailing government and revitalizing the economy.[22]

But it was not ideas in the first instance but the spectacular economic recovery of 1983 to '85 that gave reality to Reagan's economic vision: 12.3-percent real growth in the economy and a steady decline in unemployment, from the recession high near 10 percent to 7.5 percent in 1984 and below 7 percent in 1986.[23] To Reagan's credit, he held fast to his faith during the recession, and thus when the country shot upward, the public turned to him and his ideas with a new trust and openness.[24] Perhaps, people felt, top-down economics really did bring prosperity.

But Reagan's sunny economics also gained force against the gloomy backdrop of Jimmy Carter. Peggy Noonan underscored the power of the contrast; as she wrote, "There was no Reagan without Carter." Carter had left the nation confused and troubled—with an absence of any economic vision and with a purified and conservative government more in the tradition of Cleveland than in the tradition of Bryan. Carter had made no attempt to build from the bottom up or to understand the financially pressed middle class.[25]

It was not a hard act to follow. In the 1984 campaign, Reagan reminded voters of Carter's gloom, the Republican convention film observing simply, "People were losing faith in the American dream." In his TV ads Reagan offered a new possibility, "morning in America," hardworking people, good people waking up to the possibility that America was on the rise and life could be better:

> Today, the dream lives again.
> Today jobs are coming back.
> The economy is coming back.
> And America is coming back,
>   standing tall in the world again.
> President Reagan,
>   rebuilding the American dream.[26]

Touching the People

The vision Ronald Reagan inherited from the Great Republican Era had a contradiction at its core: that the interests and welfare of ordinary people would be advanced by a policy that begins by helping the most privileged. Indeed, since the collapse of 1929 and the repudiation of Hoover, few Republicans have spoken above a whisper about the virtues of wealth and corporate power. But Reagan expressed an innocent confidence in such virtues. General Electric. Progress. Americans living better electrically.

Ronald Reagan was able to elide the contradiction and
reach down to working America because he embodied and
ennobled the common experience. As a young man, he had
cleaned up at his mother's church and had worked as a lifeguard
in Dixon, Illinois; his father was fired on Christmas Eve during
the Depression, only to be saved by Roosevelt's New Deal; Reagan joined a dry fraternity at Eureka College, hitchhiked to
Chicago to look for a job in radio, and became a sportscaster,
making up all the action off a ticker; he went to Hollywood and
put his happy innocence on screen. Reagan had a special window on middle America because he represented so many of its
idealized remembrances.

But in taking his innocence into public life, Reagan also
took the people with him. The biographer Lou Cannon captured his unique place in our politics:

> He was the wholesome citizen-hero who inhabits our
> democratic imaginations, an Everyman who was slow to
> anger but willing to fight for the right and correct wrong-
> doing when aroused. It was a role in a movie—personified
> by Reagan's friend Jimmy Stewart in *Mr. Smith Goes to
> Washington*—in which homespun American virtue prevails
> over the wily and devious "special interests" that rule the
> nation's capital.

He played the role of citizen with innocence and honesty, without a touch of meanness, challenging the bullies—above all, the
establishment and bureaucrats—who make life miserable for
ordinary people.[27]

Ronald Reagan touched people, making it possible for them
to entertain his Republican top-down vision. But his window
on working America was bigger yet. Reagan warred against the
taxes and the secularism that were impinging on the lives of ethnic Catholic neighborhoods in Detroit and the white Baptist
small towns across northern Alabama. Reagan, steadfast against

taxes and abortion, opened windows across downscale America into places that affluent and corporate Republicanism had barely dared to peer.

The tax revolt caught up to Ronald Reagan, who had for years warned of the evils of the federal income tax and preached the simple gospel of lower taxes and a smaller, less obtrusive federal government. Whether it was a talk to a clutch of General Electric factory workers, a nomination speech for Goldwater's presidential bid, or inaugurations in Sacramento and Washington, Reagan found his voice on taxes: this money belonged properly to the people—and you could feel his personal indignation. Lower taxes—along with reduced federal spending, reduced regulation, and more military defense—formed his center as president. That was Reaganism and Reagonomics.[28]

So for the anti-tax revolt, Ronald Reagan was the man. It certainly was not Walter Mondale, who seemed only too anxious to pick the pockets of the middle class. Reagan used the tax issue to take himself into the economic struggles of ordinary voters and put a wedge between the Democrats and the middle class. In his 1984 stump speech, he warned about Mondale's taxes:

> He says he cares about the middle class. I think his tax plans will be a hardship to the American people, and I believe it will bring our recovery to a roaring stop. But I'll give it this: At least it gave me an idea for Halloween. If I could find a way to dress up as his tax program, I could go out and scare the devil out of the neighbors.[29]

And for the growing community of the religious faithful who felt betrayed by modernism, Reagan was their man too. He offered a clear moral direction on school prayer, busing, and abortion and thus touched the more traditional communities under siege—northern Catholics, Orthodox Jews, western Mormons, and white Southern fundamentalists, to take Kevin

Phillips's list. Reagan may not have got himself up on Sunday mornings to go to church, but he so closely identified with the traditional family and traditional America that people insisted on associating him with religious faith and sentiment. This association transported him into the lives of important segments of blue-collar and rural America, and Reagan understood the partisan opportunity. In 1977, he had urged conservatives to go beyond the traditional conservative litany and use "the so-called social issues" that "are usually associated with blue collar, ethnic and religious groups who are traditionally associated with the Democratic Party."

The clerics understood the connection. Southern Baptist ministers, who had supported the Democrats over the Republicans by 41 to 29 percent in 1980, shifted loyalties four years later, choosing Republicans by 66 to 26 percent. Born-again Christians shifted sharply to the Republicans, by nineteen points, and they have never looked back. The Democratic defections to Reagan in 1984 occurred disproportionately among those opposed to civil rights and busing, to be sure, but also among those opposed to abortion and women's rights. Phillips was right to describe such a turn as a "massive reaction of traditionalism, (white) ethnicity, pro-family sentiment and religious fundamentalism—a Counter Reformation on the heels of the Reformation."[30]

Reagan undoubtedly knew in 1980, and certainly knew by 1984, that he was in direct conversation with the Democratic base that had repeatedly felt betrayed by its party. Nixon's law-and-order campaigns had aroused the working people, but few warmed to a party of the affluent, a party without any real promise for the middle class. Reagan, however, had broadened the conversation—it was now about growth, financial struggle, and traditional values—and set a populist face against the establishment and bureaucratic bullies. He made this a conversation among Democrats, a bond forged in a common disaffection from the powerful. He honored Franklin Roosevelt's memory in nearly every speech and reminded his audience that all the Reagans had originally been Democrats.

But while he honored FDR, Reagan did not honor the Democratic president's work, and for good reason: his reach down to working America would have been cut off had the public dwelled on his earlier pronouncements about New Deal social welfare programs, particularly Social Security. Voluntary saving might fare better than Social Security, Reagan had mused. Stu Spencer, one of Reagan's key campaign advisers in 1980, pressed hard for Reagan to affirm his support for Social Security, and Chief of Staff James Baker tried to keep Reagan from even entertaining Social Security cuts—what he called Reagan's Achilles' heel. When David Stockman and the Office of Management and Budget got ahead of the administration and proposed changes in early retirement, first the Democrats, then a unanimous Senate, and finally the president himself repudiated this assault on the social contract. Stockman argued that Reagan should go before a national TV audience and make the case for sacrifice. But for Reagan, the stakes were higher than the budget: tax breaks for the wealthy and spending cuts for senior citizens were a combustible combination that could bring down the whole top-down project.[31]

By 1984, there was no sign of the old Reagan attacks on Social Security. Instead, the president reached down: "To all the good Democrats who respect their tradition, I say: You are not alone and you are not without a home. . . . We're putting out our hands and we're asking you to come walk with us."[32]

Reagan's outstretched hand was changing the political possibilities in communities across the country. Nixon had made only modest inroads into Macomb County, despite the busing furor. Ronald Reagan was another matter. The Reagan Democrats were now a phenomenon: the living, walking proof of the Republican party's renewal.

In Canarsie, a middle-class Brooklyn neighborhood, the sociologist Jonathan Rieder found a community embattled, people feeling vulnerable and betrayed. The two-family brick row houses had provided a whole post-war generation of Jews and Italians with a taste of America's dreams. But in the 1960s and '70s, busing and community-school controversies, taxes and stagnant incomes had eaten away at people's political faith. Residents felt they were losing their way of life, Rieder reported, to blacks, bureaucrats, and liberals. The Thomas Jefferson Democratic Club had made Canarsie a Democratic stronghold in the '50s—indeed, delivering 85 percent of the Jewish vote for Stevenson in 1956 and nearly 75 percent for Humphrey against Nixon in 1968. But the Democratic hold on Canarsie was being eroded locally by the profusion of tough, backlash candidates, like the 1969 mayoral nominee Mario Procaccino, and nationally by the unfolding stories of Jimmy Carter and Ronald Reagan. In 1980, Reagan carried a majority of the vote among both the Italians and the Jews of Canarsie.[33]

Sociologist David Halle discovered his own breed of emerging Reagan Democrats in northern New Jersey. They were unionized workers at a major chemical company, part of the complex of chemical production along the New Jersey Turnpike. They lived in the small bungalows and single-family wooden row houses of Elizabeth, Linden, Roselle, and Roselle Park and in the ranch-style houses farther out. More than three quarters owned their own homes. They hated property taxes and followed the New York Giants, sometimes tailgating at Giants Stadium in the New Jersey Meadowlands Sports Complex. They thought of themselves as "working men" at the workplace and as "the middle class" in their communities. That placed them "struggling" in the middle—above the poor and the blacks (the "idle" and those "who can't make it") and below the rich ("big business," "the millionaires," and "Jews"), who they felt controlled the politicians and the system. Nearly all these working men considered themselves Democrats, but Carter and Reagan upset the historic patterns. Carter gave them inflation and high unemployment, and Reagan promised something better and, in any case, hated welfare and school busing. A majority of these unionized working men voted for Reagan in 1980. By 1984, they worried that Reagan was demonstrably too anti-union, but he offered something else: a strong military and better economic times.[34]

In the fall of 1984, Reagan traveled to Waterbury, Connecticut—an older factory town at the heart of the Naugatuck Valley, a town with a large cross gazing down from the hills and where generations of Catholic immigrants had worked in the rubber-tire and brass factories. It was in Waterbury that every inhabitant, it seemed, had turned out to hear John Kennedy close his campaign. Reagan in 1984 reminded them of times past: "Even though it was the fall it seemed like springtime, those days. . . . I see our country today and I think it is springtime for America once again." And then he drew their lives together: "You know, I was a Democrat once. . . . The only abandoning I see is the Democratic leadership abandoning the good and decent Democrats of the JFK, and FDR, and Harry Truman tradition." Reagan was invading working America and holding it to his chest.[35]

In the 1984 election, Reagan won all but the District of Columbia and Mondale's home state of Minnesota—one of the biggest electoral-college landslides ever.

The bloc of Republican identifiers, which had hovered at barely a third of the electorate during the Nixon-Ford era, jumped to 43 percent with Reagan's landslide victory in 1984. The Democratic partisan advantage, which had hovered between 17 and 20 points and seemed stuck despite all Republican entreaties, suddenly plummeted to just ten points. The alienated portions of the Democratic mass base, after years of hesitation, were now explicitly identifying themselves as Republicans. In 1980, just 21 percent of white southerners identified with the party of Lincoln, but by 1986, 31 percent had crossed over; a 24-point Democratic advantage was completely erased. The number of Catholic Republicans grew steadily under Reagan—just 17 percent in 1980 but 26 percent by 1986; a 28-point Democratic advantage among Catholics was cut nearly in half, to 15 points. Even in the core of the organized working class, where Democrats once enjoyed a 33-point advantage in union households, the party balance began shifting: from a 22-point Democratic advantage in 1980 to 16 points in 1984 to only 9 points in 1988. The Reagan era was, for the first time since the Democratic crack-up in 1968, producing not just Reagan Democrats but new Reagan Republicans.[36]

The most important factor in the 1984 election and in this shift to the Republicans was Reagan's handling of the recovering economy. Personal income and Reagan's popularity moved up together to create a sense of confidence in this business-led prosperity. Optimism about the future soared almost to the level seen in 1964. (See Appendix, Figure A.3.) By the spring of 1984, the public was convinced that the Republicans would do a better job of keeping the country prosperous (a 44 to 36 percent advantage in the polls), a faith that was nurtured and expanded over the next two years. The Republican party was on the verge of reasserting itself as a modernizing force that could lead the country.[37]

In fact, starting in 1983, public confidence in all institutions began rising sharply—including more positive feelings toward the White House and Congress but also toward nearly all institutions, including colleges and universities, and toward medicine. In 1984, a near majority, remarkably, said that the government usually or always does "what is right"—44 percent, up 19 points from 1980. A striking 39 percent concluded that the government is now run for the "benefit of all"—up 10 points from 1982 and 18 points from 1980. This Reagan moment raised both the political and the civic—all the institutions that had become remote from the people. (See Appendix, Figures A.1 and A.2.)

This Reagan moment was also a personal triumph. People respected Reagan's honesty, strength, and optimism about the future: by 1986, 61 percent described him as "inspiring" and 74 percent as showing "strong leadership." But he also shaped the mood of the country, taking it beyond cynicism: 65 percent were "hopeful" (up 17 points from 1980) and 64 percent "proud" (up 32 points). Reaganism was generalizing its mood to a country that was learning to rediscover the power of a new contract.[38]

THE FAILED REVOLUTION

The Incomplete Rehabilitation of Business

By offering a compelling vision of business-led prosperity and individual freedom, Reagan stepped up to the obligations of political leadership lost for so many years. For a moment, aided by signs of national economic progress, there was a promise of restored trust, not just in Ronald Reagan but in all the institutions party to the political world broadly understood. The political world no longer seemed so remote from the people.

But this moment of faith was brief and soon dominated by the slowing and uneven economy and the Iran–Contra scandal. This restoration of trust was, after all, fragile. Reaganism brought a more positive spirit to the country, but it did not transform the standing of business, the engine of prosperity in Reagan's America. Confidence in business grew only modestly between 1983 and the end of the Reagan presidency: according to the Harris Survey, it grew only 5 points, to a high of only 21 percent in 1986; according to the Gallup Survey, it grew 11 points, peaking at 31 percent in 1985.

On the explicit principle of profitability and "trickle down"—"that profits of large companies help make things better for everyone"—gains were paltry. At Reagan's best moment, only 43 percent believed that "the profits of large corporations help make things better for everyone." Throughout the Reagan era, over 70 percent believed that the concentration of power "in the hands of a few large companies" was too great "for the good of the nation."[39]

Most Americans at the height of the Reagan era doubted that business prosperity would generalize to ordinary people. The failure to restore confidence in business despite Reagan's best efforts left this period of renewed hope vulnerable to the economic slowdown and the growing evidence of greed at the top.

Dawn in America

George Bush crushed Michael Dukakis in 1988, taking 54 percent of the vote and maintaining the firm Republican hold on the South and the West. The Reagan revolution may have dimmed somewhat from 1984, but for the casual observer the Reagan revival of Republicanism seemed to have been affirmed. Indeed, the political scientist Walter Dean Burnham, like other astute observers, looked back on 1988 and concluded, "It is hard to overestimate the damage that this sea change [the Reagan revolution] has inflicted on the Democratic party. As a presidentially viable force, this party ultimately lived and seems to have died—at least for the time—by a political economics for which the new order has little or no room."[40]

But the observers and the conventional wisdom were wrong. By 1988, the Reagan revolution had already failed. In the nights before the 1988 election, I conducted a national survey and asked 1,735 Americans their top priorities for the next president.[41] To my astonishment, given the rejection of Michael Dukakis, 65 percent placed the greatest importance on making sure the "wealthy and big corporations pay their fair share of taxes"; 60 percent placed the highest priority on

TABLE 5.1

POLICY PRIORITIES FOR THE NEW PRESIDENT
November 1988

Policy	(% Saying Policy a Top Priority)	
	All Voters	Reagan Democrats
Payment of fair share of taxes by wealthy	65	71
Stricter environmental regulation	60	64
Aid to poor and homeless	49	54
Tougher trade laws to protect jobs	47	53
Universal health insurance	44	45
Increased spending for education	38	42
No new taxes	38	39
Anti-abortion appointees to the Supreme Court	29	26
SDI, or Star Wars	12	12

"imposing stricter environmental regulations on corporations" that "produce toxic wastes." Far down was the public's interest in George Bush's number-one goal, "no new taxes," mentioned by just 38 percent as a top priority. The pattern was even starker for Reagan Democrats, 71 percent of whom were looking for higher taxes on the wealthy and just 39 percent sought "no new taxes."

These voters may have favored George Bush over Michael Dukakis and continuity over the risk of change, but they did not vote to affirm trickle-down economics, the prestige of business and markets. They shared few of Reagan's illusions about corporations and wealth. By 1988, confidence in bankers had plummeted to 26 percent from 38 percent in 1985; in business executives, to 16 percent from 23 percent. Indeed, voters wanted to check the power of those who had risen to new levels of prestige in the Reagan era.[42]

The public's discontent—not yet fully expressed electorally—reflected a growing anger with the excesses and betrayal contained in the Reagan revolution. The rhetoric about taxes was crashing against the reality: tax rates may have been slashed for the wealthy, but the middle class got no break: the effective rate for the mid-income group, 16.5 percent in 1980 (including Social Security), remained unchanged in 1988, though it was no doubt pushed upward by increased state and local taxes. Median income recovered from the 1982 recession, rising through the 1984 election until 1986, but then stopping with the average worker still earning less in 1987 than in 1980 (adjusted for inflation). There was a growing sense in the country that the supply-side promise—the golden rule of mutual advantage—was a lie. The image of the entrepreneur—investor and wealth creator—was giving way to images of Michael Milken and junk bonds. Leveraged buyouts, mergers, and stock repurchases enriched shareholders but did little to fund investment. There was diminishing fascination with television shows like *Dallas, Dynasty,* and *Falcon Crest,* which seemed only to affirm the selfishness of the era's ethic.[43]

Bush campaigned for the presidency on continuity, but he hesitated to offer a confident conservatism and defense of business in the face of growing anger about the excesses of the wealthy. Instead, he reduced the Reagan vision to "read my lips: no new taxes." That was sufficiently anti-government to satisfy some conservatives, but it was hardly an elevated discourse about bringing prosperity to the nation, and it was hardly enough to ensure his election. Republicans held on to the White House by waving their variant of the bloody shirt, with Willie Horton and flag burning as new forms of the old law-and-order and anti-busing campaigns. These were still combustible materials in 1988, and George Bush used them to hold on to power.

Lee Atwater, Bush's campaign manager, worried that the Reagan Democrats were indeed ready to return home if economic populism were allowed to resurge. Bush shifted to the tactics of Richard Nixon, in Atwater's terms, to show that the Democrats "are the party of the liberal elites who're not in touch with the mainstream of the country." Instead of running on a Republican vision, Bush sought to reassociate the Democrats with racial liberalism. Bush took the Nixon course and sought to remind voters of how Democrats had betrayed the values of the common man.[44]

The campaign stoked the fires of public cynicism in order to allow the Republicans to hold on to the presidency. While the election of 1984 had raised the public's spirits, this one depressed them. It was an alienated electorate, with a lower voter turnout than any election since 1924.

The Bush presidency was itself disfigured by the cynicism it fostered and the load it was carrying. George Bush was heir to the Reagan revolution, which had already failed. He embodied the idea of government and society for the privileged, remote from the lives of ordinary citizens, whose world was stagnating.

He personified the contradiction at the core of top-down Republicanism. The Reagan revolution had allowed the top 1 percent of the population to reap extraordinary income gains— 62.9 percent between 1980 and 1989—stripped of any elevated rationalization, while the average family saw its income stagnate—up just 2.8 percent—during the twelve years of the Reagan and Bush presidencies. George Bush lived the world of Prescott Bush while job and income growth completely stalled.[45]

But middle-class grievances went beyond the material to a sense of lost honor. In an earlier day, middle-class America was at the center of the country's story. Its values were honored and rewarded. That is what suburban America was supposed to be all about. But as political life became more elitist, the middle class became the guardians of proper values, society and politics, where greed, not work, was rewarded. Society offered an easy way out for those who ignored the rules and sought personal gain at the expense of the public at large. People were now looking for windfalls at the welfare office or on Wall Street, while working America was showing up for work every day. There was something fundamentally wrong when the powerful lacked the honest values of the working stiff: a sense of discipline, responsibility, accountability, and social obligation.[46]

The combination was incendiary for George Bush and the Reagan revival. First, it brought a collapse of confidence in prosperity. The belief that things would be better for the nation over the next five years plummeted even before the Bush recession of 1990–91. (See Appendix, Figure A.3.) In Reagan's best days, a majority of the American people could be characterized as optimists, believing in the possibility of a revitalized America, but that majority shriveled to a third as Bush took office.

Second, the combination brought a new explosion of alienation. Confidence in all institutions dropped sharply after 1989 and particularly after 1990: in major companies (to a mere 11 percent), in the executive branch of the federal government (to

13 percent) and in Congress (to the bottom, 10 percent). Belief that government could be trusted to do "what is right" headed sharply downward after 1988, from 40 to just 28 percent, the biggest drop since 1972 and 1966. A government that resists the special interests and minds the people now seemed more remote than ever, that faith dropping from 39 percent in 1984 to 31 percent in 1988 to 24 percent in 1990 to a low of 20 percent in 1992. That puts the explosion of distrust between 1984 and 1992 on almost the same historic scale as that from 1964 to 1972. (See Appendix, Figure A.1.)

The failure of Republican renewal, combined with the failure of Democratic renewal, produced a political impasse unmatched since the 1880s, what Walter Dean Burnham describes it as a "political regime," "deeply blocked and deadlocked." The public just thought of it as gridlock. This deadlock produced unaccountable government, secret negotiations—from Social Security to higher taxes—and an explosion of public debt. In previous periods of divided government, leaders had more than muddled through—as evident in the administrations of Richard Nixon and Ronald Reagan. But in this period, from 1989 to 1992, little was done to address the country's problems. Congressional leaders of both parties maneuvered for position but without hope of breaking the impasse and without any ideas that could stir the nation and alter the climate for change.[47]

The impasse left the president impotent. The public was inclined to think of George Bush, the leader of the free world, as hapless at home. At the outset of 1992, voters in focus groups accepted his diminished role:

> So what are we supposed to do, blame the president for the fact that this country is going downhill? . . . I don't think it's a president's fault.

> Of course, the president doesn't run the country. . . . Obviously—but he does set some policies. . . . He sets an impression by being there. . . . He's too busy kissing butt.

I think he's overwhelmed with what's in front of him. . . . I think he's slightly impotent in doing anything about the economy. Again, it's the political structure that won't let him do this.

George Bush and the president, no matter who he is—it's not the ultimate person who makes the decisions. The Congress is the one who appropriates. And there are many others. . . . He's the executive person.

The hapless George Bush presidency came to symbolize the elitism and excesses of the Reagan era and the failure to help ordinary Americans. It brought a crash of confidence and trust nearly equal to the explosion of the 1960s. Now people faced the world doubly betrayed—by both their bottom-up leaders and their top-down leaders, by both the Democratic party of Lyndon Johnson and the Republican party of Ronald Reagan. Both had failed their obligations to point the way toward a more general prosperity. Private corruption never proved more maddening. Politics never seemed more remote from the people.

6. THE END OF GROWTH

THE Great Society and Reaganomics were bold attempts to seize the government and the country's imagination. Each reached back to give life to historic party images and economic ideas; each sought to renew confidence in the idea that the American experience includes prosperity and progress, that there really is an American dream. Their crashing failures produced the opposite—cynicism and alienation, the product of crashed hopes.

Democratic liberalism under Lyndon Johnson reached back to Franklin Roosevelt for an imagery of people and equality and for an inspiration for governmental activism, but given the uncontainable events of the 1960s, it produced a narrow focus on the disadvantaged. There was little in the bottom–up vision about growth and a general prosperity, little that the poor and middle class could hold on to together. But there was a lot of crime, new taxes, and exploding welfare as far as most people could see. Reagan conservatism reached back to Coolidge and McKinley for an imagery of confident business and prosperity. It produced just a short spurt of growth, but in this crazy top-down world there was an explosion of rewards for the Michael Milkens and the S&L speculators and higher taxes for ordinary people.

The end of growth coincided with the collapse of the historic models for promoting a general prosperity. For two decades, beginning around 1973, ordinary Americans saw their incomes stagnate. They worked harder and struggled as the promises of the American dream—a home, dependable health care, a college education—climbed out of reach. The Bush presidency was a wasteland: few new jobs and no growth in income, political gridlock in Congress and indifferent leaders, precious few ideas for promoting prosperity and the general welfare.

In the wake of these two failed attempts at renewal, there emerged among the populace a new middle-class consciousness as middle-class dreams gave way to middle-class squeeze. Hope gave way to grievance and despair. The failure of ideas from above and below produced a middle America crystallized in its alienation—and desperate for signs of hope.

REMEMBERING

Before the 1992 presidential campaign had fully formed, I asked groups of voters to step back from the political clamor and indulge me by playing some games. I asked them to plumb their memories and make their own personal line graphs reflecting the country's economic experience since the Second World War.[1] They drew their lines carefully—upward when things were getting better, downward when worse, and level when things were stagnant or flat. Their graphs constitute remembrances of a shared history and a received wisdom.

There was a lot of skepticism among some professionals; they questioned whether ordinary people could conceptualize their economic memories in this way. But in the groups, there were not many skeptics. People earnestly worked at their graphs and produced a shared history, as one can see in the drawings.

These group exercises were conducted among voters split evenly between those leaning toward the Democrats and those

VOTER GRAPHS

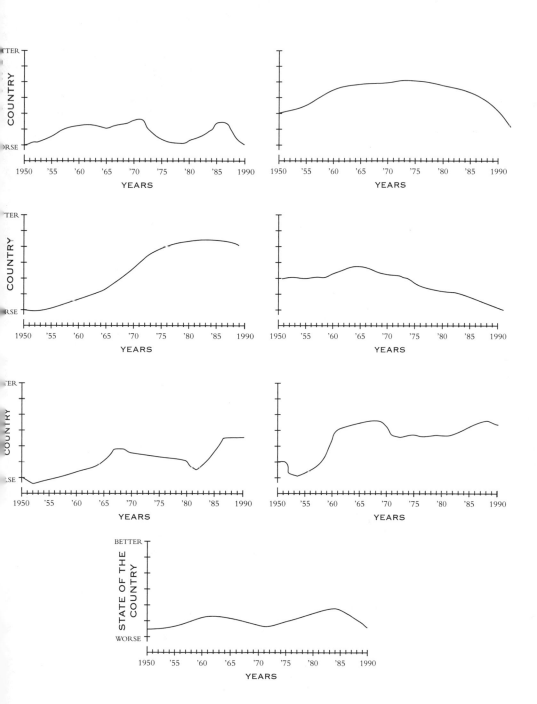

VOTER GRAPHS

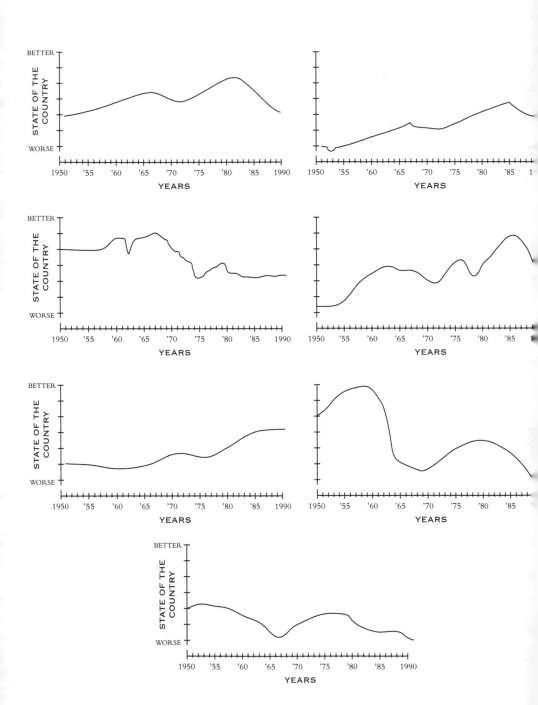

VOTER GRAPHS

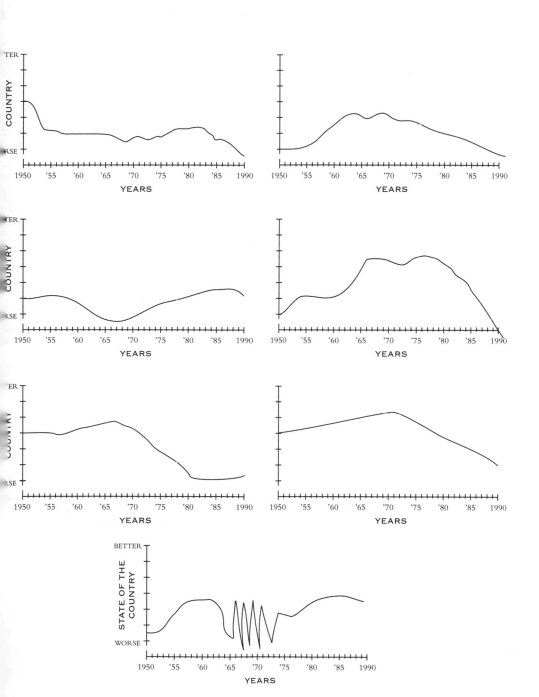

VOTER GRAPHS

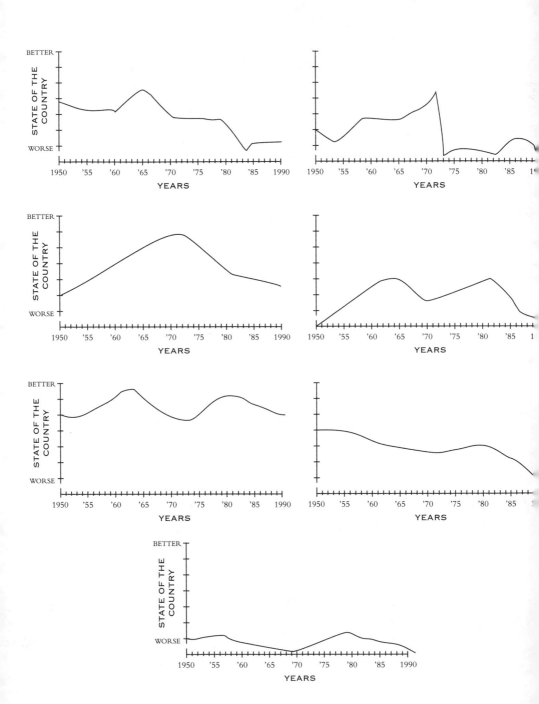

leaning toward the Republicans. Two of the discussions were held in Silicon Valley in California among younger, college-educated people, people who had experienced both the heady days of high-tech growth and the current restructuring. Men and women participated in separate groups, and all were in their thirties or forties. Two other discussions were conducted in Chicago, drawing on older people (in their late forties to early sixties) from the city and nearby suburbs who had not graduated from college and had lived through the recent restructuring of America's industrial economy. And one final discussion was held in Charlotte, North Carolina, drawing on men who had migrated from elsewhere in the South and from the North to take advantage of job opportunities in a so-called growth area.

In these small groups, people spoke open-endedly about their struggles and frustrations, discussed economic concepts, and drew graphs to reflect their sense of the country's development during four decades. Their discussions and graphs contained a sense of history and reflect an emergent middle-class consciousness.

The 1950s: The Good Years

These conversations reflected a fairly idyllic view of the 1950s—a time of building and growth, of strong families and good values, of a strong and well-led America. People thought of the '50s as fairly stable and uneventful but a good period, when sound foundations were laid for the country and for individual growth. In depicting these years graphically, more than two thirds drew lines slanting upward, thus drawing more upward-slanting lines for this period than for any period since. The lines are not steep, but they reflect a sense of steady improvement for the country and the people.

The '50s in people's minds were a period of rising productivity and growing confidence, and perhaps this carried over into the early '60s. There was "house building and stuff, and all of the expressway projects were started then. There was a lot of employment." "The country was rebuilding. . . . People were working." There were opportunities: "You could go almost anywhere and get a job." The '50s were an "optimistic time—good economy."

Nobody mentioned politics. This was a period when the New Deal promise was being realized and nationalized as Eisenhower took the country beyond politics. The country, not a party, owned the interstate-highway program and Social Security.

That these were solid times for families and values was an important part of the remembrance. Participants thought of the '50s as "fun times," when people did not get hurt and families stayed together. *Leave It to Beaver* was on TV. Some remarked, "You came home, and you knew your mother was going to be in the house." And others added: "With cookies. . . . She didn't have to work." "You had a family structure then, and today you don't." That image of the family—contrasted with the image of today's family under the pressure of work—was central to people's understanding of the '50s as a stable period.

People's imagery of the '50s was above all suburban—a house, a car, young kids and family, and television. People were not rich, but they had steady work and economic security. Problems were small, hardly worth mentioning. The Roosevelt-Truman bottom-up vision of the world had delivered for middle America in an idealized suburbia.[2]

The 1960s: The Hot Years

People were drawn back to the '60s as a decade of great change and turmoil, peace and war, great idealism and personal indulgence, growth and crash. They understood that the Great Society reforms crashed in a fit of permissiveness and unrestrained spending, but they were still drawn to the crash site. There was a separation in the public mind between the early '60s and the late '60s; people tended to think of the two as extremes and as contradictory parts of the same era. They looked back on these times with some awe, given the scale of what was happening, and they sensed that America was changed forever.

The decade kicked off with the Kennedy years, which brought to mind the space age, the Peace Corps, and Camelot. These were interesting times, and most people headed their lines upward in this early phase: "We have the Camelot atmosphere. We got Kennedy in there, and people are like, God, we're wonderful." "The '60s were interesting. There was so many things, different aspects going on in the '60s." "The blacks came in, then." For some, the early '60s were an "age of exploration," when people "talked about things in bars" and "cared."

But this all turned sour in the mid- to late '60s, with many of the lines starting to head downward by 1968 and 1969. The assassinations brought an abrupt end to the idealism; the war brought an end to the sense of progress. They saw the "Vietnam joke" beginning around 1964 and ending somewhere around 1972. In people's minds, the war was part of a cluster of excesses that would damage the country. One participant observed:

> I remember all the political arguments about Vietnam, I found tearing this country up for one. And then there were several assassinations in high school. And thought this country's going to hell. And I was just very upset by the time we reached 1969 or '70. It just seemed like there was so much political turmoil in this country, and people seemed to do nothing but put the United States down as a country.

This was a period that saw the "beginning of a lot of things": drugs, riots, "people . . . walking around with guns," hippies. One Chicago man summed it up this way: "There's a steep drop

right here, in between '60 and '69. There were a lot of assassinations in this country, a lot of turmoil, a lot of liberalism, hippies,
riots and demonstrations and roadblocks and burnings of public
buildings." This was the point when "our morals really started to
decline."

Most recognized the '60s as a period of "growth" until "disillusionment" set in toward the end of the decade. But even the
growth, in retrospect, was seen as a form of excess, pushed by
wartime and social spending: "I was thinking [at the time] we're
just fueling this economy with money, money, money and war,
war, war." "That was wartime spending, and that was artificial."
After looking at a chart showing high economic growth rates
for the Johnson and Kennedy presidencies, one man concluded,
"The Great Society spent one heck of a lot of money."

People were prepared to believe that the '60s were a period of
economic growth, a time when people had money, but they were
also prepared to discount the benefits, given the unhappy close to
the decade and the sense of excess. This was not a prosperity
rooted in a broad bottom-up vision of the world; nor was it a
prosperity that ordinary, hardworking people could depend on.

The 1970s: In Between

People had trouble characterizing the '70s, in part because the
defining events and leaders bracketed the decade rather than
dominated it. Nixon was brought up only once in these discussions and only in reference to Watergate; only one person mentioned the wage and price controls, which apparently have
passed from the public consciousness. For these participants,
Nixon was a product of the '60s and closed that decade out. His
resignation was the close of a "hot" period in our history, when
excess was the dominant theme.

Their reading of Nixon was quite sensitive to his historic
role. His tough law-and-order stands and strong opposition to

quotas closed an explosive period that furthered the racial transformation of the political parties. But in their minds, he did not
kick off some new era.

The lines at gas stations and the Arab oil boycotts of 1973
and 1979 made a big impression ("standing in those lines,"
"rationing," "like the Depression"), though there was an exter-
nal quality to these events that divorced them from our own
economic history. Gerald Ford emerged as transitional—"care-
taker," "void," "slow and cautious," "stagnant." As one man put
it, "I never took him seriously."

People had strong memories of Jimmy Carter, but the bad
economic times at the close of his presidency were barely a part
of those memories. Some of the more upscale participants
brought up the double-digit inflation and interest rates, though
in this view Carter represented more the reason for the Reagan
presidency than a period in its own right. In fact, most of the
groups were silent on the economic character of the Carter
years. Nobody could recall anything about the early Carter
years, for which many participants' charts show little movement
in either direction. The more blue-collar Chicago groups and
the Southern group barely took notice of the late Carter downturn; in fact, their graphs, for the most part, do not head downward until after Carter's presidency, or they reflect a long-term
decline beginning in the late '60s.

People had vivid impressions of Carter, but they were not
economic in character: they thought of him as "honest, too honest," as someone who "tries hard" and has "good intentions," and
as a man "without backing." Carter's presidency and America at
the time were characterized by weak leadership.

So the '70s were kind of in between: ill defined, perhaps
willfully so, by the close of the '60s and the Great Society and
the kick off of the '80s and the Reagan era. This definition led
people to think of the decade in empty terms: "From about the
early '70s to the early '80s, I think things were pretty much sta-

ble." "The '70s were nothing. . . . That's like a void. It was very stable. No major changes." "Since the late '70s, early '80s, I see the decline in all the things that are important to me." "The '50s and '70s were somewhat reflective in the sense that things pretty much went along status quo."

The 1980s: Boom and Bust

The people in these groups, even those who benefited from the rapid recovery in the mid-1980s, viewed Reagan's attempt at renewal as a boom-and-bust experiment that damaged the country, perhaps for a long time. Nearly all the participants drew their lines downward during at least part of the 1980s: for some, the downward slant reflected a longer-term decline that had begun earlier, but for most the decline began between 1985 and 1987 and accelerated after 1989. These lines reflect vivid impressions of what the 1980s were all about: a neglect of the country and "false goodness" for which we will pay "forever." One woman summarized the scope of her group's collective critique:

> Not putting money into the things that—the roads and things, education and those things that are necessary for our future. And only really concentrating on outside the country. As fast as the world is going, the U.S. has been doing a fairly decent job outside the country, staying out of war and supporting other people getting out of their bad situations. But as far as here, I think it's been the rich getting richer and the poor getting poorer.

Those in boom regions like Silicon Valley and new growth areas like Charlotte made out all right in the early '80s. There was opportunity, people could change jobs and get raises, things were being straightened out, and the country got back some of its pride. For a little while, things seemed "to get better and better."

But there was a general sense that the Reagan economic policies were "fool's gold," producing a "bubble" or a "bust" at middecade. There was a strong impression that the good times were phony, that the American people were manipulated and fooled, that the foundations of future growth have been damaged:

> I don't know if it was the Reagan bullshit or what, but there was a brief period when things—businesswise— started to get real good. Then, as you're saying, somebody figured out that this is all gloss. But for a while there, there was a bubble.

> I think it was around the '82, '83, or '84 area. . . . It seemed the economy was going up. But I think you have a lag of where we're going to start showing the effect. And from what I've read, we're going to be paying for that forever and ever and ever.

> I'd say it's slowly increasing, if you look at it in terms of the economy during that time. They were good times, especially around here. But if you look back at them . . . we're paying the price for it now.

> Well, defense growth and big budget. Well, the budget all went to hell as far as the deficit, a great increase. . . . Plus he [Reagan] really believed in what he was feeding the American people. . . . I think he fooled us all and sold out, gave away all the restraints that protected the economy from abuses. . . . His Laffer curve. No one is laughing any more.

The sense of deception and reckoning combined with fairly specific criticisms of the values of the period, compounding the disillusionment. First, it was thought that those at the top had allowed or fostered the ascendance of greed instead of civic virtues. Even in Silicon Valley, people mixed their awe of the growth of microchips, credit, and opportunity with feelings that "greed was also growing." It was a "time for moral decay . . ." when the country had "gone downhill morally . . . [and] financially." "You had runaway inflation; then the deficits kick in. And then the buyouts came along. Greed was good, greed was good." "It seems during the '80s there was no accountability for the people who were in a position to make changes—whether it was CEOs, whether it was the government, whether it was the watchdog groups that were supposed to be working for us." Elsewhere it was just assumed that "greed" was a driving force taking the country closer to a crash: "I don't even remember when Reagan first got elected. . . . There was a [period] where everybody got in bed, and greed kind of became king of this country." Clearly the private values and business leadership of the era had become an ethical nightmare.

Second, many of the participants worried that our leaders were indifferent while foreign powers were taking over our markets and our country. Part of the economic and moral decline of the country was captured for these participants in the number of foreign immigrants, Japanese products, and foreign purchases of American property: "The European and Far East, in the '80s, started creeping into our economy." In fact, "we're no longer the economic power" at home or abroad.

Finally, there was near consensus in the groups that children had been left with a bleak future, that indifference and greed had robbed the next generation of the American dream. People spoke about children unable to afford the cash to buy a house ("you're going to have $20,000 or $30,000 in cash") or the absurdly high tuition ("a school will cost you $15,000"). The kids were staring in the face of minimum-wage jobs without benefits or security. It was going to be "rough," "tense." It was "going to be real bad." "They don't have a chance." "I think there're just going to be lost dreams for them."

A NEW MIDDLE-CLASS CONSCIOUSNESS

The discussion among middle-class voters was dominated by a number of truisms. They comprised a new economic consciousness, a middle-class consciousness built out of the wreckage of Democratic and Republican economic failures:

> First, the middle class, while the center of this new world, is poised for extinction.

> Second, the middle class is being crushed by growing bills, taxes, and the cost of basic necessities.

> Third, husbands and wives are working harder and longer hours, sacrificing family life, and putting children at risk, but only to pay for basics, not to really get ahead.

> And fourth, the wealthy are making out just fine.

When asked about "the middle class," people's thinking began with extinction: "endangered," "overtaxed," "shrinking," "fading away," "declining," and "there is none." The middle class is financially pressed to the wall, struggling to survive, indeed, on the verge of extinction, as reflected in these comments from other discussions all across the country:

> They should be almost nonexistent [in the year 2000]. There should be either millionaires and the poor; there should be no in between. There should be no middle class.

> Everybody is going to be either very rich or very poor. There's going to be the rich in their little towers, and there's going to be everybody else floundering around trying to survive.

> I think the middle class might be wiped out. Half of them might go to the poverty level, and half of them might find a way to be in the upper [class].

We confronted this wisdom with a bar graph showing the changing levels and distribution of family income from 1950 to the present (Figure 6.1). The graph suggests a number of patterns: the large and predominant working-class population of the 1950s gave way to a large middle class by 1970; the low- and middle-income population remained fairly stable in size and income from 1970 to the present; a high-income segment began to emerge in 1980 and had zoomed upward by 1990.

Our middle-class voters scrutinized the bars closely, paused, and then began applying their economic truisms—sometimes using the graph to affirm them, rejecting the graph where it seemed at odds with their own sense of economic reality. The fourth truism was easy. People readily observed, to universal acknowledgment, the gains of the wealthiest Americans in the '80s, though some thought the bar should have risen to higher levels.

The bulge of middle-income earners posed something of a problem for the participants: it violated their visual sense of the rich becoming richer and the poor poorer, their sense of a more divided and polarized society. Respondents observed:

> The groups are evening out, and I don't see it that way at all. I think we're moving toward a society of rich and poor.

> [There should be a] continual widening between the top and the bottom.

> There's a stretching going on, a pulling apart between low and high.

> We're losing our middle class. We're basically going to either—there's a lot of very poor people and a lot of very wealthy. And this shows sort of an even span.

With some relief, however, the discussants began to marshal their truisms to explain away the awkward vision of a large mid-

Distribution of Family Income

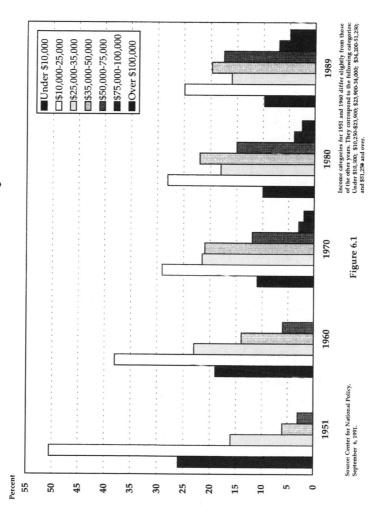

Percent

Legend:
■ Under $10,000
□ $10,000-25,000
□ $25,000-35,000
□ $35,000-50,000
■ $50,000-75,000
■ $75,000-100,000
■ Over $100,000

1951   1960   1970   1980   1989

Source: Center for National Policy,
September 6, 1991.

Figure 6.1

Income categories for 1951 and 1960 differ slightly from those
of the other years. They correspond to the following categories:
Under $10,500; $10,250-$23,900; $23,900-34,000; $34,200-51,250;
and $51,250 and over.

dle class presented by the graph. Since 1970, according to the graph, middle-class family income has remained largely unchanged: "It's gone up two thousand dollars in nineteen years? That's it?" That paltry increase affirmed the second and third truisms, that middle-class people are working harder for less. "I feel that things are getting out of control; the cost of things are going up," one woman observed; "and I say 'personally' because I have to work a lot harder too." Others observed that "*our* standard of living is going down" [emphasis added], not *the* standard of living. People believed they were "treading water" and "working really hard to do it."

Their incomes, people in other parts of the country have told us, pale before skyrocketing costs for things central to one's prosperity:[3]

> Yes, our salaries are good in this area, but everything is skyrocketing—health insurance is climbing, and car insurance is climbing, and everything is going real quick, not a little bit at a time.

> I think about when I was married, a week of groceries cost me $13 and my husband thought that was entirely too much money to spend for a week's groceries. Now I spend $150. I feel like I'm always running—and this big snowball is behind me getting bigger and bigger—and just trying to keep it from running over me.

> All of a sudden, some other tax comes in you haven't counted on. So you work a year to get a little further ahead, to get a little bit of extra. It never happens.

The inability to keep up with prices created an array of folktales heard all across the country that demonstrated a declining prosperity in the lives of ordinary people:

> We can't save like our parents did.

> The kids, they're still living at home . . . can't afford to get married . . . the cost of living.

> The children can't afford to go to college the way they used to.

> They'll have to be good to us if they want to have a home to live in, because the only way they'll get one is if we will them ours. They're never going to be able to buy a house.

> It'll be a generation mortgage. That's what it'll be. You'll end up buying a house for a hundred years.

> After struggling, holding three jobs sometimes, to keep my house, I'm not going to be able to keep it because I have to pay that higher tax.[4]

This new reality seemed quite perverse to these middle-class voters. Figure 6.1 creates an illusion of middle-class survival, but they knew the illusion was artificially produced by their hard work and sacrifice—by wives moving into the labor force and families being transformed and diminished in spite of two incomes.

> Now wives work. . . . The reason that the income is maintained is that you put your wife to work.

> We need more money to live. . . . It takes two people bringing in an income. . . . In the '50s, you had one person basically bringing in the income to sustain the family. And it's not practical anymore to assume that one person is going to.

> Think of both spouses in those households—15 percent were employed in 1975, and in 1990 it's probably well over 50, 60 percent. If you look at it from that perspective, it's incredible where the middle class stands.

Satisfied with the analysis, respondents settled back into their original observations about economic realities: "I think in the past twenty years the squeeze has been on the middle class basically." In one group, the wrap-up conversation went like this:

> The middle fifths are the ones that are really suffering, though.
>
> Exactly.
>
> Would that be us?
>
> Yes, that's us.

It is important to note that nearly all conversation about economic truisms took place with hardly a mention of political events or periods or presidencies. The sense of a declining middle class, of people and families working harder and not getting anywhere transcended perceptions of Bush, Reagan, Carter, and Nixon and represented the "the way things are" compared with the way things were in the '50s and '60s. This middle-class consciousness is the product of failed politics, but it now transcends those politics.

FAILED DEMOCRATIC ECONOMICS

By the early 1990s, Americans had lost confidence in the Democrats' ability to assure economic prosperity.[5] Before the 1992 presidential campaign, there was little sign that Democrats understood the new "facts" and truisms about the unique squeeze facing middle-class families. The Democrats rarely spoke of the middle class, lest somebody be offended in the cacophony that formed the Democratic party. There was no evidence that Democrats understood how to change things—how to raise incomes or make things affordable again. Democrats had policies and programs but no "vision."

When Michael Dukakis ran for president in 1988, the country was in an anxious mood. A large majority thought the country was headed down the wrong track, yet the out-of-power Democrats could do no better than establish parity when it came to inspiring confidence on handling the economy. A year into the listless Bush administration, the Democrats trailed the Republicans by 15 percentage points (39 to 24 percent) in the public's assessment of their ability to keep the country prosperous. Indeed, on the eve of the 1992 presidential contest, with the country in recession, the Democrats could barely muster a 9-point economic advantage. None of this resembled the heady days when voters turned naturally to the Democrats for prosperity and national leadership: Democrats had enjoyed healthy advantages on prosperity when they succeeded in electing presidents—15 points when John Kennedy was victorious, 32 points for Lyndon Johnson, and 24 points for Jimmy Carter. (See Figure 6.2.)

The collapse of the Democrats' standing on the economy was evident in the traditional realms, like prosperity and, predictably, inflation and the federal-budget deficit, but it was also evident in the new world of economic challenges: being tough with countries that trade unfairly, making America "economically strong," and putting America's economic house in order. (See Table 6.1.) Even blue-collar workers and those worried about unemployment now put more trust in the Republicans' ability to keep the country prosperous (by 28 and 14 points, respectively).

After all, what is "Democratic economics" today? Democrats used to share a macroeconomic common sense, rooted in Keynesian assumptions, that linked government spending with economic security and a rising economic welfare for working people and the nation. But Keynesian assumptions were in retreat, and now Democratic pronouncements on spending

Political Parties and Prosperity

Net Democratic advantage: percentage who say Democrats will do a better
job minus the percentage who say Republicans will do a better job

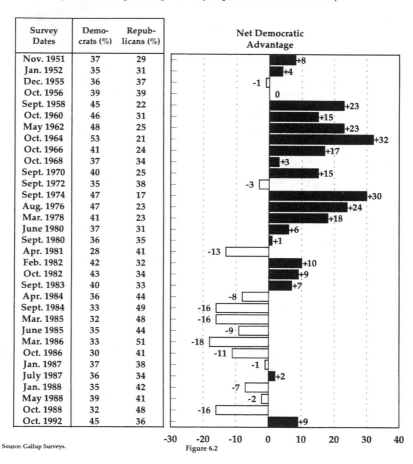

Survey Dates	Demo-crats (%)	Repub-licans (%)
Nov. 1951	37	29
Jan. 1952	35	31
Dec. 1955	36	37
Oct. 1956	39	39
Sept. 1958	45	22
Oct. 1960	46	31
May 1962	48	25
Oct. 1964	53	21
Oct. 1966	41	24
Oct. 1968	37	34
Sept. 1970	40	25
Sept. 1972	35	38
Sept. 1974	47	17
Aug. 1976	47	23
Mar. 1978	41	23
June 1980	37	31
Sept. 1980	36	35
Apr. 1981	28	41
Feb. 1982	42	32
Oct. 1982	43	34
Sept. 1983	40	33
Apr. 1984	36	44
Sept. 1984	33	49
Mar. 1985	32	48
June 1985	35	44
Mar. 1986	33	51
Oct. 1986	30	41
Jan. 1987	37	38
July 1987	36	34
Jan. 1988	35	42
May 1988	39	41
Oct. 1988	32	48
Oct. 1992	45	36

Source: Gallup Surveys.   Figure 6.2

TABLE 6.1

THE PARTIES AND THE ECONOMY
March 1990

	(% Saying Phrase Applies to Party)		
	Democrats	*Republicans*	*Difference*
Overall			
Can keep the country prosperous	24	39	−15
Older Realms			
Will keep inflation under control	27	40	−13
Can best handle the federal-budget deficits	25	34	−9
Newer Realms			
Tough with countries that sell goods here in America but that unfairly restrict the sale of American products overseas	24	32	−8
Can put America's economic house in order	30	35	−5
Can make America economically strong	27	39	−12

seemed timid, lacking an economic rationale. Democrats used to speak of equity and fairness, but such economic values had become too narrow and partial to encompass the Democrats' potential diversity; those values, literally applied, seemed mindlessly hostile to wealth without an evident public purpose. Finally, Democrats used to speak of government, collective purpose, and a vital public life that inspired confidence in Democratic leadership. But in the Reagan era, Democrats joined with Republicans in diminishing the public sphere and narrowing their specific claim to being the stewards of the economy.

It is hard to imagine how voters could think otherwise. Jimmy Carter gave them "malaise" and inflation combined with a conservative fiscal austerity. Walter Mondale offered them higher taxes and special interest groups run amok. Michael Dukakis offered the mantra "good jobs at good wages" but disdained talk about the middle class and populism. He was willing to champion ethnic Americans, their heritage, and their journey, but he never championed people's lives against the powerful forces that disrupted them. On Labor Day 1988, he strode off the stage and, before his chastened campaign aides, ripped up his new populist campaign speech with the warning, "I don't want to see this divisive shit anymore."[6]

Indeed, the Dukakis campaign stood dumbstruck before the new economic realities and the new economic consciousness. There was certainly enough evidence in 1988 that the public was fundamentally uneasy about the economic world, yet the Democratic campaign remained inarticulate on the economy. Dukakis did conventional things, like climbing into a tank in Warren, Michigan, to reassure people of his stand on national defense, but he never ran for president as if the world had changed and as if people were troubled.

Voters in 1988 may not have read Paul Kennedy's bestselling book *The Rise and Fall of the Great Powers,* but they did have an acute sense that the United States, once the envy of the world, was in danger of decline. Two thirds of the public believed that the American economy had gotten weaker compared with the economies of other countries; over 60 percent believed America was "slipping dangerously" or in "long-term economic decline."[7] Despite macroeconomic indicators that seemed to satisfy the elites, voters wanted a new president who would bring economic change: around 60 percent listed as their first or second criterion for president "someone who can strengthen our economy"; a similar proportion wanted "someone who will address our country's social problems, like education, health, and poverty." Only a third of the voters indicated that it was important to have "someone who will protect our national security interests."[8]

Dukakis's campaign dissolved into a thematic mess, believing it was still fighting old wars, not American economic decline. Some of the candidate's key advisers thought the Democrats were stalled primarily before the "gateway" of U.S.-Soviet relations. They believed Democratic presidential candidates were perceived as "naysayers to a strong America," and that situation "effectively prevented the Democrats from passing through the gateway" to national office. Though their surveys found that 62 percent of the public believed economic strength to be more important than military strength for a nation's influence in the world, Dukakis's advisers asserted only that the public is of "two minds, that economic and military strength have achieved roughly *equal* importance." They urged the Dukakis campaign simply to play both sides—emphasizing America's economic strength as "equal in importance to its military strength in protecting America's national security."[9] The net effect of this caution was a Democratic party still muddled before the growing economic despair.

None of the national Democratic leaders in the 1980s, from Carter to Dukakis, had come to terms with the wreckage created by the failure of party renewal. The crash of the Great Soci-

ety had left the Democrats a narrow party without a vision of
middle America that could encompass the disadvantaged as well
as the middle class. The crash of Reaganomics had left the
Republicans ever more narrow, preoccupied with the privileged, also with little promise for those in the middle. The old
economic ideas that excited imaginations—from the New Deal
to a business-led prosperity—also lay shattered. But perhaps
worse, none of the political leaders, certainly none of the
Democrats, seemed to understand the scale of the economic
challenge.

Yet for all their troubles, the Democrats were still alive on
the economy. They were alive because voters have a sense of
history—modern Democratic presidents, after all, generally
presided over periods of strong economic growth. But Democrats were alive as well because of the historic imagery that associates Democrats with the common person. Bereft of ideas and
without a shred of positive results in recent years, the Democrats
still seemed less beholden to lobbyists, the rich, and the powerful and perhaps more likely to side with the people. In 1990, survey respondents gave the Democrats a 5-point advantage (37 to
32 percent) over the Republicans when asked, "Which party do
you consider on your side?"

Indeed, that remembrance was powerful enough that the
Democrats still had the chance to recapture the attention of the
public—if they could have acknowledged the middle class, if
they could have found a new approach to the people, one that
would have brought together the less privileged and the struggling middle class. The acknowledgment in itself would have
signaled a new understanding and a new direction, perhaps a
new bottom-up route to progress. After the collapse of Reaganism, this desperate electorate was looking for another way.

In March 1990, I offered a national sample of Americans a
stark choice: if you are coming to the aid of the middle class, do

you lower taxes (the essence of Bushism and Reaganism), or do you take government initiatives to address the financial squeeze?

> The Republicans say the middle class carries too heavy a burden of taxes, and tax cuts are the best approach to helping middle-class people keep up with the rising costs of things.

> The Democrats say the middle class faces rising costs for basic things, health care, education, and housing, and the government should do more to bring these basic needs in reach of middle-class families.

There was no contest: by 62 to 26 percent, voters opted for a government activism with the breadth to reach the middle class. Under this umbrella, Democrats carried white-collar, blue-collar, and clerical-sales workers (66 to 24 percent), white Catholics (60 to 32 percent) and white moderates (62 to 27 percent) as well as liberal Democrats (85 to 6 percent) and blacks (79 to 7 percent).[10] The appeal to middle America appears to be a big umbrella.

Voters were clearly looking for an acknowledgment of their struggle, and Coolidge-like tax cuts now seemed disingenuous, given the Reagan experience. They no doubt despaired that the tax-and-spend Democrats would in reality offer more of the same, just taxes and welfare, but the survey suggested a surviving glimmer of hope that Democrats would offer a more direct attack on today's people problems, like jobs and income, health care and education. Voters were looking for a broader and more purposeful political response to the lagging living standards of ordinary people. One East Coast voter referred to such a response as "hopefully pulling us out of the hole financially so that people can start enjoying their little raises again. There would be a little more money for us."

This was all wistful in 1990 because Democrats were still largely silent in the face of the end of growth and this new middle-class consciousness. The party was still silenced by its own demons.

FAILED REPUBLICAN ECONOMICS

Our middle-class voters in the focus groups, graphs in hand, did not think much of George Bush. They knew he was a product of something bigger—the failure of Reaganism. I asked them each to write a postcard to George Bush, discussing anything they wanted about the nation's economy. The postcards were poignant and underlined the collapse of Reaganism. There was no confidence that business would lead us out of our problems, no respect for life at the top. These were people who felt lost and wondered whether the president understood. They called on the president to discover the recession, to do something, to stand up for America, to take care of problems at home and stop giving breaks to the rich. The postcards, represented by the sample below, captured the economic consciousness and despair that now dominated the political landscape.

Dear President Bush:
I think the present economy stinks right now. I think it's time to step back, take a look at where we are heading and do something, i.e., stop trying to squeeze the breath out of the middle class. Start taxing the rich. Put in regulations that will curb the appetites of the wealthy industries.

Dear President Bush:
"Either lead, follow, or get out of the way," good advice. Get the "vision thing" or get another job (and get your greedy friends out of my government).

Dear President Bush:
Pay more attention to what American businesses are saying. Why is the standard of living continuing to decrease? Why can't you balance the budget? Why do you continue to point fingers and blame others for the economy? You were voted into office because you convinced people you could handle these problems. What happened?

Dear President Bush:
Wake up, there is a recession. People are out of work. Too many getting by free. Seniors need to eat also. Higher raises in Social Security checks. More jobs, keep jobs in America.

Dear President Bush:
The "trickle-down" theory has worked: what has trickled down is a tragic state for the poor, the working poor, increasingly the middle class. What has not trickled down is economic resources to make changes in the way we help maintain human dignity and respect. We are headed toward a disaster of class warfare.

Dear President Bush:
The economy favors the wealthy. America's economic strength of the past favored the middle class and the small business. To resolve our economic problems, we need to legislate laws that bring the balance of favor to the middle-class worker.

Dear President Bush:
Take a leave of absence! Using the James Earl Carter disguise. Walk the streets, tour the country as a cameraman. Develop an understanding of results of a consolidation of wealth. The strength of small business is creating employment. Understand the inability of a service economy to create wealth.

Bush's indifference to the recession and problems in America placed a curtain of indifference over Reaganism. Trickle-down economics, in the absence of growth, was now just cynical. There was nothing in this economic appeal to Bush to suggest any desire to return to Republican economics.

In fact, these voters seemed lost. They called for balanced budgets, help for the middle class and small business, national health insurance, more taxes on the wealthy, and more spending at home; they appealed to their president to get moving and do something, to take care of America. But they were lost because America's leaders were lost, getting by on failed ideas.

7. THE CLINTON SOLUTION

BILL Clinton announced his candidacy for president of the United States on the front portico of the Old State House in Little Rock, Arkansas. It was noon on October 3, 1991.

Clinton spoke immediately and directly to the people of Macomb County, Michigan—and to the people like them all across the country whose dreams had been dashed and whose contract with the country's leaders had been broken. There was nothing indirect here. Clinton declared that these people provided this new candidacy with its sense of purpose. He would take this step "beyond a life and job I love, to make a commitment to a larger cause, preserving the American Dream . . . restoring the hopes of the forgotten middle class . . . reclaiming the future for our children."

The forgotten middle class—the phrase seems almost trite in retrospect, but at the time no Democrat in decades had so directly linked his political life to the lives of ordinary Americans. "That is why I stand here today, because I refuse to stand by and let our children become part of the first generation to do worse than their parents."

The New York Times described his speech as "relentlessly focused on the strains of the middle class." Indeed, Bill Clinton rooted his political life in the values of middle-class America—

"solid middle-class values of work, faith, family, individual responsibility and community"—values that were now "threatened by an administration that refuses to take care of our own, has turned its back on the middle class, and is afraid to change while the world is changing." Clinton charged the Republican administrations of the past twelve years with sitting on the sidelines while middle-class life was deteriorating: "Middle class people are spending more hours on the job, spending less time with their children, bringing home a smaller paycheck to pay more for health care and housing and education. Our streets are meaner, our families are broken, our health care is the costliest in the world and we get less for it."

Bill Clinton declared his candidacy in their name: "That is why today I am declaring my candidacy for President of the United States. Together I believe we can provide leadership that will restore the American Dream, that will fight for the forgotten middle class, that will provide more opportunity, insist on more responsibility, and create a greater sense of community for this great country."

"This is not just a campaign for the presidency," Clinton concluded, but "a campaign for the future, for the forgotten hard-working middle class families of America who deserve a government that fights for them. A campaign to keep America strong at home and around the world."[1]

THE LABORATORY, 1974 TO 1984

Bill Clinton forged his own solution for reaching middle America, and he did so in the most challenging laboratory possible almost two decades before running for president. In his first Arkansas campaign, he brought together populism, education, and reinvented government in a vision for a bottom-up party struggling to show ordinary Americans the way to a better future. The intellectual roots of the "new covenant" that Clinton offered America lay not with his presidential advisers but with the yeoman farmers and their heirs who paused to listen to this young congressional candidate in 1974.

That year Clinton came within 6,000 votes of defeating a four-term Republican congressman, John Paul Hammerschmidt, who had won his two previous races with 67 and then 77 percent of the vote. The Third Congressional District was not especially hospitable to Democrats; support for Humphrey and McGovern had sunk to barely a quarter of the vote in 1968 and 1972. But Clinton took 48.5 percent and surprised all the political pundits, including the incumbent, who watched the results until sun up the next morning and claimed victory just before noon in a written press statement. Clinton's extraordinary achievement created, according to the local AP bureau chief, "an aura of inevitability" around this man.

Two years later Clinton was elected the nation's youngest state attorney general, and in 1978 he became the youngest governor. For the Arkansas press and for many across the country who watched with fascination, this was the story of a wonder kid who took the unsuspecting by storm. The press wrote of a "real comer," a "star," a man of "extraordinary credentials, an unusual intellect and a dazzling personality," and "one of the brightest figures on the state's political horizon."[2]

But for the nation, that was not the real story unfolding in Arkansas. The real story was the test of ideas: conceived in the contest for Congress, muddled in the first campaigns for attorney general and governor, and then forged into a unity in the bitter battle to put Bill Clinton's stamp on Arkansas. The Clinton solution was developed, against the odds and under the most unlikely circumstances, in what was likely America's best laboratory for a new bottom-up vision.

The Ground Rules

When Bill Clinton declared his candidacy for Congress, he entered a world with ground rules that underscored the Democrats' remoteness from their roots: Hubert Humphrey had received only 27 percent of the vote in Arkansas's Third Congressional District and 30 percent statewide in 1968, while George Wallace carried Arkansas and ran second to Nixon in the district as well as in the state. This was downscale America, not some country-club suburb. While some of the towns had benefited from an influx of retirees, this remained a district of mountain counties where hardworking farmers and townspeople struggled for their subsistence. The soil was thin and the land was rocky, so hard work was the rule if you were to win out over the unproductive land. The pine forests in the Ouachita Mountains allowed some scattered sawmills, but northwestern Arkansas was dominated by the life of small-scale farming.

In fifteen of the district's twenty-one counties, per capita income did not reach $2,000 in 1970; in only two did the per capita income top the princely figure of $2,300 a year, and even then income fell well below the statewide average of $2,822 a year. In a third of the best-off counties, less than half of all residents had graduated from high school; in the rest of the district, two thirds or more never finished high school. These were white people of humble means and traditional values. In the core northwestern counties in the Ozarks, 99.4 percent were white, rising to 99.5 percent in the western counties along the Oklahoma border. Statewide, Arkansas was home to the poorest white people in the United States: in 1970, white per capita income was just $2,410—lowest in the nation. Between 1974 and 1978, the state hovered between forty-seventh and forty-ninth in per capita income (both black and white)—always above Mississippi and sometimes above Alabama and South Carolina.[3]

People here took their Bible seriously, with fundamentalist evangelical churches in nearly every hollow. In Carroll County, at the heart of the district, tourists would soon come to see the Bible Museum, the Christ of the Ozarks statue, and a performance of The Great Passion Play.

These counties had supported the Confederacy only reluctantly and voted Republican after the Civil War. But their Republicanism was shaped by the peculiarities of southern politics—a common man's politics, counterpoised to the dominance of the slave and plantation oligarchy in the Delta and big business in Little Rock. The poor whites of the Ozarks backed Jeff Davis, the populist turn-of-the-century attorney general and governor who attacked corporations for monopoly pricing and attacked the "high-collared roosters" and "silk-stocking crowd" of Little Rock. But the agenda of the common man was suppressed in Arkansas, as it was across the South. The poll tax and literacy test disenfranchised the black and the poor white alike, while the state's economic elite moved comfortably in control of a white supremacist Democratic party. The populist current was diverted into a one-party politics devoid of issues, enduring factions, or popular leaders.[4]

It was an arrangement that favored the economic establishment and shortchanged the poorer classes, both black and white, who were served badly by government. Taxes were low, to be sure, but the benefits of life in Arkansas were few. In 1978, when Clinton ran for governor, Arkansas ranked fiftieth among the states on spending for public education and on the percentage of college graduates.[5]

The ground rules began and ended with low taxes. The state's constitution barred any increase in broad-based taxes—income, business, or sales tax—unless approved by a three-fourths vote in the state legislature. But that formalism does not quite capture the state's anti-tax culture that bracketed Clinton's first campaigns. In 1970, Governor Winthrop Rockefeller lost his bid for reelection, to Dale Bumpers, in part because he had raised taxes. And David Pryor succeeded Bumpers in 1975, having campaigned on the "Arkansas plan" to cut taxes by 25 percent. After Clinton was defeated in his bid for reelection as governor in 1980, he gave a farewell address underscoring the social cost of this principle: "The state will have to come to it [broader taxes], sooner or later, meantime settling for the barest minimums in the services expected in the American society."[6]

The First Campaign: "Beans and Greens"

If you're tired of eating beans and greens
And forgotten what pork and beef steak mean
There's a man you ought to be listening to

Bill Clinton's ready, he's fed up too.
He's a lot like me.
He's a lot like you.
Bill Clinton's going to get things done
So we're going to send him to Washington.

Clinton campaign tune,
1974 congressional race

In early 1974, at age twenty-seven, Clinton got into his 1970 Gremlin and began searching for any gathering of people that would hear him out. Later he switched to a little Chevelle truck with AstroTurf in the back and drove from Hot Springs, where he had grown up, to Clarkesville and Prairie Grove. He was known to have hit ten rural towns in a day, as the *Arkansas Gazette* observed, "dropping in at hardware stores, barber shops, banks, second-hand stores and stopping people on the street."[7]

He began this campaign, and his political life, by attempting to rebuild the Democrats' association with the common person,

working with a remembrance clearly faded and tarnished in
northwestern Arkansas. With the battle over racial liberalism rag-
ing nationally, there was little room for the poor whites of the
South. In the dominant culture of the day, these were racists at
worst and hillbillies at best; in any event, they were hardly the
heart and soul of the national Democratic party, which would
be embarrassed by their presence.

But Bill Clinton, who had grown up in Hot Springs, knew
that Arkansas and the mountain counties were not the Black
Belt, where a virulent racial politics crowded out new possibilities. While membership in the White Citizens Council had
grown to 300,000 in neighboring Mississippi, in Arkansas there
were no more than 20,000 members. Race had not fully obscured the politics of the common man.[8]

Clinton's radio ads aired in the final three weeks of the campaign brought home the association with the common man as
first principle.

Clinton's campaign was infused with a commitment to
change the direction in Washington, where government neglected the economic needs of "average people." He said, "The
good Government we love has too often been made use of for
private and selfish purposes. Those who have abused it have forgotten the people."[9]

Clinton made clear his populist leanings by regularly attacking corporate power and tax advantages. He called for public
disclosure of oil-company operations and an excess-profits tax
on their income. In fact, he proposed excess-profits taxes on
"every industry reaping unwarranted profits during inflation."
American tax dollars, he believed, should be used to address "real
needs" at home, not to promote and underwrite corporate
expansion abroad: "Congress has to blame itself for allowing
corporations to build plants overseas instead of at home and
then taking tax write-offs. The Congress even has its approval on

an insurance policy paid by you, the taxpayer, to pay these corporations if they lose money in their overseas ventures."

Clinton opposed the Ford administration's tax surcharge
that was intended to contain inflation and proposed instead that
Congress pass excess-profits and minimum corporate taxes and
reduce tax credits for companies investing overseas; and he
added, "We don't need foreign investment by American businesses at this time." Clinton drew the populist contrast that associated him with the lives of average Arkansans: "The economic
policy of this administration has been to make the middle sector
of this economy suffer and tighten its belt while large, multina-
tional companies such as Gulf can use tax loopholes to avoid
paying its fair share of taxes."[10]

Clinton maintained a drumbeat for tax relief for average
Arkansans. He strongly opposed proposed taxes on gas and
income to control inflation: "I think it's just more of the same.
They want to fight inflation by hurting the little people. How
can you propose tax relief for middle- and lower-middle-
income people and then turn around and do worse to them by
making them pay 10 to 30 cents more a gallon of gasoline."
What Clinton supported was tax relief for ordinary people,
funded by higher taxes on corporations and by closing loopholes in foreign investment.[11]

Clinton identified his campaign with everyday people. In a
telegram to President Ford, urging him to adopt the Clinton
approach, Clinton described his "economic advisers"—"small
farmers, small businessmen, working people, retirees and almost
anyone you can imagine." His campaign manager recalls a Bill
Clinton who remembered the working people he met along the
campaign trail, the people who gave his campaign purpose.
Clinton would recall "the words of a friend of mine who works
on the Scott County road crew, 'the people want a hand up, not
a hand out.' "[12]

The Clinton economic program centered on education, which the candidate felt had to be funded if the people were to be better off. He strongly supported increased federal funding for education, particularly for "less-wealthy states like Arkansas." The federal role was important because Arkansas could not make sufficient progress on its own "without taxing working people, small farmers, small businesses and retirees too harshly." Clinton wanted increased federal support, without strings, for education in general but also for career, vocational, and adult education. He considered this to be money well spent because "money invested in education" produces an educated people who "get good jobs and pay far more taxes over a lifetime."[13]

But Clinton's call for government activism on behalf of the people was infused with hostility to big federal bureaucracies and wasteful federal spending. This opposition was evident in a range of policy postures—from breaking up the federal education bureaucracy and taking away the limousines of federal bureaucrats, relieving "small businessmen of much of the burden of government paperwork" and changing the course of the deficit to achieve a balanced budget. Clinton declared at one of his weekly press conferences, "We need a congressman who's not afraid to say no to the unnecessary government spending that has been going on and has hurt the economy of the country."

Clinton wanted to reorient public life, putting the people's interests and feelings center stage. At the heart of this race, Clinton said, was "a feeling of general helplessness on the part of the voters about the federal bureaucracy. It's unyielding, distant and not responsible. And the people feel the same about the big oil companies. They want a strong Congress to stand up and do what it's supposed to do."[14]

Congressman Hammerschmidt attacked Clinton for his immaturity, for his big-labor support, and above all, for his "radical left-wing philosophy." Even so, he did not unravel the Clinton solution: the challenger took 48.5 percent of the vote but, more important, succeeded in building from the bottom up. Hammerschmidt took the five counties with the highest incomes and the lowest rural populations (Sebastian, Washington, Boone, Benton, and Garland). Clinton, however, won big in ten counties—nearly all of which ranked at the bottom on per capita income, education, and rural population; he won three other counties, all of which scored low on education. In the process, he won four of the six Wallace counties in the district. The Clinton solution had clearly opened up the heart of downscale America to a revitalized vision of Democratic purpose.[15] (See Table 7.1.)

From Politics to Governance

It was supposed to be rosy from there. Bill Clinton had done the impossible and impressed all those who anoint rising stars. Governor Bumpers, along with every top Democrat, campaigned for Clinton in 1974 and described him as the "kind of man this country needs to turn things around." With the remarkable performance in 1974, Clinton's rise to high office was deemed inevitable, and indeed, he quickly became a candidate for attorney general. He won the position outright in 1976, taking 53 percent of the vote in a three-way Democratic primary, thus avoiding a runoff. The Republicans did not bother to field a candidate, so Clinton was declared attorney general on May 25. Before completing his two-year term, he became a candidate for governor. Again he swept a multicandidate field, with 60 percent of the vote and again avoided a runoff. This time the Republicans ran a candidate against him, but he won in a landslide, with 63 percent.

In the absence of tough electoral battles in 1976 and 1978, the Clinton solution became somewhat diffuse in presentation.

Important elements remained, to be sure, but Clinton's political life no longer hung on finding just the right balance between an activist government for the common person and the burdens of paying for it. The fiscal requirements of a program to uplift Arkansas imposed new policy and political challenges, but they also demanded an evolving vision that would keep working- and middle-class Arkansas engaged in the project. None of that seemed obvious, however, as Clinton moved into the governor's mansion.

Bill Clinton had built his statewide identity by taking on the utilities—the symbol of private monopoly power counterpoised to the interests of the ordinary consumer—a cause that was the centerpiece of his low-key campaign for attorney general. As a candidate, he supported intervention on proposed utility-rate increases, toughening amendments to the Clean Air Act opposed by state officials, and toughening amendments to the Consumer Protection Act. As attorney general, he intervened with the Public Service Commission to allow people a month to pay their utility bills; and when he declared that he was running for governor, he pointed to that record: "I have fought utility policies and rate increases I thought were wrong. I have worked to protect consumers and small businessmen from those who abuse the marketplace." As attorney general and as a gubernatorial candidate, he called for an investigation of the Arkansas Power and Light Company because it had contracted for more expensive Wyoming coal "at the expense of Arkansas utility customers." His radio advertisement, disputed by his opponents, declared that as attorney general he had intervened in every major electric, natural-gas, and telephone rate case.[16]

And after his relatively easy win in 1978, Bill Clinton proceeded to antagonize almost every powerful corporate interest in the state. His proposal for part-time doctors in rural health clinics raised bitter opposition from the state's medical organiza-

TABLE 7.1

THIRD CONGRESSIONAL DISTRICT

Arkansas, 1974

County	Per Capita Income 1974	Less Than High School Education 1974 (%)	Non-urban Population 1974 (%)	Clinton 1974 (%)	Presidential Winner 1968	Democratic 1968 (%)	Democratic 1972 (%)
Downscale							
Newton	$1,308	73	100	58	Nixon	30	30
Searcy	$1,537	76	100	59	Nixon	22	21
Madison	$1,569	11	100	57	Nixon	32	36
Perry	$1,693	72	100	67	Wallace	28	36
Marion	$1,707	41	100	54	Nixon	30	32
Scott	$1,733	73	100	62	Wallace	29	24

Middle

Logan	$1,801	70	58	50	Nixon	31	28
Franklin	$1,801	65	77	48	Wallace	25	25
Montgomery	$1,803	66	100	63	Wallace	26	30
Polk	$1,874	65	66	51	Nixon	25	23
Johnson	$1,876	67	65	54	Humphrey	34	33
Crawford	$1,901	64	67	44	Wallace	22	18
Yell	$1,995	66	77	60	Wallace	29	34

Upscale

Pope	$2,071	71	59	52	Nixon	30	32
Carroll	$2,147	60	100	55	Nixon	26	28
Baxter	$2,185	54	74	52	Nixon	28	28
Boone	$2,240	56	62	47	Nixon	26	25
Garland	$2,262	55	34	49	Nixon	28	25
Benton	$2,281	57	55	41	Nixon	25	22
Washington	$2,367	51	39	49	Nixon	28	29
Sebastian	$2,636	50	18	36	Nixon	23	19
Total/Average	$1,942	60	74	48		27	28

SOURCES: U.S. Bureau of the Census, 1970 Census data in *County and City Data Book* (Washington, D.C., 1972); Kelly Bryant, Office of the Secretary of State of Arkansas (Little Rock, 1968, 1972, 1974); Richard M. Scammon, *America Votes*, vols. 8 and 10 (Washington, D.C.: Congressional Quarterly Press, 1970, 1973).

tions. But their ire hardly matched that of the timber interests, who saw Clinton take the first tentative steps toward addressing the problem of clear-cutting. Trucking interests, including those involved in the poultry industry, rebelled against the taxes and fees for upgrading the state's highways. Steve Smith, Clinton's first campaign manager and senior adviser in his first term, suggests in retrospect that perhaps use of phrases like "corporate criminals" probably "did not really endear the governor" to business interests.

Clinton had run for governor as an activist, as a "worker and a doer." But his activism was short on specifics, and some in the press described a "front runner's campaign," cautious and not very controversial. He committed himself to education as his highest priority for any state surplus, proposed modest salary increases for teachers, and suggested the possibility of a bond issue for road construction and repair.[17]

When Clinton took office, however, the activism proved more than stylistic. He proposed increasing state aid to the public schools by 21 percent in one year, raising teacher salaries by $1,200 in each of the next two years, and giving teachers health and life insurance. He matched the spending increase in the following year, for a 40-percent increase in school spending during his first term. Clinton worked aggressively to recruit new industries, established a Department of Energy paralleling President Carter's national energy initiative, created a network of rural health clinics, and offered the first major road-building program in fifteen years.[18]

But Clinton did not balance his populism and activism with any serious discussion of disciplined or reinvented government, as he had in his 1974 race for Congress. Once during the gubernatorial campaign, before a high school audience, he mused that "there are an awful lot of people who work for the state who aren't busy every day," calling that "a different sort of welfare."

But he later clarified his remarks and dropped the theme. After the election, he affirmed his fiscal prudence and the need for more efficient government, even as he committed himself to activist government:

> The people want us to take Arkansas off the bottom in education spending and improve the quality of education, to promote economic development and to improve the quality of life for our senior citizens and others who are working to make do on limited incomes. But they expect us to do these things while maintaining our commitment to fiscal conservatism, cutting work, promising responsible management, and demanding performance, not rhetoric, from government.

But the prudence seemed more a reassurance than a passion. There was no anger about "uncaring government," out of touch with the values and interests of ordinary people.[19]

With all of these spending initiatives, it should not be surprising that the Clinton governorship crashed against the rocks of taxes. In order to finance his highway program, Clinton proposed raising the gasoline tax by a penny and offering a new schedule of vehicle-registration fees. The proposal reflected his overall populist orientation—a 50 percent increase on heavy trucks, a $20 fee on the least expensive cars, and $50 for the most expensive ones. Clinton observed, "A person who can afford a Cadillac or a Mercedes can afford a $50 license plate." But organized interests beat back the trucking fees, shifted the costs to passenger vehicles, and shifted the formula to weight rather than value. Clinton's car-tag tax was now a tax on working people who tended to own the older, heavier cars.[20]

Clinton's Republican challenger ran under the banner "car tags and Cubans." The former reflected Bill Clinton's increase in car-registration fees; the latter reflected public disquiet over Clinton's handling of the riot of Cuban refugees sent to Fort

Smith by President Carter. But it was the car tags that really mattered, as the issue reflected a fundamental breakdown of the Clinton solution in the difficult laboratory of Arkansas. Clinton's Republican challenger, Frank White, pledged to roll back the tax increases and empathized with the "great pain" felt by ordinary Arkansans, particularly the senior citizens. Clinton lamented, as the *Arkansas Gazette* put it, that White was stuck on "emotional issues" while failing to talk about the "valid issues—jobs, housing, education, roads, taxes and programs for the elderly."[21]

Through the summer of 1980, Clinton gave a number of addresses around the country in which he lamented the sense of drift and lack of vision, but the Clinton solution was nowhere in evidence. There was no sign that Clinton was fully sensitive to the breach developing between ordinary people and himself. Before the state Democratic convention in Hartford, Connecticut, Clinton warned of the "deeply entrenched alienation" and deep pessimism about the country's economic future. He warned that people feel "powerless to do anything about it" and "do not see where we are going." But then he observed that "Republicans say that government is the problem," and he parodied their litany: "Give us less government. Cut the taxes. Balance the budget." And he concluded, "I don't believe the American people believe that." The answer for Clinton in 1980 was a government that would respond to economic crisis, that "promotes growth and the health of the economy." There was a passing mention of waste as bad—"that is not to say there is not waste in government"—though his rhetorical energies were devoted to a government that would restore prosperity.[22]

He took the same message to the Democratic National Convention at Madison Square Garden in New York City. Again he highlighted the alienation, economic woes, and lack of vision. He said that "it is not enough" to put together "the old elements of the Democratic coalition" and suggested looking to

a new generation of Democrats who would lead the way to a
new and broader coalition. He called for an "economic revital-
ization of America," and "of our basic industrial structure." He
ended by saying his home remained within the party that
offered "a better hope for a safe, and prosperous, and good, and
decent world than the alternative." In the summer of 1980, Clinton had lost the combination of activist and reinvented government that had proved so powerful just a few years earlier.[23]

Apparently, even as he was giving these speeches to a
national audience, Clinton was beginning to hear something
different at home. During the summer, he came back from a
campaign trip to southern Arkansas, where he had visited a
number of factories, and confided the bleak mood to his chief of
staff: "They're killing me out there. I go into these factories
where people have always been kind to me and they tell me I
kicked them in the teeth." It was not the amount of money—
just $25 for a new license plate—"no, they said I kicked them
when they were down."

The reality of Clinton's woes had become evident as election day neared. The state's established interests—the timber
companies, the truckers, and two of the biggest utilities, Arkansas
Power and Light Company and Southwestern Bell Telephone—
rallied to White, who outdid Clinton in fund-raising and ultimately defeated him by 32,000 votes.[24] It was a tough year for
Democrats: Jimmy Carter lost the state after racking up his
biggest win here in 1976. But Clinton lost in what is best characterized as a rural rebellion: downscale, rural counties that
mostly voted for Wallace in 1968 and stuck with Carter in 1980
now singled out Clinton to vote no. In the old Third Congressional District, four of the Wallace counties that Clinton had
carried in 1974 with at least 60 percent of the vote—Mont-
gomery, Scott, Yell, and Perry—supported Carter and White in
the 1980 downscale rebellion.[25]

Two weeks after his defeat, Clinton confessed in a newspaper interview that he had "failed at a fundamental level"—"I simply didn't communicate to the people that I genuinely cared about them." And then he focused in on the "emotional" issue— the increase in car-license fees—that cut away at his standing:

> That's my one regret—that some person in Yell County, for an example, who is from a family much like the one I grew up in, lower middle income, is sitting there thinking that I just stuck it to him on his car taxes for no reason. Ironically, those were the people who I thought good roads would benefit the most.

Post-election polls showed that anti-Clinton voters were concerned above all with the car-license fees (26 percent), followed by a general discontent with taxes and government spending (15 percent); 11 percent mentioned the handling of the Cuban refugees.[26] As the smoke of defeat cleared away, Clinton was able to see how the car fees and bad economic times had left people angry and trapped: "A lot of wage-earning people get up every day and feel that they're standing in a small room with the walls closing in." That identification and understanding had slipped from the Clinton solution but clearly remained central to Clinton's identity.[27]

From Populism to Responsibility

Clinton made his peace with the people of Arkansas in 1982. In February, at the outset of the next campaign, he aired TV spots, acknowledging mistakes and apologizing for having lost touch: "My Daddy never had to whip me twice for the same thing." He set down the theme that Clinton would repeat all across the state: "You can't lead without listening." In the reflection of his defeat, Clinton determined that he had to understand the people and that he had to strike the right balance between change and tradition, as he described in this 1992 interview with David Maraniss of *The Washington Post:* "I realized that when we got in trouble it was when the need for change conflicted with people's most deeply ingrained habits or most cherished values. If you want to be for change, you have to render that change in ways people can understand and relate to."[28]

In 1982, that meant a focused populism. It included the right fights, of course, against the utilities, but also a populism grounded in personal style and approachability, in biography and personal commitment. The Bill Clinton of 1982 was a candidate of ordinary people, not that distant governor who raised fees on the old Chevies of rural folk. This was an aspirant governor who "came up through the public schools" and whose daughter would go there too. With unemployment approaching 10 percent, voters began to turn back to Clinton.[29]

On the campaign trail, Clinton said the race was about three issues—"jobs, education, and utility rates"—but it was the last that became defining. Clinton focused on Governor White's close identification with the utilities that had raised rates. Indeed, Clinton called White a "country-club governor" and an "errand boy for the utilities." The issue turned dramatic when newspapers broke the story that Governor White had sent prospective appointees to the Public Service Commission to be interviewed by officials of Arkansas Power and Light—appointees who soon after voted a $104-million rate increase and helped make possible a 47-percent profit for the utility. For Clinton, the issue was defining, "almost unbelievable." This corruption, Clinton's ads declared, had produced $227 million in rate increases, and now White was "using utility company money to run for re-election." The state, Clinton declared, will not tolerate this "reactionary, special-interest-dominated, backward-looking White administration." Clinton advanced his proposals for utility reform, including the direct election of commissioners and a phase in of rate increases when people faced tough economic times.[30]

The media campaign in 1982 offered flat-out class warfare. While Clinton's spots spoke of the recession and jobs and education, the focus was above all on the utility companies and their rate increases. High rates kept jobs from coming to the state and hurt people in the midst of a recession. Clinton depicted White as completely owned by the big utility companies, which were themselves completely out of control. Clinton's television ads said he proposed to change things:

> It's wrong for utility profits to go way up while
>   the rest of our economy is down.
> But last year, our largest electric utility's profits
>   increased 47 percent because of a huge rate
>   increase.
> To control utility rates, you've got to control utility
>   spending.
> I'll audit that spending and require utilities to publish
>   the salaries of their top executives.
> I'll review other costs too and cut wherever we can.
> I'll rebuild the system of utility rate control my
>   opponent tore down.

In the homestretch, Clinton launched a broader attack on Republicanism and Frank White, whose budget cuts, he said, came "out of the hides of the poorest [and] weakest." He attacked the national Republican policies that hurt the elderly and threatened Social Security.

> Oh, Frank White may have let utilities raise their rates.
> But when it came to the elderly and the medicine they
>   needed, he really put his foot down.
> Frank White—soft on utilities, tough on the elderly.

Clinton continued to emphasize education, without which there could be no economic growth. "If we want lower unemployment and higher wage paying jobs," his ads declared, "we've got to invest in education."[31] But he remained careful on taxes: "I would have to have a clear indication from the people that they agreed with me that there was a pressing need for more revenues sufficient to justify an increase in taxes." There would be no car-tag issue in 1982, though Clinton would soon address the missing piece in his solution—the role of government and its relation to people and society.[32]

Clinton won handily, capturing 54.7 percent of the vote. Immediately after the election, he committed himself to a bold initiative in behalf of education, promising to increase funding, improve retirement benefits, and protect teachers against unfair dismissals. But as governor, Clinton took a somewhat different course: he combined the concept of expanded services and spending with that of standards; he combined government activism with accountability. He created an Education Standards Committee to make recommendations on raising the level of Arkansas's schools, and he placed his wife, Hillary, at its head. After extensive field hearings and visits to every Arkansas county, the committee recommended enriched education, higher salaries, and higher standards. "We Arkansans," Hillary Clinton said, "have to quit making excuses and accept instead the challenge of excellence once and for all." The combination of education and accountability re-created and elevated the concept first introduced by Clinton in 1974, the concept of anti-bureaucratic activism. Clinton was trying to reinvent government to make it accountable to ordinary citizens.[33]

On September 19, 1983, Clinton gave a thirty-minute address on education reform, which was carried by every Arkansas TV station. The governor proposed higher standards and higher taxes combined with a broad effort to make education accountable. The philosophical battle lines were drawn. He proposed a series of tax increases to address the stark failings of an education system that left over a third of the school districts without instruction in physics, advanced mathematics, art, foreign language, or music; he also proposed increased spending for teachers' salaries, which would go up $4,400 by 1985. But he also insisted on a competency test for teachers. The last proposal was explosive. The Arkansas Education Association fought bitterly in the legislature and at the polls to defeat the testing proposal. When Clinton went to address its convention, the members sat in silence, later giving standing ovations to anyone who promised to work for Clinton's defeat. The National Education Association condemned the new law and declared an "educational crisis" in Arkansas. But between 60 and 65 percent of the Arkansas public supported Clinton's approach, and in 1984 they gave him 63 percent of their votes despite a one-cent increase in the sales tax. Ultimately the competency test led to the firing of 1,315 teachers.[34]

Some observers looked at the combination of spending on education and accountability and saw just compromises and deal making; Clinton had merely created a combination that made it possible to pass educational reform through the Arkansas legislature. The teachers in particular saw it as a betrayal by a politician in pursuit of "political popularity, to secure his political base." Both views, however, fail to recognize that for ordinary people the combination makes government action possible and positive. It is not a compromise. It is a necessary link if ordinary citizens are to see their values and interests in government initiatives. It is the difference, in Clinton's words, between getting "the government off our backs" and having it "by our sides."[35]

The Clinton solution—populism, investment, and responsibility—was an electoral coup de grâce. In 1984, Clinton took 62.6 percent of the vote and carried sixty-seven of Arkansas's

seventy-five counties, recapturing all but one of the rural swing
counties despite the Reagan landslide that left the national
Democratic party near death.[36] Prominent national Republicans
came to Arkansas to attack the "liberal" Democratic party, but
their "liberal-bashing" ads produced few tremors and few defectors in the governor's race. The Clinton solution, refined under
fire, allowed the people and the Democrats to find each other
again. The Arkansas laboratory was ready to offer the nation the
product of its best work.[37]

THE YEAR OF THE DLC

The Bloodless Revolution

Al From believed that the moment had arrived for a "bloodless
revolution" in the Democratic party. He had just watched
Michael Dukakis go down in defeat, demonstrating one more
time to From and his allies in the Democratic Leadership Council that Democratic liberalism was bankrupt nationally. From
was the tough-minded and controversial president of the
DLC—a haven for mostly moderate southern elected officials.
In 1988, many of these leaders had helped create Super Tuesday,
simultaneous state Democratic primaries across the South,
which was to give voice to "mainstream" thinking and break the
hold of northeastern liberalism on the party. But the moderate
hope, Senator Al Gore, failed to win decisively in the South or
anywhere else.

    That left the party's flag to Michael Dukakis. A bruised and
nearly defeated Dukakis, seeking to revive his campaign in its
last week, embarked on a whistle-stop tour through California's
central valley. At Bakersfield, he stood at the side of the railroad
tracks and made his confession. He was a liberal after all, a liberal

perhaps in the tradition of Franklin Roosevelt, Harry Truman, and John F. Kennedy and one who believes in "balancing budgets" but a liberal nonetheless. And yet Dukakis did not articulate any set of principles, leaving the public with no image to counter Republican strategist Lee Atwater's savage caricature: a liberal short on patriotism, weak on defense, soft on criminals and blacks, indifferent to work, values, and family, and inexplicably infatuated by taxes. By the end of the campaign, Dukakis was seen as even more liberal than Ted Kennedy. He was swamped by Bush on election day despite the mood for change. Dukakis managed only a draw among Catholics and those earning between $10,000 and $20,000 a year and lost every income group above that.[38]

In the year after the Democratic defeat, From wrote to his board members—Senators Sam Nunn, Chuck Robb, and John Breaux and Governor Bill Clinton—and urged a new and more urgent course. Forget taking over the party process; instead, focus on becoming a "full-fledged political movement" energized by ideas, ideology, strong leadership, and grassroots organization. The Republicans had run "out of ideas at the end of the 1980s," he wrote, and the Democrats remained in the grip of the "liberal fundamentalists." He offered a call to arms:

> Make no mistake about it, what we hope to accomplish with the DLC is a bloodless revolution in our party. It is not unlike what the conservatives accomplished in the Republican Party during the 1960s and 1970s. By building their movement, nurturing it with ideas from conservative think tanks, and with Ronald Reagan as their standard bearer, they were able to nominate their candidate for President and elect him, and in the process, redefine both the Republican Party and the national public policy agenda.[39]

The starting point was to be the DLC New Orleans conference in March 1990, at which From hoped to issue a statement of policies and ideas that would captivate the nation. The United States would see a new Democratic party with a "clear sense of direction," offering "a new course, grounded in mainstream values." To lend weight to the effort, the conference would be dominated by prominent elected officials.

There were two other elements in the From plan, not immediately evident in the New Orleans strategy. First, From almost immediately began to think of this as a decisive one-year period, kicked off by the New Orleans declaration of principles and culminating a year later in the ratification of a final declaration at the May 1991 annual conference in Cleveland. The year would become a "high-profile platform project" advancing the DLC's ideas, revitalizing the party, and setting the stage for the presidential race. The DLC would become the intellectual center of the Democratic party. From, not given to understatement, described the DLC's goal: "to make the Mainstream Movement the dominant political force in national politics. The first step toward that goal is to make it the dominant force in the Democratic Party."[40]

Second, From recruited Bill Clinton to chair the organization during this critical period, because Clinton "could deliver this new message better than anybody I'd heard." In fact, the issue had been posed to Clinton as far back as 1987, but the discussions got serious only after Dukakis's defeat. The conversations started in April 1989 but took almost a year to bear fruit. In a January 1990 memo to Clinton, From set out the case:

> We need a charismatic leader willing to get on the road himself and equally important willing to ask other DLC leaders to do so, as well. And in my view, it would be very helpful if our next chairman were from outside Washington. A political movement needs to be built out in the country, and it's hard to excite rank and file Democrats when playing within the constraints of the Congressional caucuses.

Clinton finally accepted the chairmanship at the end of February and was inaugurated in New Orleans in March. He immediately embarked on a speaking tour across the country and helped found DLC chapters in almost half the states.[41]

On the Road: From Responsibility to the Middle Class

Clinton had found common purpose with the DLC on a key concept—government that is accountable to people, that respects their values and demands responsibility. That theme was at the center of the teacher-testing controversy in Arkansas and had legitimated Clinton's use of government to uplift his state. The theme ran through a series of Clinton initiatives after that—from welfare reform to deadbeat dads to school dropouts losing their driver's licenses. In the National Governors' Association, Clinton had taken the lead on welfare reform and education standards. Indeed, from his comeback in 1982 to the present, Clinton would never again run or govern without the theme of responsibility. That is where Bill Clinton and the DLC joined forces.

But the Arkansas governor knew deep in his soul that the Clinton solution required opportunity as well as responsibility. When battling for his political life in 1974 and 1982, Clinton engaged in what some called class warfare, making clear that his ideas were inspired from the bottom up. The battle with the utilities underscored his motivation and perspective. In 1990, however, he would eschew the concept, though with an important ambiguity. "While we favor tax fairness and think the middle class is overtaxed," Clinton said, "we don't think the Democratic Party should *lead* with class warfare" (italics added). He was suggesting that class warfare might appear further down in the lineup.[42] For the moment, Clinton and the DLC pushed middle-class tax relief, including the earned-income tax credit and a Social Security tax cut—as a signal to disaffected Democrats.[43]

But Clinton's principal focus in New Orleans was on responsibility. At the conclusion of his address to the conference, Clinton recalled visiting the grave site of his great-grandfather and great-grandmother by an old wooden church, and he told the audience of a "picture in my office of my great-grandfather holding my hand when I had my leg broken." But then he recalled another less idyllic visit, this time with his wife, Hillary, to a public school in a gang-infested neighborhood of Los Angeles. For an hour and a half, he told his audience, they talked with a dozen eleven-year-olds. "Their number one fear," he said, "was being shot going to and from school—not by people who wanted to kill them, but by crack-crazed kids who didn't know right from left and would just shoot for the heck of it." As he recalled, all but two of the kids had raised their hands in answer to the question of whether they were prepared to turn in their parents to the police if their parents would then get treatment for drug addiction. And then Clinton drew his audience back to its own mainstream experience: "Now, it's a long way from a kid who can remember holding his great-grandfather's hand to a child who will never have a picture of a grandparent in the house and thinks that he or she ought to turn their parents in because they can't fulfill the most basic responsibilities."

Most of the initiatives in the New Orleans declaration focused on government tempered by and infused with personal responsibility: "equal opportunity, not equal outcomes"; a mission "to expand opportunity, not government"; a social welfare system to "bring the poor into the nation's economic mainstream," not to maintain dependence; a demand for citizenship with rights as well as responsibilities. National service emerged as an important vehicle for expressing these new Democratic values. The declaration set out the new course: "It is time to replace the politics of entitlement with a new politics of reciprocal responsibility." In his speech, Clinton identified himself with the DLC project, focusing on restoring government legitimacy through responsibility. To be a Democrat in "the emerging century," he stated, requires two basic things. First, "you have to believe there's a role for government in solving common problems." And second, government must "empower" the people who are being helped, and "whenever government does something with or for individuals who are irresponsible, it must require responsibility of them."

Clinton's speech and the declaration broke with longtime Democratic squeamishness and raised the question of investment and growth. The declaration affirmed a belief in free markets as the "best engine of prosperity," while emphasizing the importance of investment and training. Clinton deplored the decline of investment in education, the environment, and infrastructure and declared, "We need a national investment strategy."

The declaration committed the organization to a progressive tax system as the "only fair way to pay for government," but there was no populist touch: there was no critique of the ethics of Reagan's golden age, and there was no championing of a struggling middle-class America. There was instead a commitment to honoring the life of work in social policy. The declaration affirms: "We back a proposed Guaranteed Working Wage that would enable all full-time, year-round workers who support a family to lift themselves and their families out of poverty"— thus the centrality of the earned-income tax credit, a social policy that placed the government on the side of work and responsibility.[44]

Fourteen months later, Bill Clinton stood at the podium to deliver the lead-off speech at the DLC's 1991 Cleveland convention. This was the first national stage for prospective Democratic candidates contemplating challenging George Bush, who was basking in the success of the Persian Gulf War. Outside there was a host of minidramas: an offended Jesse Jackson with striking workers at a union hall just blocks away and UAW workers leafleting outside the convention hall, protesting the DLC's support of the proposed North American Free Trade Agreement.

Clinton's Cleveland DLC speech was above all a discourse on middle-class Americans; rarely had any modern Democratic leader so clearly identified with their lives. Clinton began with irresponsibility, as he had in New Orleans, but this time he cast his net much more broadly. He looked back at the 1980s and saw a decade that "glorified the pursuit of greed and self-interest." He highlighted the "explosion of the number of poor women and their little children," which was paralleled by the behavior at the top: "In the 1980s our competitive position eroded, but the CEO's of this country gave themselves pay raises that were four times as much as they gave their employees and three times as much as their corporate profits increased."

The middle class, for its part, saw its material situation decline: "Middle income families' earnings declined for the first time in our memory, and not because we are a lazy people. Working class families put in more hours at work and less time with their children in 1989 than they did in 1979."

Yet Democrats, Clinton warned, had failed to honor their struggle or advance their interests: "Too many of the people that used to vote for us, the very burdened middle class we are talking about, have not trusted us in national elections to defend our national interests abroad, to put their values into our social policy at home, or to take their tax money and spend it with discipline."

Clinton called on Democrats to give a broader meaning to opportunity, which "first and foremost" means a "commitment to economic growth"; it means "more investments in emerging technologies, and more incentives to invest by U.S. companies in their own country"; it means "world-class skills for people who live here while money and management may fly away." Finally, Clinton affirmed, "opportunity for all also means that the government ought to help the middle class as well as the poor when they need it."

It is not enough, Clinton reminded his audience, "if you give opportunity without insisting on responsibility." He repeated his support for national service, welfare reform, tough child-support enforcement, and reinventing government to make it work. Opportunity and responsibility must move forward hand in hand.[45]

The platform adopted at the Cleveland convention, the New American Choice, elaborated the program first endorsed in the New Orleans declaration, but it also reflected Clinton's discourse on the middle class and his populist tone. It declared: "America doesn't need two Republican parties, two establishment parties, or two parties from Washington, D.C., but it does need a Democratic Party that will stand up for ordinary people." For the first time, the DLC formally emphasized "higher taxes for wealthy persons" as well as "reducing the tax burden on moderate-income and middle class families."[46]

At the end of his address, Clinton came back again to his great-grandparents—just as he had in New Orleans. He recalled a "two-room shack up on stilts" and "the best room" in the house, the "storm cellar . . . where I used to spend the night with a coal oil lantern and snakes." What Clinton chose to emphasize this time were the "government commodities," the "help from the government." His great-grandparents "did a heck of a job with what they had," and they had good values: "They believed in personal responsibility. But they also believed that the government had an obligation to help people who were doing the best they can."

As in New Orleans, Clinton reflected on Los Angeles and those kids who had never met their grandparents, who worried about "getting shot going to and from school," who feared "when they turned thirteen they would have to join a gang." Their plight and the contrast with his own idealized experience led Clinton to an emotional conclusion about a government that must address people's needs:

> Now let me tell you something, friends. Those people do not care about the rhetoric of left and right and liberal and conservative and who is up and who is down and how we are positioned. They are real people, they have real problems, and they are crying desperately for someone who believes the purpose of government is to solve their problems and make progress.[47]

Activism, responsibility, and populism had been joined again under the banner of the Democratic party.

Clinton developed this train of thought as he moved closer to a declaration of his candidacy for president. At Sioux City, Iowa, on September 6, he unfolded a strong populist line of argument, one that took the concept of responsibility right to the top. He touched on welfare reform, child support, and his traditional litany, but then he embarked on a sharp populist critique: "Democrats should insist that those at the top of the totem pole be responsible, too." He repeated his conventional statistics, used in Cleveland, about corporate pay but then began talking about "financial abuses" from "the S&Ls to Wall Street" and "golden parachutes." The president, he believed, has a special responsibility to define what is wrong in society:

> When Harry Truman was president, he jawboned powerful people into behaving. When Jack Kennedy was president and corporate America abused its position, he jawboned them into behaving. I'm still waiting for George Bush to say the first word about what Salomon Brothers did the other day, about the S&L ripoff, about all these things that have happened in America where people on the top have taken advantage of the people on the bottom. The people

on the bottom watch the same television news you and I do. How can you tell people to be responsible? How can you tell the farmers who till the soil to be responsible while the people whose hands are in the till do well by behaving irresponsibly.[48]

Before the Democratic National Committee on September 20, Clinton introduced another powerful idea: an aspiration for unity across race lines that would allow America to face its problems. He challenged a Democratic party afraid of its diversity and burned by race-baiting to assert a new confidence before a predictable and perverse Republican course:

> I am a fifth generation Arkansan. A Southerner born and bred. I embrace it proudly, but I tell you something, folks: this argument over quotas that they're setting up for the next election, this is not a new argument. Those of us who come from the South, whatever our race, know that they've been running this old scam on us for decades now. Whenever things get really tight and they get really worried, they find the most economically insecure white Americans and they scare the living daylights out of them and get them to leave their natural home and run away from the unity that is the only source of strength in this country.
>   If we permit the Republicans to keep people staring at each other across racial divides, those people will never be able to turn their heads and look to the White House and look to Washington and say, "Why have you let all of our incomes go down for the last 10 years?" We cannot permit that division because that is what they want.[49]

On the eve of his prospective presidential run, Clinton broadened his purpose and his appeal. He challenged the policies and ethics of a Republicanism that had threatened the public good. He challenged the old Democratic course that had failed the middle class. And now he challenged bottom-up

America—both black and white—to find common purpose before the real threat to their values and interests. In the Clinton solution lay an aspiration to unity that could reshape the nation.

THE NEW COVENANT

On October 23, just three weeks after declaring his candidacy, Clinton kicked off a series of speeches at Georgetown University that became known as the New Covenant Addresses. It offered the sharpest critique of the ethic that guided the top-down years of Reagan and Bush. They had "exalted private gain over public obligations, special interests over the common good, wealth and fame over work and family. The 1980s ushered in a gilded age of greed, selfishness, irresponsibility, excess and neglect." The speech offered a sharp warning to those at the top, "but," Clinton said, "I want the jetsetters and the feather bedders of corporate America to know that if you sell your companies and your workers and your country down the river, you'll get called on the carpet. That's what the President's bully pulpit is for."

Clinton offered the strongest identification with middle America: "And through it all, millions of decent, ordinary people who worked hard, played by the rules and took responsibility for their own actions were falling behind, living a life of struggle without reward or security. For twelve years, the forgotten middle class watched their economic interests ignored and their values run into the ground." He then delivered a stirring critique of government and business as usual in Washington: "Government, which should have been setting an example, was even worse. Congress raised its pay and guarded its perks while most Americans were working harder for less money." Democrats, Clinton believed, had a special responsibility to "put

Congress in order," since "they want to use government to help people." The address challenged Washington to "revolutionize government and fundamentally change its relationship to people. People don't want some top-down bureaucracy telling them what to do anymore. That's one reason they tore down the Berlin Wall and threw out the communist regimes in Eastern Europe and Russia."

The answer for each of these areas is "a New Covenant, a solemn agreement between the people and their government, to provide opportunity for everybody, inspire responsibility throughout our society and restore a sense of community to this great nation. A New Covenant to take government back from the powerful interests and the bureaucracy and give this country back to the ordinary people."

In the spirit of this new covenant, people will "assume responsibility and shoulder the common load":

> When people go to work, they rediscover a pride that was lost. When fathers pay their child support, they restore a connection that they and their children need. When students work harder, they find out they all can learn and do as well as anyone else on Earth. When corporate managers put their workers and their long-term profits ahead of their own paychecks, their companies do well, and so do they. When the privilege of serving is enough of a perk for people in Congress, and the President finally assumes responsibility for America's problems, we'll not only stop doing wrong, we'll begin to do what is right to move America forward.

This is what this election was about, Clinton concluded, "forging a New Covenant of change that will honor middle-class values, restore the public trust, create a new sense of community, and make America work again."[50] The Clinton solution had now been elaborated on a national stage.

8. THE BATTLE FOR MACOMB

MIDDLE America had not fared so well as the 1992 election year began. Median family income, which had risen under Reagan until 1987, had faltered, falling sharply from 1989 to 1991. As Clinton observed in stump speech after stump speech, people were working harder and longer hours and earning less. At the outset of the Bush years, people were working more hours each year than they had before Reagan took office in 1979, yet under Bush wages and salaries fell 2.2 percent. The drop was even more pronounced for those who had not gone beyond high school, particularly men. To keep up, more wives were working ever longer hours, particularly those in lower- and middle-income families. Still, the cost of sending a kid to college, of health care, of a car and a house all went up.[1]

In Macomb County, Michigan, where middle America had rebelled against the Democratic betrayal, evidence of a second explosion was accumulating. The new contract with the better classes had not paid off. Unemployment jumped sharply after 1989, hitting 9.1 percent in 1991 and remaining high, at 8.5 percent, in 1992. The growth in personal income, which had been respectable between 1987 and 1989, stopped suddenly after George Bush took office.[2]

The voters of Macomb watched George Bush and saw a president adrift and out of touch and a country and economy heading downward—as one voter put it, "regressing instead of advancing." In focus groups in the summer and fall of 1992, voters shook their heads and shared a common recognition: George Bush was too distant to entertain any compact with struggling middle America; he combined inaction with indifference, born of upper-class remoteness and trickle-down ideas. The president "doesn't seem to care," one focus-group participant observed. "He doesn't realize that people live on $20,000 a year." That is the way it is "on the upper-crust level, with the elite people." Bush is "not down with us. He's superman, and he's looking down." "He's too aloof," another participant said. "He doesn't know what's going on with the whole society." They shared an observation, underscored by one participant, that the president was "unconcerned for the American people, period."

From their vantage point, there was not much universality in Bush's economic principles: "The trickle-down has only gone down to the top two ladders [i.e., rungs]; the trickle down hasn't trickled down far enough." For the common person, that meant no agenda. One participant observed that "he seems like he doesn't have a plan right now," to which others added, "He's out fishing" and "golfing" and has "no sense of direction to go in." "As far as I'm concerned," one voter concluded, "he doesn't have any policy," and that leaves the average citizen in the cold: "As far as our economy, he is a do-nothing. And as far as the senior citizens and all this, he does nothing. The jobless, the homeless—I mean, you know, he doesn't care. He puts his money overseas, so we know."

President Bush left these Macomb voters without a faith that the nation's leaders could point to something better.

THE BUSH CAMP

George Bush gave his long-awaited State of the Union speech in January 1992. Bush had patiently waited out the recession, but declining poll numbers and painfully slow recovery forced the president to publicly set out his economic ideas and plans. But voters in Macomb could not connect those ideas with a vision or a set of principles that might give the ordinary citizen heart. George Bush hesitated to make the case for a revitalized American capitalism.

Bush began with an explanation for his indifference to matters at home—not indifference after all but a preoccupation with winning the war against communism:

> Even as president, with the most fascinating possible vantage point, there were times when I was so busy helping to manage progress, and lead change, that I didn't always show the joy that was in my heart.
>
> But the biggest thing that has happened in the world in my life—in our lives—is this: By the grace of God, America won the Cold War.

That allowed Bush to pivot off the Cold War and turn toward home: "I mean to speak this evening of the changes that can take place in our country now that we can stop making the sacrifices we had to make when we had an avowed enemy that was a superpower. Now we can look homeward even more and move to set right what needs to be set right."

The bold rhetoric of the Persian Gulf War turned cautious as Bush discussed the country's economic problems: "Unemployment is too high," and "growth is not what it should be." Little wonder frustrated Macomb County voters paid little attention to the president's Persian Gulf bravado on the economy: "This will not stand."[3]

Bush's economic plan was based on the principle "that people will do great things if only you set them free." This was more reminiscent of Goldwater than of Reagan and produced a package of negative prescriptions: an end to "the obstacles to growth—high taxes, high regulation, red tape, and yes, wasteful government spending." Bush's answer for the recession was to get government out of the way, but without mentioning the entrepreneurs who would rev up the engine of growth. Even the discussion of the capital-gains tax cut failed to mention investors and business. With trickle-down principles out of favor, Bush was afraid to ennoble the privileged or the market.

Instead, he offered some paltry tax shifts in the form of reduced or deferred withholding, a moratorium on government employment and regulation, and expanded trade combined with a grab bag of contradictory measures: accelerated federal spending, new highway-construction projects, and "common-sense investments" in research and development. If this was not confusing enough, the president threw in an initiative on crime and drugs and another one on health care. That night he proposed to increase the personal exemption for families with children but then failed to submit the proposal to Congress. The Reagan legacy was stillborn.

THE CLINTON CAMP

By early March, Bill Clinton had swept the Super Tuesday primaries across the South and was rolling into Michigan and Illinois. But the primaries had been brutal. Clinton was viewed unfavorably by about 30 percent of the primary electorate and by about 40 percent of all the voters in the country. The situation was worst in the West and the Northeast, the two areas hit hardest by the Bush recession. Both Bush and Clinton lagged far behind the billionaire independent candidate Ross Perot in the public's assessment of their ability to handle the economy.[4]

Clinton's earlier triumph of ideas was but a faded memory. His principles for rebuilding the contract with middle America were lost now amidst the tabloid frenzy of personal allegations in the New Hampshire primary.

On the evening of March 12, just two days after Super Tuesday, Bill Clinton made a crucial trip to Michigan. He was about to reaffirm the scope of his bottom-up vision by challenging the white voters of Macomb County and the African American voters of Detroit to unite behind the Clinton solution. The candidate and the campaign had decided to make Clinton's earlier victories produce more than just electoral momentum. By challenging the people of Macomb and Detroit across the racial divide, the campaign hoped to elevate Clinton's ideas for a new Democratic majority.

The gym at Macomb County Community College had been reconfigured, set up with a Donahue-style stage, rows of chairs on all sides, and a big blue college banner on the wall. There were some students, but most of the audience seemed middle-aged and from the white heartland of the county. Clinton worked his way around the front rows, shaking hands, as the audience stood to applaud him. He adjusted his microphone and warmed to the crowd.[5]

Clinton came right to the point. Macomb, he told his audience, is a "very famous county" because the "native Democrats" have turned to the Republicans—not unlike the situation in his own state of Arkansas. He combined the acknowledgment with a shared sense of grievance: Arkansas voters too felt let down by Washington, which did not share their values and no longer rewarded "middle-class effort and middle-class values." Clinton understood Democratic defection, acknowledging the Democrats' failure to keep their bargain.

Then Clinton asked Macomb County voters to ponder the deal offered them by the Republicans: "So what has happened in this decade in which the American people voted for people who promised to honor their values and stand up for everything that was best in this country?" The top 1 percent had won 60 percent of all the income gains, while the next 19 percent got all the rest. "The middle class is working harder, making less, we've lost our economic leadership," Clinton observed. Meanwhile, big companies, like General Motors, were pocketing concessions and tax breaks without reinvesting "a lot of that money in the production process." "Executives continue to raise their pay and their perks while the workers got the shaft."

Clinton offered Macomb County voters a new bargain, based on the Clinton solution, starting with "people-first economics": "Our economic policy ought to put our own people first again," he declared. "It ought to reward work and family and effort, and not just wealth and power."

But the new bottom-up bargain had an important caveat: black and white must unite with a sense of common purpose. Clinton knew something about this historic division between black and white. "Arkansas and Michigan were approved for admission into the union at the same time. Did you know that?" he asked. "One would be a slave state, mine, and one would be a free state, yours." But Michigan, he believed, got the better deal, because across the South racial divisions held everybody back. To move ahead now, Michigan must revisit its politics and racial sentiments, which is why Clinton had come back to the Reagan Democrats. For his part, Clinton said, " 'I'll give you your values back, I'll restore the economic leadership, I'll help you build the middle class back.' " But, in turn, "you've got to say: 'Okay, let's do it with everybody in this country.' "

At the end, Clinton appealed directly to each audience member to "embrace a Democrat again based on opportunity, responsibility and people-based politics." He said, "Let's forget about race and be one nation again."[6]

The next morning, Bill and Hillary Clinton went to the Pleasant Grove Baptist Church in Detroit, where more than two hundred mostly black parishioners jammed into the pews, waiting to hear from the man they hoped would be the next president of the United States. A succession of ministers warmed up the congregation with testimonials about Clinton—"one who ministered to all." One speaker announced the Baptist pastors' endorsement of Clinton, which he brought home by singing "The Battle Hymn of the Republic," concluding with this call to action: "March on Bill Clinton, our next president."

Clinton arrived at the side door and was immediately ushered into a crowded, private meeting with the ministers and their family members before going out to speak to the congregation. After the whole congregation had risen to sing further choruses of "The Battle Hymn" and welcome in Governor and Mrs. Clinton, Reverend O'Dell Jones (himself a former Arkansan) welcomed the candidate, whom he called no longer "a southerner" but "an American" who "came from the bottom" to lead the nation.

Clinton faced this congregation—standing and rocking and ready to embrace his candidacy. He began by asking his audience to join "a new partnership to change this country," a partnership with the most unlikely of partners, white Macomb County:

> I went to Macomb County in Michigan, and I said something politicians don't normally say in Macomb County. I said, "I want you folks to come home to the Democratic Party. . . . I want to tell you that we didn't do right by middle America for awhile, but I have a program that will restore the middle class, without regard to race. You have rewarded Ronald Reagan and George Bush, and they have punished you."

He told his audience to look north to Macomb because it "is basically full of people who did right and were done wrong, just like the rest of us."

Clinton described the bargain he offered those white disaffected voters: join this people-centered investment approach, but only when "all of you folks decide that race is not the problem." The problem instead is "economics and education, and public morality that is frayed at the edges." He described the challenge: "If you want a new America, you have to be willing to talk with your brothers and sisters of others races, and find pure value in common ground and make a new coalition for change to honor work and family and faith in the future."

"Today," Clinton told the congregation, "I come here and challenge you to reach out your hands to them, for we have been divided far too long."

Clinton gave voice to the opportunity in his program, but then he visited the theme of responsibility, which resonated strongly in the church, punctuated by amens. Clinton observed, "We have forgotten something else in the 1980s, too, and that is the responsibility of ordinary citizens to take control of their lives and do better." He warned his listeners not to be "misled by politicians who come here asking for your votes and pretending that we can do something for you if you don't do things for yourselves." That is the core of the new bargain: "What I offer is a chance to give you the opportunity to assume responsibility that every American should assume for his or her own life." "I know I'm speaking overtime," he said, "but this is important. I cannot do for you what you will not do for yourself."[7] And the congregation applauded and seconded his bargain.

Clinton's bottom-up solution reached across both sides of Eight Mile Road, the Berlin Wall separating Detroit and Macomb, separating people who had held firmly to their own versions of the American dream. He offered them both a "new covenant" that would cement them politically and morally and give them faith in the belief that America can change.

The Manhattan Project

And yet even after victories in Michigan, Illinois, and New York, a central problem remained: distrust trumped the message. After

months of Clinton's being pounded in the press, skeptical voters
had come to view Bill Clinton as a "politician" and therefore
were not prepared to listen to the Clinton solution, no matter
how elevated it was. Voters were increasingly angry and desperate for change, and they wanted to believe there was a way out
for them and for America. Among the Reagan Democrats, two
thirds wanted to vote against George Bush, but only a handful
(less than 10 percent) had any idea what Bill Clinton stood for
or cared about.

To address the problem, the Clinton campaign created the
"Manhattan Project"—a general election strategy group outside
the regular organization. Clinton's principal campaign strategist,
James Carville, believed from the outset that the answer lay in
advancing a "big idea" that would associate Bill Clinton with the
rising demand for change. The country, he believed, had moved
from being moderately upset about the direction of the country
to deeply disturbed and on the edge of desperation. In that context, Clinton offered "no real departure from the status quo" and
no idea powerful enough to get the public's attention.[8]

A small group of Clinton advisers, pressed by Carville's
obsession, assembled to talk about the "change message" and
nothing else. Carville declared that the "big idea" must reflect
the fact that this is "not the same country" as the one that witnessed Clinton's announcement. "This is a fundamentally different atmosphere. People are pissed off [because] everything is
rigged."

Unknowingly the group ended up disaggregating Clinton's
earlier solution as its members looked for something that would
stand on its own. Those with the DLC perspective—Al From,
Will Marshall, and Bruce Reed—proposed an emphasis on
"radically changing government" under the banner of "no more
something for nothing." Among the targets of their bomb
throwing were special interest politics (abolishing PACS, taxing
lobbyists, opening up the airwaves), programs lacking responsi-

bility and proper values (the education and welfare bureaucracies), police forces that do not deter crime, schools that fail to educate, and welfare that fails to bring people back to the mainstream.

Media consultant Frank Greer and campaign adviser Paul Begala championed middle-class populism. They proposed a straightforward "on your side" tack, taking on the "big interests," like insurance companies. Begala described a broader target, the "system that is stacked against the working stiff."

That the "Clinton problem" was the absence of a big-change message was far from the dominant viewpoint in the Manhattan Project. Media consultant Mandy Grunwald and I (as campaign adviser and pollster) advanced the idea, tentatively at first but with increasing certainty, that the problem was rooted in the absence of biography. Voters did not know the real Bill Clinton. They knew nothing of his humble origins, his work to improve education and to uplift Arkansas. In the world created by tabloid journalism, Clinton was simply a politician, saying whatever was necessary to get elected, without any history or grounding in principle. How could voters put their faith in him to fight the special interests, champion the middle class, and change America when he seemed so embroiled in the system they hated? Voters were not ready to listen to a message of change from a politician.[9]

We organized two sets of focus groups—one in the San Fernando Valley of California and the other in Allentown, in the Lehigh Valley of Pennsylvania—to test the power of biography and message.[10] Each participant was presented with a one-page listing of facts about Bill Clinton, including such simple items as "born in a small town called Hope, Arkansas," "worked his way through Georgetown," "makes $35,000 a year—never had a pay raise in 11 years," and "introduced sweeping education reform."

The result was breathtaking. After hearing the "facts," voters began to speak of Clinton in radically different terms: "down to

earth," a "middle-class boy," "self-made," "earned it," "the opposite of Bush," "has some values," "honest, hardworking man,"
"he's a human being," "worked his way," "had to struggle," "no
silver spoon." Many were angry with the press for withholding
information and distorting the national debate. Indeed, there
was an evident presumption that this was a man who could offer
a genuine bottom–up vision for America.

The Reich-Osborne Solution

While biography was important, it still was not sufficient to turn
the tide. The search for power and simplicity of message next
gravitated toward Clinton's commitment to invest in people. That
was the commitment closest to his heart and to his life's work—
raising up people by enriching their education and skills and
empowering them to prosper. That was the commitment central to the economic ideas he had worked through with Robert
B. Reich of Harvard University—giving people the skills and
capacity to prosper in a changing world. This "people first" message most clearly exposed the indifference and partiality of Bush's
elitist Republicanism.

   Clinton's advisers struggled with a number of the candidate's
ideas—the importance of welfare and work to the middle class
("move people from welfare to work"), the desire for a country
that would unite ("begin to work together"), the irresponsibility
of the rich ("eliminate tax breaks for corporations that ship our
jobs overseas"), and contempt for politics ("the special interests
that dominate Washington"), as well as investment in people
("devote ourselves to educating our people"). The goal, Carville,
Grunwald, and I told a May 11 meeting in the governor's mansion in Little Rock, was a message that distilled these elements
and was optimistic, understandable, and big, one that would draw
a sharp contrast to Bush, was rooted in the core beliefs of the
candidate, and would be validated by the experts and the press.

Though there was no doubt about the continuing power of the different elements, the advisers reported two weeks later that there was still no progress on the overall message. Research in California and Ohio showed about an equal and strongly positive reception for reinventing government, middle-class populism, and Reich's investment proposal, but there was little inclination to translate receptivity into votes for Clinton: his support rose only about 4 percentage points and left him trailing the pack. Bush was surely in trouble, but Clinton could not capture the wave of change.

A few days later I had an epiphany. It was so simple. Why not combine the message of anti-politics and reinventing government with the message of investment in people? That Clinton had himself harnessed the power of that combination almost twenty years earlier was a history none of us appreciated at the time. The DLC strand in the campaign was blinded by its desire to revolutionize government, and the middle-class populist strand by its desire to use government. Only Clinton had realized these are not contradictory positions. Reforming government is a precondition to using it.

The campaign's communications director, George Stephanopoulos, convened a meeting on June 12, at which I distilled the message of joining the two intellectual strands that were so important to Clinton: essentially, a David Osborne critique of government for failing the people and a Robert Reich strategy for investing in the people. Osborne had studied Clinton's early innovations in Arkansas and emerged an apostle for the idea that government could do more for less, that government could be re-invented. The proposed campaign message used Osborne's criticism of an inefficient and out-of-touch bureaucratic government while shunning the more arcane—even if sensible—solutions, like increased choice and decentralization. It used Reich's economic focus on initiatives for the people while eschewing any propensity to big-government spending pro-grams. The anti-political argument was, in effect, the opening for the investment argument.

We could tell we were on the verge of a breakthrough—a message with power that made sense to people and reflected the deepest feelings of the candidate. Grunwald and Begala urged a popularization of the message, linking the failure of government with the failure of trickle-down economics. Government re-warded excess and irresponsibility and failed to reward work. Government failed not because it spent too much but because it did not address the needs of ordinary citizens, for health care, education, and a growing economy. The final element of the synthesis was Clinton's biography, which showed a committed leader ready to use government to help people.

Carville and Stephanopoulos pushed for an immediate national test. Starting Sunday night, June 14, a thousand respon-dents across the country listened to a message, dubbed for our purposes "the people-first profile." It began with a bold assertion that government had failed the average person while taking care of the wealthy; but worse, the middle class was working harder and paying more for a government that did little about the economy or health care. The answer: Bill Clinton, a man of humble origins who worked for what he got and who believes "we need a government that puts people first again," a man who proposes a national economic strategy that invests in our own people—in welfare reform, education, vocational training, and health care.

When people heard the profile, the race changed, at least in the context of our surveys. Clinton moved into a tie for first place, and after an attack on Bush, he surged in front. The people-first message—combining the themes of government failure and government initiatives for the middle class—proved twice as powerful as any message we had tested in the past.

"Reinventing government" and "investing in people" were twice as powerful in combination as each was on its own.

This was the Clinton solution. The campaign had finally caught up to the candidate's understanding and vision.

THE WINNOWING OF TRICKLE DOWN

With the economy on a slow track and his economic initiative dead in Congress, the president tried to change the subject. Before arriving at the Republican convention in Houston, he told the Knights of Columbus in New York that America's "moral compass had gone awry" and that he offered leadership with "the courage to stand up for the changes that are morally right for America." At the convention, he paraded his military exploits before the delegates and scorned this "leader of the National Guard." So, "while I bit the bullet, he bit his nails."[11]

But 1992 was not 1968 or even 1988. The battle could not be waged on the battlefield of the 1960s, and it could not be waged against the ghosts of Lyndon Johnson, Hubert Humphrey, and George McGovern. George Bush would have to get on the economic battlefield, where he was but a raw recruit. Clearly the contradictory and limited proposals of January would be insufficient in this battle.

Bush and his advisers decided to employ the biggest weaponry in Reaganomics—an across-the-board tax cut. That was the simple but powerful concept through which Ronald Reagan was able to make the case for top-down incentives and generalized prosperity. But Bush's proposal was minimalist, defensive, and uninspired. At the convention, he said, "I will propose to further reduce taxes across-the-board—provided we pay for the cuts with specific spending reductions that I consider appropriate, so that we do not increase the deficit." He was not specific about the amount and, astonishingly, said no more about it in the speech. At the Detroit Economic Club in September, he launched his economic plan and added specificity—a 1 percent across-the-board reduction in the income tax rate, a reduction in the small-business tax rate from 15 to 10 percent, and a reduced tax on capital gains. But again he said no more about it, not a single sentence.[12]

In the wake of public discontent with Reagan's policies, Bush was afraid to make the case for business and capitalism. But by putting the proposal into the battle, he left trickle down undefended. Indeed, Bush took the safe course. First, he took up the common denominator of Republican politics: less government. He offered his personal mantra: "Government is too big and spends too much." That was the choice in the election: George Bush, who spent his life in the private sector, versus Bill Clinton, who lives and breathes government. Bush proposed cutting taxes and spending, and Clinton proposed raising them.

In his belated economic plan, "Agenda for American Renewal," Bush offered a second approach: small business as the engine of economic growth. Here Bush found some rhetoric about "entrepreneurial capitalism": "We have always preferred an entrepreneurial capitalism that grows from the bottom up, not the top down, a capitalism that begins on Main Street and extends to Wall Street, not the other way around."[13]

Finally, Bush declared that he would work to make America an "economic superpower" by aggressively expanding trade. It was this last point, emphasized in Detroit, that seemed to energize the campaign. The first Bush general-election campaign commercials to air immediately after the Detroit Economic Club speech declared, "We must be a military superpower, an economic superpower and an export superpower." The ad offered military imagery as a large press stamped Bush's name, letter by letter, on the screen. The entire tax proposal was reduced to two words, *tax relief,* nearly lost in a sentence crowded with proposals.

Just four days after the Detroit Economic Club speech and the launch of the Bush media campaign, we asked the Macomb County voters what they made of all this. As it turned out, this winnowed trickle down produced hardly a ripple across Eight Mile Road. The Detroit newspapers had emboldened Bush's timid proposals under the headline BUSH'S NEW TAX PLEDGE: A BIG CUT.[14] But for most of these voters, there was not much worth noticing: "He supposedly has an economic policy, but he doesn't go into any details on it." "He doesn't have any clear-cut domestic vision." "As far as I'm concerned, he don't have any policy." Bush had trouble finding an audience for his limited Reaganism: "If he had a plan, then why hasn't he implemented it during his four years as president?"

For those who noticed what he said, particularly about the across-the-board tax cut, the results were worse. Some noted the hypocrisy, "cause he had already raised them," and "he's going to do it again." For others, it sounded like more of the same Reaganism that had betrayed suburban Macomb: "OK, 1 percent across the board, and who's it going to benefit the most? The little guy? One percent of what? Of his wages? And here's the guy that's making, what is it, over $200,000. . . . It's going to give the very rich a much better tax break." Another of Macomb's disaffected was more to the point: "Well unfortunately when I heard his speech the other night, I listened to some of it, and I thought it sounded like a repeat of whatever, and I switched the channel."

9. THE PEROT
DISSOLUTION

AFTER three decades of growing middle-class grievances and political distrust, America was ready for dissolution. The Democratic idea had lost its hold years ago, and now the Republican idea had failed too. The collapse set adrift new segments of the electorate. This was Ross Perot's moment. Perot mounted a crusade against a corrupt political system, and despite throwing a tantrum on national television and accusing the president of the United States of conspiring to disrupt his daughter's wedding, he received 19 percent of the vote. Perot expressed a compelling and simple idea, that the political elite of the country is corrupt and that the people should reclaim the government.

The Perot bloc of 1992 was a diverse collection of political refugees, though among them the most important were disaffected Republicans who rejected Reaganism and independent-minded younger voters who could find no future in the major parties. These were self-consciously middle-class, populist, and anti-elitist voters who expressed scorn for the country's political and economic establishment. Their disconnection from the mainstream world revolved around two symbols: the deficit, whose growth spelled doom for the country, and Congress, whose arrogance represented the elite's indifference to the fate of ordinary citizens.

This dissolution gave Perot his opportunity. He scorned the historic debates that have dominated our politics for the last century. He did not try to revitalize a bottom-up vision. He attacked the political elites, to be sure, but not the economic ones; he championed people as citizens, not as workers or as the middle class. His economic program was a collection of pragmatic fixes. The only red meat he threw to downscale America was a jingoistic attack on foreign lobbyists and interests.

Nor did Perot try to revitalize a top-down vision. He did not place business or entrepreneurs on some pedestal as creators of wealth. He saved his emotion for the project of purifying the political system, symbolized by the elimination of the deficit, an act that was to save the country from the abyss and assure prosperity. He was as likely to showcase bold government initiatives to finance new technologies and found new industries as he was to promote business investment and prerogatives.

Although Perot's project was distinct from the historic party projects, it would not have existed without their failure. The collapse of the dominant ideas for organizing America and assuring prosperity gave us our own distinct forms of alienation—middle-class consciousness and political distrust. They gave us the Congress, the symbol of paralysis, debt, and failed representation. More than any other institution, Congress has fallen in public esteem as paralysis has overtaken our leaders. So the rubble of failed Democratic and Republican renewal provided the building blocs for the Perot project. Despite all his personal failings, Perot succeeded because the party solutions no longer allowed people the dreams that America had promised them.

Antonio Gramsci, the Italian Marxist who was imprisoned by the Fascists and observed the dissolution of the political order around him, wrote from prison: "the old is dying and the new cannot be born; in this interregnum a great variety of morbid symptoms appear."[1] Perot is such a symptom, though he would like to believe that he has created a new force outside the parties that will hold the country's leaders accountable. And indeed, some observers believe that this new "middle-class radicalism" is creating a new center politics outside the dominant parties.

The Republicans are hopeful that these mostly conservative, mostly Republican voters will find their way back home— much as the Democrats hoped that those who defected to Wallace and Nixon would return after 1968. The Republicans pin their hopes to the Perot voters' hostility to government and the federal deficit, which the Republicans read as a support for limited government and conservative economic principles. That Perot voters supported Republican congressional candidates in 1994 by two-to-one seems to give some credence to those hopes.

The Perot voters find themselves in an uncomfortable political position, reminiscent of that of the Wallace supporters in 1968. Then a disaffected bloc, hostile to both the rich and the poor, found itself at odds with a Democratic party that championed the disadvantaged and a Republican party that was aligned with the wealthy. For nearly all of Nixon's first term, the Wallace voters remained conflicted until the Democrats turned to George McGovern. Today similar contradictions are in evidence. The Perot voters are strongly populist and anti-establishment, similar in their thinking to Democratic presidential voters. At the same time, the Perot voters are strongly anti-government, much like Republican presidential voters. That anti-establishment and anti-government sentiment leaves them estranged from all the power centers in society, and in an important sense indigestible for the conventional parties. Indeed, at the center of the consciousness of Perot voters is an ongoing struggle between their deep cynicism about government and a strong desire for government action. Perot himself embodies the struggle. So how can such contradictory views be accommodated when the choice is between one party that hates government and another that loves it?

The original Clinton solution was forged to address just such a contradiction—and the frustration and anger that result from it. Though Perot voters were wary of Clinton at the outset of his term and mistrustful of politicians, most of them were listening. Perot voters were motivated by a sense of middle-class grievance and shared populist disdain for the politically and economically powerful. While Perot himself concentrated his fire on the political establishment, his supporters hated power generally. And while the Perot voters were angry with politics and politicians, they were hardly in favor of small and limited government. They were looking for an activist leader, a doer who could break the impasse, clean up government, and address the needs of ordinary citizens. Perot himself reflected that spirit: he wanted to reform government so it could do the right things for the country.

All his political life, Bill Clinton struggled to bring together a populist spirit with accountable but activist government. Whether the Perot voters would remain a "morbid symptom" or fade into a remade political world would depend on Clinton's ability to bring these ideas together again.

PEROT'S REFORM PROJECT

The Ross Perot candidacy focused above all on reforming a corrupted political system that had become a captive of the political elites. This system no longer worked for the "owners of their country," who, Perot hoped, would use the 1992 election to "reassert" their claims.[2]

A powerful wrong was taking the country to the brink of another Great Depression, Perot asserted. Government was piling up a tremendous national debt, requiring ever growing and ever more burdensome interest payments, while the political elites were enriching themselves. Ordinary citizens, who would be forced to pick up the tab for such perfidy, could no longer afford the price of admission into government circles. The people were pushed aside by the lobbyist who "walks in the door with a fat check from the special interest political action committee." The "Washington lobbyists, political consultants, and lawyers are selling to their clients . . . the access you aren't allowed anymore." It is a powerful image: the country goes to hell while the politicians and lobbyists closet themselves in privilege and ordinary citizens are locked outside.[3]

Perot's analysis of the federal deficit had little to do with the economy, though he linked the deficit's growth to economic decline and doom. The deficit's growth was produced by corruption and government practices that were "impoverishing ourselves"; its reduction meant sound government and good times. The national debt was thus just the most outrageous symptom of traitorous leadership, and its reduction would serve to restore honest government, tempered by the interests of ordinary citizens.

Addressing the debt was a question of right and wrong, and common sense said the country must do the right thing: "We have to face up to our debt." "Our first priority is to balance the budget." "The United States must pay its way." To contribute to the debt means "borrowing our children's money to finance a lifestyle we haven't earned and can't afford," Perot observed. "It can't go on." The discussion of the debt in the Perot platform was full of moral urgency but contained almost no analysis of the deficit's impact on the economy. Indeed, in his book, Perot filled an entire chapter on how to achieve prosperity yet manages to never mention deficit reduction as a relevant policy prescription.[4]

Perot's prescription was to "take back control of our government that has been taken from us." His platform was an exposé of elite excesses: from big consulting contracts with foreign governments and foreign interests to the mobilization of special interests to cover up the S&L scandal to members of Congress lining up for perks and superpensions. Together these excesses underscored a shocking failure of representation. Perot's campaign sought to expose the "betrayal by the elites" and to "restore a sense of ownership to our people."[5]

The Perot project was populist in its anti-elitism, but its anti-elitism was confined to the world of politics, as Perot offered no bottom-up view of the world. When Perot addressed the economy, he depicted a looming Armageddon, but his prescriptions were religiously pragmatic and instrumental. He did not champion people in their economic or industrial lives. He offered no critique of economic power or inequality. His economic program included ending interest and health-care deductibility for upper-income individuals, but that was more about reforming government than attacking economic power. While his plan showed concern for education, it was not about investment and empowerment; it was about fixing broken schools.[6]

Nor did Perot view the world from the top down. He paid a dutiful respect to small-business entrepreneurship, which he saw as creating the vast majority of new jobs, and he favored a number of conservative policies, like investment-tax credits and tax breaks for long-term capital gains, though without much romance. There is no "magic cure-all" here, he says. Perot, in fact, seemed much more fascinated by government and the possibility that it can lead society. He looked at our economic competitors and concluded, "They know how to use government to promote their growing economies." With some wonder, he observed, "We can target, stimulate new industries, applications, and inventions that have not even been conceived of yet. . . .

We can put all our muscle behind industries that produce jobs and a higher standard of living for all Americans." The Perot platform proposed big public investments and government initiatives to create new industries, reflecting our success in promoting the aerospace industry, the interstate highway system, and the satellite communications industry.[7]

The Perot project gained its force from the scent of failure all around it—the failed ideas, the bankrupt parties, gridlock, economic stagnation. Ross Perot rushed into the lead in the presidential race—peaking (at 38 percent) in June—when the only thing he had promised was to clean up the mess in Washington and give the place back to the people. His purpose was not smaller government or bigger government but simply a government properly led and properly accountable, one that would promote a changed America.

THE DISCONNECTED

Who are these people who seemed so intent on escaping politics, the dominant parties, and our party history?

Kevin Phillips tempts us by labeling the Perot voters as the latest twist of "middle class radicalism." The Perot voters were middle American, to be sure, and they were certainly radical in their rage about the political system. But the concept is much too simple and all-embracing to accurately represent the Perot force in our time. Phillips, for example, equates the candidacies of David Duke (white supremacist candidate in Louisiana), Senator Harris Wofford (health-care candidate in Pennsylvania), Pat Buchanan, Jerry Brown, and Ross Perot. But all that these candidacies had in common was populist anger—and even that is a stretch. They offered radically different programs, attacked different villains, and appealed to fundamentally different groups in society. Their supporters were not interchangeable. Phillips is struck that Buchanan's pollster "soon turned up taking surveys for Ross Perot."[8] It would be more interesting, however, had his voters traveled that course as well, which they did not.

The suggestion that the Perot bloc may have been heir to a "center extremism" of the early 1970s is more interesting. In that period, Pat Caddell, Jimmy Carter's pollster, and Donald Warren, director of the Middle American Project, each identified a disaffected bloc, comprising 20 to 30 percent of the electorate, which was left leaning on economic issues and right leaning on social and racial ones. Many of these voters responded to the insurgent third-party candidacy of George Wallace, and others moved over to the law-and-order Republican, Richard Nixon. This disaffected bloc was hostile to both the rich and the poor and thus had trouble fitting comfortably into the conventional political parties—one of which favored the poor and the other, the rich.[9] But this "center extremist" bloc of the 1960s and '70s was the product of the failure of Democratic renewal as the Great Society and the civil rights revolution alienated large segments of middle-class America.

The Perot bloc was created by a different political moment but by a like collapse in our time—the failure of Republican renewal and Reaganomics. This time the sense of betrayal was exaggerated by the continuing economic stagnation and the impasse born of two broken parties. The cries of anger with the establishment sounded something like those of past alienated blocs, but it was a different anger with a different establishment. The "Perot dissolution" was a refuge for disaffected Republicans and younger, detached voters who saw little future in the established parties.

There was a Perot movement in 1992 because of the collapse of the Reagan Republican idea after 1988. Feelings about the Republican party deteriorated sharply after 1988. (See Appendix, Figure A.4.) Indeed, the collapse of positive feeling toward the Republican party after 1988 has been matched only by the Democratic collapse after 1964, the last period of failed renewal. The Perot bloc was a direct product of failed Republican renewal in our time.

A diverse collection of disaffected voters assembled under the Perot banner, but it is hard not to notice the predominance of an alienated Republicanism. Our national survey of Perot voters, sponsored by the Democratic Leadership Council, found that excepting those younger than thirty, these voters shared a Republican voting history in recent elections. Among those older than fifty, three quarters (73 percent) had voted for either Reagan or Bush; and for those aged thirty to fifty, a very respectable two thirds (67 percent) had voted for one or the other. Among all Perot voters, 62 percent voted for Reagan at least once, and 62 percent voted for Bush in 1988.[10]

These were alienated Republicans: they had walked away not just from George Bush but from the Reagan idea that the wealthy should be rewarded in order to promote prosperity. Perot voters held Ronald Reagan in low esteem: just 31 percent expressed positive feelings toward him, and 49 percent expressed negative feelings; among the large center bloc of independent Perot voters, positive sentiments fell to just 25 percent, and negative sentiments rose to 56 percent. Virtually every survey shows that had Perot not run, half these voters, despite their Republican history, would have supported Bill Clinton.[11] These voters were refugees from a national Republican ascendancy that they had largely rejected.

The failure of Republican renewal had set loose a large number of downscale baby boomers (thirty to fifty years of age), who, along with under-thirty voters, dominated the Perot bloc. Perot, then, offered at least a temporary home for many of the non-college-educated voters who were struggling financially

TABLE 9.1

COMPOSITION OF THE PEROT BLOC, 1992

Key Groupings	Percent of Total	Vote for Bush/Clinton Had Perot Not Run
Young voters (under 30)	19.6	39/38
Non-college-educated younger men (30–50)	17.2	41/33
Non-college-educated younger women (30–50)	14.8	32/41
Non-college-educated older women (over 50)	12.8	33/33
Non-college-educated older men (over 50)	10.2	33/33
College-educated younger men (30–50)	8.9	51/30
College-educated younger women (30–50)	8.2	36/43
Older college-educated voters (over 50)	8.2	46/29

and who found themselves, probably uncomfortably, in a top-down party of business led by Ronald Reagan.

The non-college-educated younger men comprised 17 percent of the Perot electorate and embodied the intense alienation that characterized the Perot bloc as a whole. They were the most opposed to the elite establishment and to government and believed middle-class America was getting the shaft.[12] Absent

Perot, the male downscale voter would not have made it all the way over to vote for Bill Clinton: by 41 to 33 percent, these voters would have opted for Bush had Perot been out of the race. The non-college-educated younger women comprised 15 percent of the Perot bloc and were prepared to move to the Democratic side in 1992. They were upset about the economy and their living standards, and they resented the privileged elites, both corporate and governmental.

The under-thirty voters joined the Perot bloc in large numbers as disillusionment with both major parties grew. Overall, feeling about the Democratic party also fell in this period, no doubt reflecting the impasse in the country as the economy stagnated. Among voters under thirty, half now rejected any identification with the two major parties. These younger voters were one fifth of the Perot bloc and together with the downscale baby boomers comprised half the Perot electorate. They were deeply distressed about the economy and their financial prosperity; unlike other Perot voters, 60 percent of them had never voted Republican, but they remained politically rootless: they distrusted the powerful, though they had not come to hate government.[13] (See Table 9.1.)

THE POLITICAL WORLD OF THE PEROT VOTERS

The U.S. Congress

In our national survey, Perot voters reserved their deepest and richest criticism for the Congress, which seemed to represent everything they disliked about our politics in this age. Upon hearing the simple word *Congress,* the Perot participants in the focus groups offered rapid-fire negative associations:

Spending

Crooks

They don't live in the real world

Greed

Rich men

Jerks

Insensitive jerks

Spending money

I think of them as a big block wall

Stopping everything from happening

Thieves

Waste

Bad checks

Special interests

Total waste of money

Payola

Ineffective

Corrupt

Overpaid

Not in touch

Perot voters thought the Congress was dominated by special interest groups, gridlocked in the face of the country's problems, peopled by members who were enriching themselves and out of touch with the lives of average Americans. Little wonder that the Perot voters had so little confidence in Washington's ability to address the country's problems. Instead of addressing real problems, it was thought, members of Congress bickered and fought to a stalemate and offered the country just more bureaucracy and wasteful spending. A Perot voter in Akron summed it up: "They're out of touch with reality. There's no common sense." And the final indignity, pointed out by a man in San Bernardino, was that they "give themselves a raise, and then tax us for it."

The Perot Antidote

For these voters, Perot was the antidote to Congress. He was more than simply the champion who would have challenged Congress; they associated characteristics with Perot that diametrically opposed those of Congress. If one maps out the Perot worldview, as in Figure 9.1, two axes emerge: the Democratic-Republican axis and the Congress-Perot axis. On the map, Democrats and allied institutions are to the left (defined by Bill Clinton), and the Republicans and their institutions are to the right (defined by Ronald Reagan). That places Perot as the positive pole of an axis defined by the negative pole, Congress.[14]

It should not be surprising, then, that Perot voters ascribed to Perot a whole range of traits that counter what they disliked about Congress. First, they believed Perot to be honest. He was "sincere" and a "straight shooter, tells it like it is, exposing special interest groups." He "speaks his mind" and "didn't seem to be bought." Union members surveyed in Akron believed that "he doesn't seem like he's a puppet, like somebody's going to control him." Another responded, "He's his own man." In San Bernardino, the women reiterated that sense of honest independence: "He had the guts enough to do it without all the favors."

Second, they believed Perot cared about people. These voters thought of Perot as somebody who was "concerned about the people." One man in Bangor personalized it: "He seems to be for us." That contrasted with the prevailing practice: "He's

Perceptual Map of Perot Voters, 1993

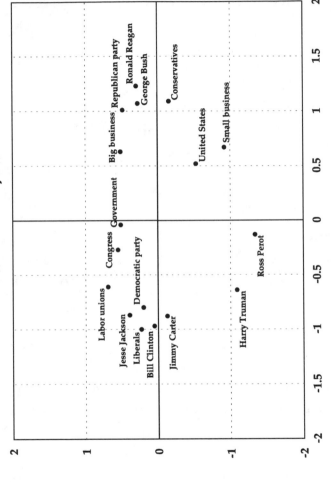

Figure 9.1

Source: Democratic Leadership Council, "Road to Realignment. The Democrats and the Perot Voters," 1993

more for the people, understands what the people are trying to say, versus the other ones that really aren't so much for the people. They've been so high up for so long that their heads [are] in the clouds." A man in Akron said that Perot's actions would have shifted the balance, "taking it out of lobbyists, taking it out of the people that are in there that are making hundreds and hundreds of thousands of dollars to make decisions that, you know, we should make" and putting "the power in the people's hands."

Third, they believed Perot could have broken gridlock and got things done. Perot was seen as "aggressive," "takes charge," "hard driving," indeed, as somebody who was "not afraid to take on Congress" and "gonna get in the trenches and make something happen." There was a real sense of hope in these discussions: "I really think he'd have a great opportunity to break the gridlock because he's not one of them."

Fourth, they believed Perot would have cut out the frills, waste, and overspending. These voters thought of him as "down to earth," bringing business sense to spending. He "knows how to handle money." He would have "cut waste" and "cut government spending." He would have "cut off . . . these Congressmen [who] take all these free trips and stuff. He'd cut all that out." He would "take them off of pork barreling and government spending, one-hundred-dollar toilet seats and stuff like that." He "would cut spending where we need it cut in the White House, get rid of some of that loose rubbish."

Finally, they believed Perot would have stood up for America. His voters thought of him as "patriotic," "puts America first," and "wants to help the people in the U.S.A." He was "totally for the country," concerned for "the welfare of the country," "cares about the American people." One man observed, "He's trying to bring the pride back to America." Specifically, that meant Perot would have tried to "keep the money here to help our own." "He would really take a real good look at foreign aid." These voters thought Perot would have given priority to America, something that Congress had repeatedly failed to do.

The Perot voters thought of their candidate as a "good businessman." That meant above all that Perot was "not a politician," that he embodied "change." Unlike the politicians who now run Washington, D.C., Perot would have respected the tax dollars people pay, tackled the country's problems, and helped people; and against the tenor of the times, he would have succeeded at governing. The politicians who tell people what they want to hear always break their promises, but Perot, they thought, was different, was somebody who would "keep his promises" and restore the public trust.

For all the positive sentiment about Perot, however, the doubts were close to the surface. They centered on the very attributes that made him different from Congress. He was inexperienced and independent, a member of no party. His independence was personalized as a "temperamental" rigidity, "somewhat dictatorial" and "paranoid." A Perot presidency, even these Perot voters feared, could have produced a political mess and a new form of gridlock. "Perot has zilch to fall back on if he got in," one man from San Bernardino observed. There "might be total chaos in the government and in Congress because of his inexperience in dealing with politicians." One of the men in Bangor summed up the underlying concern:

> I think . . . there seems to be some of a dictatorial attitude there, and that will never work in the political field in Washington, D.C. . . . You can try anything you want to try, but unless Congress and the rest of the politicians and the lobbyists and the business and the special interests will let you do it, he's gonna get hurt really quick.

Perot's quitting the race in July 1992 reflected his temperamental quality. That was the most frequently mentioned doubt:

"quitting and coming back like that." A Bangor woman observed, "When he backed out of the campaign, I lost a little hope." Right below the surface was a fear that Perot's temperament would lead him to quit and to fail to keep his promises.

The National Debt

The federal deficit is a powerful symbol of the mess in Washington and had a great deal of meaning to Perot voters. They used the deficit to talk about a broad range of things that are wrong in the country. But we should not confuse symbolism with policy prescription. The deficit is very important, but it was not the first policy concern of Perot voters: nearly three quarters failed to mention the deficit as either the first or second most important problem facing the country. More important for Perot voters, as for other voters, was the economy in general. Almost four in ten mentioned the economy, compared with the 27 percent who cited the deficit. But other problems, like health care (25 percent) and jobs (23 percent), received virtually the same level of attention. These voters had broad policy concerns that belied Perot's near total preoccupation with the deficit.

Still, nearly all Perot voters believed the deficit was a serious problem: 78 percent said the federal-budget deficit was one of the most important problems, or a very important problem, facing the country. The deficit was not so much an immediate policy focus as an expression of something very wrong in the country. It was not so much about austerity as it was about responsibility, and was not so much about limited government as about liberating government to work for the people.

There were, of course, some Perot voters who thought of the deficit as a bottom line, an inability of government to think sensibly about money and to operate in the black. These voters sounded like the fiscal conservatives that give Republicans heart: "wasted money," with "poor control"; they "overspend on everything"; "it's just like they've got a plastic card, and they can go crazy." Some of the Perot voters were just hostile to taxes, and a growing deficit constitutes a steady pressure to raise taxes.

But the "green-eyeshade" view of the deficit was subsumed by more emotional assessments, in which the deficit emerged as a metaphor for broad problems facing the country. For many Perot voters, the deficit represented the country's problems growing out of control and beyond the capacity of anyone to solve. They were left, consequently, feeling overwhelmed and scared and impotent, calling the deficit "too overwhelming," a "bottomless pit," "a deep hole," "astronomical, absurd, and out of control."

For many, the rising debt presaged not only national bankruptcy but also the decline of the country: "The country will run out of money and go into a total depression real soon, real soon." "We're gonna be a third world country." "It's just making us a weaker nation." That Congress watched the problem worsen yet failed to act only heightened their alienation, as it seemed the politicians simply wouldn't take responsibility.

There was, however, a very strong current among Perot voters that bemoaned the reckless spending because it created an incapacity of government to address genuine human needs, to do the right things. These voters believed the growing national debt swallowed up money that could be used to make things better in society. For them, concern with the deficit had little to do with a philosophical aversion to government. Instead they wanted the government to do more, but felt its hands were tied by mounting taxes and interest payments:

> The money's so staggering with the taxes that we're putting everything back to the deficit to pay it off. You're taking away from everything else.

> We pay millions every day just in interest that we wouldn't have to pay that could go to create jobs and good schools.

We'd have money for the elderly, the hospitals. We'd be able to educate our people better; we'd have a cleaner environment.

If we didn't have the deficit, we could take care of our elderly and health care stuff.

We could invest a lot more money in our children and in our future and wouldn't have to worry about getting old.

For this important segment of Perot voters, cleaning up the deficit was a precondition for a renewed government that is better able to address important needs. Political reform offers the prospect of political possibility.

THE MIND OF THE PEROT VOTER

The Perot voter is kind of a canvas on which the political perversity of the last few decades has been painted. Voters have lost interest in political parties—there are more independents (38 percent) now than adherents of either major party—and Perot voters are the most detached of all. If voters in general have become more distrustful of the goodwill of the country's leaders, the Perot voters, with their weakened political commitments, have become the most distrustful of all. The Perot voter has emerged as a kind of caricature of our distorted age, experiencing and feeling its failings.

For Bush and Clinton, the 1992 election was a clash of two stories, both told for this audience of rootless and cynical voters. Clinton's story began with a critique of the political and economic leaders and a government that had failed middle-class America and ended with a program to invest in people to bring about growth and jobs. George Bush's story told of a president who hated taxes and big-government spending programs and who had faith in the resurgence of American business and American prosperity.

It is easy to imagine that Perot voters would have been more attentive to Bush's top-down tale; after all, 71 percent were self-described moderates or conservatives, and nearly 100 percent believed that government would mess things up, not from a philosophical conservatism but from a pragmatic state of mind about government competence. Political economist Albert O. Hirschman identifies three such lines of argument that, in practice, buttress conservative thinking: the "perversity thesis," which says proposed changes, whatever their good intentions, produce the exact opposite of their intended result; the "futility thesis," which says changes do nothing but touch the surface and therefore are not worth the effort; and finally, the "jeopardy thesis," which says change may put in jeopardy other important things.[15] All three came together in the Perot voters' frustration with government.

But since so many Perot voters were contemplating voting for Clinton in 1992, we have to imagine that there was something in the Clinton story countering such pragmatic conservatism.

Using an extensive battery on values and attitudes, we sought to identify the primary dimension of political thinking among Perot (as well as Bush and Clinton) voters. The battery of questions represented an updated version of questions used by the University of Michigan and by the *Times-Mirror* to explore the thinking and consciousness behind political choices. (See Appendix, Table A.1.) Our research used a factor-analysis methodology to explore which opinions correlated with one another, enabling us to identify five distinctive attitudinal dimensions:

> **Middle-class consciousness:** a sensitivity to middle-class grievances; a belief that a well-behaved and industrious middle class gets a raw deal, particularly as the poor and others use special claims to get around the rules and gain advantage.

Anti-government: a feeling that you cannot trust the government to do the right thing and not screw things up; a belief that politicians are corrupt.

Anti-establishment: a belief that the system rewards those who get around the rules and that public officials and corporations are indifferent to the public interest.

Secular: a belief that government should be tolerant of different views and lifestyles and that government should not interfere with abortion.

Financial pressure: a sense of economic distress, particularly the inability to keep up with prices and make ends meet.

The Perot voters stand out from the Clinton and Bush voters in their simultaneous alienation from government and from all other powerful institutions in society. (See Figures 9.2 and 9.3.) That is what defined the group and set the tone for its politics. In terms of these dimensions, the Perot voters were strongly anti-government and anti-establishment. They did not trust the government to do the right thing, and they did not trust the private and public wielders of power to act in the public interest.

The Perot voters seemed to carry on their backs the whole burden of middle-class America, as they scored very high on middle-class consciousness; those who play by the rules, they believed, get little recognition today.

Perot voters were also markedly libertarian, distinguishing themselves from the Bush-Republican bloc that many of them had left behind. Their scores on the secularism and tolerance dimension suggested a strong individualism and a reluctance to see government get involved in moral questions. Indeed, on abortion, Clinton voters and Perot voters held almost identical views, distinguished from the Bush voters, who stood strongly opposed to legalized abortion: 68 and 72

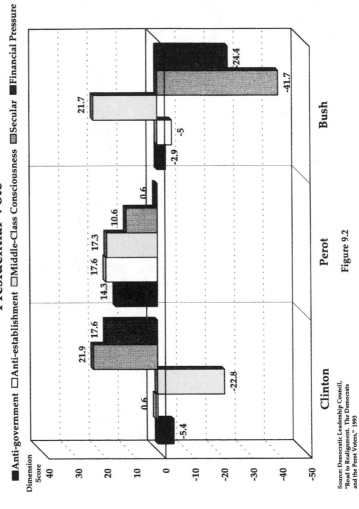

Political Consciousness: 1992
Presidential Vote

■ Anti-government □ Anti-establishment □ Middle-Class Consciousness ▨ Secular ■ Financial Pressure

Clinton   Perot   Bush

Figure 9.2

Source: Democratic Leadership Council,
"Road to Realignment: The Democrats
and the Perot Voters," 1993

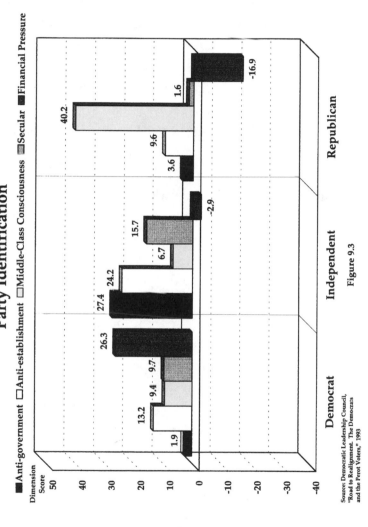

Political Consciousness: 1992

Party Identification

■ Anti-government □ Anti-establishment □ Middle-Class Consciousness ▨ Secular ■ Financial Pressure

Dimension
Score

Democrat   Independent   Republican

Figure 9.3

Source: Democratic Leadership Council,
"Road to Realignment. The Democrats
and the Perot Voters," 1993

percent of Perot voters and Clinton voters, respectively, believed abortion should be legal, compared with just 44 percent of Bush voters. In the focus groups, Perot voters repeatedly said that government should keep its hands out of such private matters. A typical comment was "It's not the government's business, and it's not the neighbor's business, and it's not anybody's business."

About one fourth of the Perot voters (24 percent) leaned toward the Democratic side; that is, they identified as Democrats or voted for them at the local level. This was the first audience for the Clinton bottom-up story. These voters stood out from the other Perot voters by virtue of their pronounced economic worries and by the pattern of their alienation: they were anti-establishment but not particularly anti-government.

The Bush top-down story likely reached about a quarter of the Perot voters (28 percent), those who leaned to the Republican side. These voters felt fine financially, they were not particularly secular, but they did score very high on middle-class consciousness.

In the middle were the straight independents, who constituted 43 percent of the Perot voters. They were secular voters, not particularly concerned with personal financial issues. They stood out, however, in their intense anti-government and anti-establishment views. Neither Democrats nor Republicans will reach these voters unless they find a way to break through the fog of populist, political alienation. Republicans have positioned themselves against taxes and against government, but as we saw, that hardly captured the complexity of these voters, who were quite populist, eager to break gridlock and reform government, and looking for major changes in society. But Democrats will find an audience only if they can combine their populism with a fervor for reforming government.

UNWELCOME REFORMERS

At the outset of the Clinton administration, these Perot voters wanted a government that would be efficient and do the right things. They supported proposals to restrict lobbying severely and cut the bureaucracy. They reserved their strongest endorsement, however, for proposals to "radically change government": 72 percent were much more likely to support a candidate who will change the way government does things, "cut bureaucracy, make government more efficient, and give ordinary people better service and more choices." Among the independent Perot voters—the most important swing segment—intense support for a candidate who would revolutionize government jumped to 76 percent.

Obviously Perot voters wanted to clean up government and cut bureaucracy and privilege, but their passions lay with changing a government to make it more efficient in delivering services for ordinary citizens. Support for radically changing government was 21 points stronger than support for simply cutting bureaucracy (72 versus 51 percent), suggesting that the Perot bloc was looking to make government work rather than looking simply to make it smaller. The Perot voters were strikingly more supportive of political reform than either the Clinton or Bush supporters: the pro-government Democrats resisted the critique of government, while the anti-government Republicans would have cut government rather than reform it. But the Perot voters wanted to change government so it can do the right things for the people who pay the bills.

It was clear by election day 1994 that Perot voters were dissatisfied with the spectacle in Washington and Clinton's reform project. Their worst fears about government were only being confirmed, as four in five now believed "government always

TABLE 9.2

REFORMING GOVERNMENT

Reform Options	Percent
The government should be given back to the people by reducing the influence of special interests and lobbyists.	59
The government should be made more efficient so it delivers services for less money.	45
The government should be made smaller so it will cost and do less.	27

manages to mess things up"—up almost 10 points during Clinton's term. By more than two to one, they had concluded that Bill Clinton was pursuing big government, rather than less bureaucratic approaches to addressing the country's problems.[16] Their anger was evident at the polls.

One might imagine that disillusioned Perot voters would set aside their reformist instincts and just give up on government and Bill Clinton. One can hardly fault Republican observers for reading just such intentions into the Perot voters' overwhelming support for Republican congressional candidates in 1994. That interpretation, however, underestimates the depth of conviction and the depth of alienation that motivate the Perot voter.

Even as they were voting to reject the Democrats' hold on the political world, Perot voters were affirming their commitment to radical reform in a national survey I conducted after the election. They specifically rejected the Republican idea that "government should be made smaller so it will cost and do less."

Instead, they affirmed their quest for a government that belongs to the people and one that delivers services more efficiently and for less money. At the center of their political project is not gutting government but reclaiming it for ordinary people and making sure it does the right things with less bureaucracy. Those goals were reflected in their agenda for the new Congress—cutting spending and the federal bureaucracy to be sure, but also protecting Social Security and Medicare, reforming health care, and limiting the influence of lobbyists. (See Table 9.2.)

The Perot voters' support for Republican congressional candidates in 1994 is only a partial guide to Perot voters' evaluation of the president. Even with the midterm upheaval, they were more inclined to see President Bill Clinton as a New Democrat who wants to "help people equip themselves to solve their own problems" than as a traditional Democrat who believes "government can solve problems and protect people from adversity"; more said they are "hopeful" that Clinton will succeed than said they have "given up" on him.

The 1994 election did nothing to resolve the contradictions that leave the Perot bloc unassimilable for the national political parties. These voters remain more anti-government than Bush voters and Republicans—creating the current shift to the right. But at the same time, Perot voters are intensely anti-establishment, indeed, more anti-establishment and populist than Clinton voters and Democrats. And on the secular dimension, they are closer to the Democrats than to the Republicans at a time when Republicans are coming to highlight their strong bonds with the religious right. (See Figure 9.4.)

That leaves these reformist Perot voters in a position reminiscent of the Wallace voters of an earlier period. After the 1968 collapse of the Democratic idea, the party system struggled with how to cope with a disaffected bloc that resented both the poor and the rich. These voters did not fit comfortably in either of the

258

Middle Class Dreams

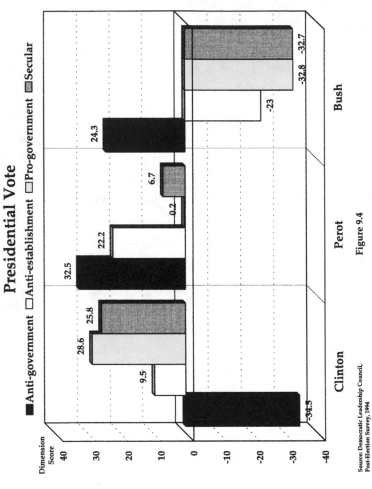

Political Consciousness: 1994
Presidential Vote

■ Anti-government □ Anti-establishment □ Pro-government ■ Secular

Dimension Score

Clinton

Perot

Bush

Figure 9.4

Source: Democratic Leadership Council,
Post-Election Survey, 1994

dominant parties, and this showed in their volatility and anger. The question today is whether the political system can accommodate these detached voters who both hate government and demand government action, who resent both political elites and economic elites. Their world view is not easily accommodated by the dominant parties—one associated with political elites and government activism and the other with economic elites and government indifference—a situation that may yield yet another harvest of angry alienation. But that contradiction is at the very heart of the Clinton solution, which aspires to deliver accountable and activist government to working- and middle-class America. That contradiction is now one of the principal dramas at the heart of our politics.

10. NEW CONTRACT

THE major parties dominated the political landscape for a good part of a century, but now they have fallen into disrepute. Each in turn crashed spectacularly as disillusioned voters turned elsewhere, to radical reformers and all manner of outsider parties and movements.

This sounds like the drama that gave us failed Democratic liberalism and failed Reagan Republicanism, indeed the drama that gave us Ross Perot and the politics of alienation. But the drama that played out in America does not stand alone. It shares the stage with the fiery crash of the established parties in developed democracies around the world.

Top-down conservative parties in Canada, Japan, and Italy nearly disintegrated in the year following America's party crash of 1992. In July 1993, Japan's Liberal Democratic party, which had ruled Japan without interruption and without serious challenge since 1955, splintered and lost its iron-clad hold on the Diet. Three months later, Canada's Progressive Conservative party was nearly obliterated: its national vote fell from 43 to just 16 percent; and whereas it once held 169 seats in Parliament, it now holds just 2 seats. And in March 1994, Italy's Christian Democratic party, which had helped form every centrist coalition government since 1948, won only 11 percent of the vote, a third of its previous standing.

Bottom-up socialist parties shared in this ignominy. In 1993, the French Socialists saw their vote cut nearly in half (from 54 to 28 percent) and their seats in the National Assembly reduced to a fifth (from 275 to 54). The Communist party, once poised to compete for national leadership, slipped quietly into oblivion. In the countries where conservative parties were collapsing, social-ists lacked the standing to benefit. The Socialists lost ground in Japan, despite the massive defeat of the conservatives. In Italy, the Socialists virtually disappeared as the corruption scandals en-veloped all the governing parties. The socialist New Democratic vote in Canada fell from 20 to less than 7 percent—its worst per-formance in sixty years.

The breathtaking collapse of the established parties opened up the political world to Perot-like candidacies and radical reformist and ethnocentric regional parties—all innocent of the corrupted national politics and all prepared to sweep out the sta-bles of their respective national regimes. They based their claims on their disassociation from old-party divisions. The result was a cacophony of political expression. In Canada, Bloc Quebecois, the French separatists, won in Quebec, and the Reform party swept all the western provinces, the latter running against taxes, budget deficits, bureaucracy, and immigration and for more direct democracy through referenda and recalls. The neo-Nazi National Front firmly found a place on the French political scene, as the neo-Nazi Republicans found a place in Germany. In Japan, an odd assortment of seven parties and independent members formed a new reformist bloc and elected its own gov-ernment, only to be followed by a new unlikely and unstable coalition of old guard Socialists and Liberal Democrats. The most dramatic change came in Italy, where the dominant parties were crushed by a coalition of the separatist Northern League, the neo-fascists, and Forza Italia ("Go, Italy"), led by a billionaire businessman, Silvio Berlusconi, who soon found himself in seri-ous political difficulty.[1]

This mix of angry and alienated voices shouted down the historic political parties as a gloom descended on the developed

democracies. The traditional social contract that had allowed
ordinary citizens to find their place in a developing industrial
world was under siege. Since the late 1970s, parties of both the
right and the left had supported the retrenchment of social welfare spending on health care, unemployment benefits, and housing, yet taxes remained high. During the 1980s and early 1990s,
economic and income growth slowed everywhere, with unemployment rising across Western Europe to double-digit levels,
undercutting the promise and ideas associated with Europe and
Asia's postwar miracle. Even Japan, leader of the postwar boom,
watched its economy sink into recession and periods of negative
growth in the 1990s.[2]

The idea of a contract—with its obligations, mutuality, inclu-
siveness, and solid values—may have lost its economic foundation.
The days when an expanding "Fordism" in the advanced democracies could bring ever-expanding production, rising income and
consumption, leisure and suburbanization now seemed quite precious. The successful entrepreneur was struggling to throw off
these old contracts and obligations. The "reciprocal relations that
bound big labor, big capital, and big government" together, writes
sociologist David Harvey, has become "a dysfunctional embrace."
This new age was rewarding mobility, flexibility, speed, change,
and information; it was rewarding educated workers who could
master the new forces. More and more workers found themselves
in unorganized, uncertain, and lesser-paid service positions that
allow people to make fewer claims on employers and society. In
this new age, growth furthered fragmentation and seemed to
diminish prospects for some social compact.[3]

The middle-class bargain—growth, work, and a better life—
had come undone, yet the major parties appeared paralyzed
before the challenge of forging some new contract with working people. With the dominant ideas and parties in retreat, all
kinds of macabre political forces rushed to the fore, campaign-

ing against taxes, immigrants, corruption, elitism, bureaucracy, gridlock, the national government. At the same time, increasing numbers of people turned away from the political community and modernism to find meaning in fundamentalist religious communities and politics.

This may be America's fate too—nothing exceptional, just one more bleak example of century-old political traditions faltering and crashing before the forces bearing down on the advanced democracies. America may be doomed to a failed politics, one fully capable of expressing rage but incapable of recapturing the public's imagination.

That certainly sounds like the story of America's 1994 midterm elections. As the authors of the *Times-Mirror* survey put it immediately before the election, "the American electorate is angry, self-absorbed, and politically unanchored."[4] It expressed its anger by voting against a Democratic-dominated national politics that seemed tangled in partisan bickering and special interest lobbying and that crowded out the needs of ordinary citizens. The electorate voted its disappointment with the spectacle of a Democratic president and a Democratic Congress promising change, but seemingly unable to produce it. The vote was less about Bill Clinton or presidential politics than about their disappointment in the nature of our politics. When asked in the DLC post-election survey to describe the "mess in Washington," a near majority of the independent swing voters (48 percent) mentioned this corrupted political world; only 8 percent mentioned Bill Clinton. (See Appendix, Table A.2.) When asked what their protest message is about, 45 percent said it is about "politics as usual" and another 15 percent, about "Congress."[5]

I went back to Macomb in the days after the election to listen to people talk about what they had done at the polls.[6] In the focus-group discussions, these swing independent voters spoke of people and a country still in trouble, and a political system that seemed capable only of producing turmoil. The voters were intent on sending a message about politics and the Democrats. They were intent on using their vote to hold the current political class accountable for the failure of politics:

> I don't even know what to change, but we need something changed. No, we're not getting anywhere. We're at a standstill or it's getting worse. It's not getting any better.

> The Democrats have been in there for a long time. They've had the majority rule. They haven't gotten anything done. Give somebody else a chance and see how they do. And if they don't, then we can throw them out and put the Democrats back in.

> They've had the majority vote and they haven't done enough. Give the Republicans a chance.

> They don't listen to the people and then they wonder why they're thrown out. I think that this last election is a perfect example of it yesterday where masses were thrown out of office because they're not listening to what the people are telling them.

> I don't know if there was a message as much as there's just a deep sense of anger. People are just upset, they don't know how to change things, and so they're going to do it in the only way that they know how, and that's to remove some people. I think essentially that what they're saying is listen to our interests and be accountable to us.

A voter in a similar focus group in Riverside, California put it bluntly: "It was like a Nike commercial. Just do it. Do it now, do it quickly, just do it. Enough is enough, just do it."

The 1994 election brought a collapse of confidence in the Democratic party—matching the Republican collapse of 1988 to

1992. (See Appendix, Figure A.4.) The mean thermometer score for the Democratic party fell from 58.5 in 1992 to 52.5 today—with 100 degrees meaning a very warm feeling and zero degrees meaning very cold and with 50 degrees being neither warm nor cold feeling. But one should not lose sight of the character of the current partisan reality: both national parties are in trouble. After the election the public gave the Republican party a mean temperature score of 53.1 degrees, virtually unchanged from the time of its defeat in 1992, when its mean temperature was 51.7 degrees. That places the Republicans only a half degree above the Democrats. Indeed, the two parties stand at a kind of bleak parity, compared with their historic positions.

These independent voters could barely muster anything positive to say about either party, despite recent gains for the Republicans. Some of the men volunteered that the Republicans were "conservative," but that was overwhelmed by other images that suggest a largely unreconstructed party:

For the rich

Big money, big business

Conservative, money, greed

Reagan, peace

Big time, business and investments

More military-minded, unemployment

For big businesses

Big business

Cut government size, benefits and taxes and take care of the big business

It depends on where you are on the economic ladder.

The open-ended comments about the Democrats were even more scathing and the compliments even more backhanded:

Money, spending, Clinton

Working people, blue collar, small business

Clinton spending our tax dollars unwisely

For the little people, haven't been that successful

Working to help the little people, but sometimes go too far.

They don't have the power.

Taxes, benefits

Clinton, disappointed, idealists

Kennedy, liberal, spenders

Big spenders, supposedly for the people

They're out of touch with us.

After the crash, people find it hard to be charitable about the parties and our national politics. That is an inducement for our national parties to maneuver for advantage within this shattered politics, without creating something that the citizenry can believe in, without giving the middle class any hope for a new contract. Republican presidential candidates would attack the Democrats for their aging failures—taxes, spending, and big government—and Democrats would attack the Republicans for theirs—favoring the wealthy and indifference to the common person. Each would try to create ad hoc coalitions that might momentarily break the impasse, but neither party would successfully articulate a core idea on how to organize and change the country. Both parties would come under attack from the radical reformers impatient with corrupt and arrogant political leaders and parties that neglect the people and offer little promise of change. Democratic and Republican candidates would obviously still win office, but they would win little appreciation or respect. Politics without vision is a formula for further dissolution.

Such despair hardly suits the American experience or voters' current inclinations. Americans are still innocent enough to seek a politics that could make their lives better and restore confidence in the country. Many voted for Ross Perot specifically to get the government to do the "right thing" with the people's money. In 1992, people flocked to the polls—a 5.5-percent increase in turnout after three decades of almost inexorable decline—because they believed they could affect government and this was an election that mattered to their lives.[7] In the end, over 60 percent voted for candidates of "change," and on the eve of Clinton's inauguration over two thirds described themselves as "optimistic" that the president would succeed in creating something new; over 60 percent expected Clinton to "make significant progress on reforming health care, improving education and creating jobs."[8]

The din of negative news and the grueling battle to enact major legislation have sapped a good deal of that optimism, but people are not looking to become "alienated, middle-class radicals" in a declining country. Even after the 1994 congressional election that swept out so many Democrats, two-thirds of independent voters said they are "still hopeful that Clinton can succeed." People continue to look for a restoration of the public trust and middle-class dreams. The future lies with those political leaders who understand the frustrations and aspirations of the majority of Americans, who have seen the crash and have not been crippled by it, and who have the vision and the will to rebuild the social contract.

THE REPUBLICAN GAMBLE

The starting point for Republicans has been to minimize the crash of '92 and the amount of reconstruction necessary to rebuild their party and the country. Their electoral gains in 1994 seemed to justify that course. They have focused almost exclusively on the Democratic heresy of taxes and big government, and they have given only passing attention to Republican economic ideas, the so-called Republican "Contract with America" notwithstanding. Rather than aspiring to transcend the failed party order of the 1960s, the Republicans have been hard at work trying to resuscitate it. They cannot imagine a politics not dominated by taxes, race, crime, and cultural wars, the combination that separated the Democratic party from its downscale base and enabled Republicans like Ronald Reagan to bring together the more secular upper classes and the Godfearing lower classes under the same political umbrella.

The Republicans, however, despite their recent gains, are in no position to renew America's politics or rebuild the hopes of a frustrated middle class because they deny the crash: there is nothing to renew; there is just the task of putting George Bush and his heresies out of mind and reclaiming Reaganism. For all their success in fanning the flames of protest, the Republicans are oddly out of touch with this political moment. They can win elections, to be sure, but not change America's political course or raise its spirits.

The Republicans have been busy demystifying the 1992 election: it cannot be allowed to signify a historic change. Everett Carll Ladd, a leading conservative political scientist associated with the American Enterprise Institute, rejected 1992 as a "realigning" election in social science terms. Instead, he wrote, it should be considered a "deviating" election, in which "the prevailing balance of power in presidential electioneering, was rocked by short-term demands for change strong enough to give the out-of-power party control of the Executive Branch for the first time in a dozen years." Ladd detected no change in the "structure of groups' political loyalties" or in the expectations about public policy. The Republicans, he believes, entered the 1992 election with "most of their assets intact."

According to this analysis, Bush lost because of "short-term" factors that are not replicable and leave no long-term implications for the party. The public remained stuck in their bleak feelings about the economy—77 percent characterizing it as in "bad shape"—largely because of the press's "sustained, unremitting emphasis on problems and failures." Perot's television blitz compounded the problem, underscoring the perception that "the sky had fallen economically on the watch of George Bush."[9]

Bush himself is seen as an aberration who failed to carry the banner of Reaganism in the 1992 election. Indeed, John Podhoretz, a disillusioned Bush speechwriter, described his apostasy: "George Bush's recessions and ineffective leadership allowed the Democrats to succeed in 1992 at something they had failed to do throughout the 1980s—invalidating Reaganism in the eyes of the American people." When Bush walked away from his no-new-taxes pledge in 1991, the staunch Reaganites saw him walking away from the "Republicans' central unifying principle." Bush never understood that Clinton's attack on greed was an "attack on the low tax, deregulatory strategy of the modern Republican Party."[10]

Republicans have come to see Perot voters not as an expression of political dissolution but simply as "Republican voters who couldn't stomach George Bush." Ladd gave that position intellectual respectability by asserting that the "Perotists resembled the Bushites, though with a more libertarian coloration." He concluded that "disproportionately, they were demographic and attitudinal Republican voters." Thus one anti-tax leader concluded, "The party should . . . stop acting as if [the 1992] election were a repudiation of conservatism—rather than of one politician who abandoned it."[11]

Underlying the Republican discourse is an unquestioned and unexamined assumption: that Reaganism is a vital concept in the country, respected and in no way repudiated by the electorate in 1992. None of the Republican think tanks that have cropped up since the election—Project for the Republican Future, National Policy Forum, or Empower America—has raised any questions about the values, success, consistency, or appeal of Reaganism. It is a truth that need only be reaffirmed.

The denial of the crash allows Republicans to avoid facing some very difficult electoral realities: the defection of non-southern lower-middle-class voters to Clinton, the defection of more secular and better-educated Republicans to Perot, and the weakened Republican presence among younger voters. Even with Republican gains in 1994, the lower middle class remained contested and younger people voted Democratic. The emergence of the religious right highlights all these unresolved problems, which together undercut the post-1960s Republican formula for national dominance.

Reagan and Bush had successfully built a national majority by appealing to upper-income voters on growth and to working-class voters on values (as well as growth). For the latter, the uneven economic rewards of Reaganism were more than compensated for by the Republicans' heightened commitment to family and religious values. Thus, Reagan and Bush were able to join upscale and downscale America under a common program of low taxes and religious sentiment, a program opposed to a free-spending Democratic party that is seen as soft on taxes, indifferent to crime and family breakdown, and hostile to religion. The evangelical segments of downscale America, particularly in the South, took the Republicans' moral claims to heart and voted overwhelmingly for Bush, as well as for Reagan. They now constitute the most loyal element in the Republican base, comprising more than one in three of all Republican presidential voters, and they are Bill Clinton's strongest critics. With the Republicans in defeat, the religious right has moved to assert its claim on the Republican party. Before the summer of 1994, it had taken control of the state Republican parties in South Carolina, Texas, Virginia, Oregon, Iowa, and Washington and was banging on the doors in Minnesota, California, Florida, and many other states. While Oliver North's unapologetic religious right campaign lost in Virginia, Senate candidates of similar views won in Oklahoma, Minnesota, Missouri, Pennsylvania and Tennessee.

The "cultural war" has put the Republican party on a collision course with the more secular growth-oriented segments of the country and underscores the limits of the Reagan-Bush solution. Among Republicans in 1992, almost a third of pro-choice and more secular voters defected—the large majority of them to Ross Perot. Clinton also won big among the more libertarian and secular younger voters—by 9 points over Bush, widening to 13 points among those eighteen to twenty-four years old. Secular voters have grown in number, rivaling the number of white evangelical Protestants, and they are strongly Democratic in their leanings.[12] In choosing to escalate the "cultural war," the Republicans are betting that downscale America can still be divided along the battle lines of the 1960s, but in the current context, that may only compound the problems that endanger the Reagan-Bush formula for achieving a national majority.

The Republicans have united around a demand for lower taxes and opposition to big government, though stripped of Reagan's loftier rationale and vision. In the first two years of the

Clinton administration, they made themselves the bulwark against Clinton's "big government" solution to health care and against his tax increase, the "biggest tax increase in history." By attacking government and taxes, Republicans were able to identify with genuine voter anxieties and further elevate the public's skepticism about government. In the Democratic Leadership Council post-election survey, two-thirds concluded that the government "always manages to mess things up" and half, that "you really can't trust the government to do the right thing." This relentless Republican attack on government advanced the conservative premise, mentioned earlier, that well-intended, purposeful government initiatives will only make things worse, have little effect, or endanger things we cherish. While the attack did little to advance a new top-down compact, it did compound the citizenry's skepticism about government and about its capacity to change things. In the political battles of the day, that is a big tactical success.

Yet the approach has done little to allay the public's deep skepticism about Republican tax and economic policies that begin by enriching only the few. In 1994, the Republicans studiously avoided the subject by declining to propose any rollback of the Clinton taxes on the wealthy. Their platform included a cut in the capital gains tax, but they never mentioned the subject above a whisper. After the election, when voters were asked about their priorities for the new Congress, such breaks for the upper strata fell near the very bottom—along with other popular ideas like cutting Social Security. The Republicans laid no foundation for a return to Reaganism.

The straightforward attack on government ignores the public's longing to reclaim the government—to make it more efficient, respectful of the ordinary citizen and not the special interests, to make it more mindful of middle-class values and needs, and to make sure it does the right things to address the country's problems. The approach weakens the public's sense of capacity, but it provides no alternative view of how life can be better. Perhaps that is why voters prefer by 52 to 38 percent a New Democrat who believes "government should help people equip themselves to solve their own problems" to a Republican who believes "government should leave people alone to solve their own problems."

The Republican discourse, consequently, has been reduced to a collection of wedge issues. Republican politicians can be seen rushing to demonstrate their bona fides as anti-gay, anti-alien, anti-criminal, anti-politician, anti-tax. They have moved to the front of the parade on "term limits" and other anti-political and anti-Congress measures. They have pinned their hopes on a rising tide of alienation and anger and on their ability to associate the Democrats with values hostile to mainstream America. They seek power on the cheap—by attacking corruption, foreign elements and modernity, not by rebuilding public confidence in a top-down view of the world. And they will soon appreciate that America is in trouble not because of corruption but because of the failure of ideas.

THE DEMOCRATIC CHALLENGE

For all the flaws in doing so, there is a certain security in denying the crash and relying on old formulas. For the Republicans, this course may well spare the party a wrenching and divisive reexamination of its purpose.

But Bill Clinton and the Democrats stand at a different moment in history. Voters are watching to see whether Clinton and his administration will create something that middle-class America can believe in or whether they will fail and breed yet more feelings of disappointment and betrayal. Frankly, the citizenry has lived with decades of disappointment and finds it hard to imagine any other outcome. That cynicism makes it that much more difficult for the Democrats to succeed.

There are large forces at work that will impede Democratic efforts to remake our politics. The economy, even in recovery, seems unable to generate real income gains. During Clinton's first year in office, for example, the median income edged downward and stood 7 percent below the level when George Bush had taken office. The great majority of people without college degrees, particularly the men, have watched their incomes decline for a decade.[13] Little wonder that working people's faith in economic progress has proved so fragile.

The Democrats' association with the Congress has made them part of the problem. Many voters have come to see them as defenders of the interests that keep government large, wasteful, and outdated and of the privileges that place the political class above the people. At the same time, President Clinton came to office pressing for reform but with only a small Democratic majority in the Congress, one so fractured that it seemed to resemble, as Walter Dean Burnham put it, "a holding company of diverse and often warring interests."[14]

Moreover, voters who seemingly want a bigger governmental role promoting investment, educating people, creating safer neighborhoods, and assuring better health care and a secure retirement are, at the same time, deeply skeptical about the government's capacity to do any of this. As far as most voters can tell, the government appears to be bankrupt, wasteful, perk-laden and expensive. It is prone to mess things up, and indeed, most voters can barely recall anything that the government in Washington has done for them. The politicians who run the government respond to special interests and organized pressure groups and all but ignore the ordinary citizen. Until voters experience something visibly different in politics, their support for purposeful change will be tempered by doubts and skepticism that easily turn to caution and opposition.

The capacity of our presidents to remake the country's politics may also face increasing limits. The failed party renewals of Lyndon Johnson and Ronald Reagan underscore the point. Reagan set out to remake our politics, repudiating Great Society liberalism and restoring the ethos of Coolidge. But as Stephen Skowronek observes in *The Politics Presidents Make,* Reagan had but one year of reconstruction at the outset of his term: "The Reagan Revolution turned out to be a single-jolt affair." The modern president may dream of past reconstructions, but the reality of an independent Congress, the budgeting process, slow economic growth, fiscal constraints, the modern bureaucracies, the proliferation of power centers, political fragmentation, organized special interests woven into the complex of existing programs—all conspire to limit the modern president's ability to move the nation in a new direction. Reagan paid little heed and produced gigantic budget deficits and a crisis of legitimacy, but he did not produce a new party order. Perhaps, as Skowronek argues, modern presidents must abandon unrealistic claims to remake our politics in favor of a more pragmatic and less heroic course.[15]

These limits and the public's skepticism combine to shape conventional wisdom into a presumption of failure. That is the backdrop for the Clinton presidency, which aspires to use this experience to motivate a new kind of politics. These aspirations are not rooted in tactical maneuvering simply to win the next election. Since his first run for office in 1974, Bill Clinton has contemplated something more radical: a denial of the whole party order of the 1960s, a radical critique of government, and the formulation of a new vision that would allow the rebuilding of the American community.

Beyond Stale Orthodoxies

Before reaching the presidency, Bill Clinton held to a strong conviction that the established party divisions had divorced politics from the lives of ordinary citizens. The people, he asserted, "do not care about the rhetoric of left and right," what he called "stale orthodoxies." The real people, he said, "are crying desperately for someone who believes the purpose of government is to solve their problems and make progress." Clinton offered people a "new choice" that "plainly rejects the old categories and false alternatives," neither liberal nor conservative. "The truth is, it is both, and it is different."[16]

The press never paid much attention to Bill Clinton's rejection of false alternatives. Most reporters and columnists thought of it as a sleight of hand whereby Clinton tried to compromise what could not be compromised, trying to have it both ways— a bit of slipperiness that did not matter very much in politics. In any case, nobody took it very seriously.

But Bill Clinton's anger about false choices remains a cry of liberation from the restraints and distortions of the party order of the 1960s that associated Democrats with government and that blocked the Democrats from successfully representing America from the bottom up. The racial and cultural polarization of that period had changed the imagery of the parties, giving the Republicans access to working- and middle-class voters and making many of them inaccessible to the Democrats. Not only did this party order divide black workers from white workers, segregating and marginalizing black concerns in the process, but it also prevented the middle class in a stagnant America from finding political expression for their growing frustration.

What's special about the moment today is the shared determination of the president and the citizenry to put an end to this political misery even as Republicans struggle to breathe new life into it. As E. J. Dionne points out, the "great American middle felt cheated" by a liberal creed that "demeaned its values" and a conservative one that "shortchanged its interests." Clinton's presidency, however, is premised on the simple idea that such a separation is unnatural, and the citizenry has since embraced the radical and unlikely idea of a politics that advances both their values and their interests.[17]

Under political fire, however, the gap between the premise and the reality has grown dangerously wide. The Clinton solution was always reformist and anti-bureaucratic, skeptical about government and insistent on accountability, even as it advanced populist goals and sought to uplift people. The "Reich-Osborne" message during the 1992 Clinton campaign declared first, that government had failed, and second, that it was time to invest in people. But after two years of political battle, the president is more associated with "big government" than with "less bureaucratic solutions": by 53 to 36 percent in the DLC post-election survey. That is a difficult place from which to advance both the values and interests of the middle class.

This is all reminiscent of 1980 in Arkansas when Bill Clinton lost his first reelection for governor after two years of political turmoil—energetic and activist government, increased education spending, fights with the big utilities and timber companies, increased car taxes, and most important, little mention of changing the way government does things. Clinton was reelected in 1982 and for the rest of the decade after he rejoined his support for public investment in people with a demand for accountable government. Then it was teacher testing and education spending that symbolized changing government so it can work for the ordinary citizen. The approach allowed for a Democratic party that could once again represent people in the broadest sense. It is the promise of such a vision that allows most Americans two years into his presidential term to say that

Bill Clinton is a "new kind of Democrat," not a "traditional liberal" one; that he is "trying to change the Washington establishment," not part of it; that he is "trying" to move the country in the "right," not the "wrong" direction.[18]

The Clinton solution represents a personal revolt against the lines and categories that blocked the formulation of a broad bottom-up vision. Such an approach challenges the organizing idea of the party of Lyndon Johnson. The plight of the poor and the unfinished business of civil rights are no longer the first principles of Democratic politics. Instead, Bill Clinton is seeking to reassociate his party with the American dream. That idea is itself a first principle that could potentially unite the poor and the middle class and change the face of politics in the United States.

Some commentators look at this transformation and see a Democratic party now silent on race and intent on pushing African Americans and the traditional Democratic base to the sidelines. They see this new consensus on race as a decision to elevate the concerns of suburbia and "bury race as an issue" and, perversely, to allow "society at large to absolve itself from responsibility for the conflict and turmoil of race."[19]

Such a critique misses the cooling of the fires of racial politics in 1992 that allowed many white working and middle-class voters to discover just how uncomfortably they fit into Reagan's top-down coalition. A large majority of whites now accepts that discrimination must be barred in employment, housing, and schooling. The public is divided on quotas, to be sure, but that division should not obscure the areas of normative consensus that allow whites and blacks to rediscover each other in politics.[20]

The critique also romanticizes what the Democratic preoccupation with race has meant for African Americans. A politics organized around race and civil rights was critical to the transformation of American life in the 1960s and '70s, but then became unproductive. A segregated politics is a stigmatized politics, one that has marginalized both African Americans and the coalition that would advance their interests. Black America is struggling to progress against forces that by the outset of the 1990s had produced fewer intact families and a growing majority of black children born out of wedlock; almost one third of black Americans were poor. Whatever the legitimate triumphs of the civil rights revolution for the black middle class, William Julius Wilson writes, the "life chances of the ghetto underclass are largely untouched by programs of preferential treatment based on race."[21]

As Jesse Jackson has observed, "If you're in a game in which you lose if you lose and lose if you win, it's time to enter another game." When the discourse enables your enemies to enjoy the political fruits of Willie Horton and quotas and you and your allies are further marginalized, win or lose, it is time to change the terms of the debate. "The issue," Jackson says, "is not quotas. It is not reverse discrimination. It is not welfare queens. It is the need for a new American agenda to restore the country's economic base."[22] That is indeed a formula for reconstructing the Democratic party from the bottom up.

A Renewed Bottom-up Vision

With the dominant party traditions in ruin, one might imagine that this is the time to reject both top-down and bottom-up views of the world and seek a political future that encompasses parts of both or rejects both, that forges something wholly new to meet the challenges of the times. After all, Bill Clinton did call on voters to reject the false choice of liberalism and conservatism. It may be the moment to bring the curtain down on this drama and open a new one for the new century. Indeed, putting an end to both party traditions has a kind of symmetry and finality that would recommend it as a conclusion to this work.

But to detach the Democratic party—or the Republican for that matter—from its history and historic imagery would leave the party dangerously ungrounded. The Democrats are still the party for the little people, and the Republicans are still more business-oriented. Politics without these historic traditions and images is littered with all manner of fragmented and personalized movements of uncertain durability.

Bill Clinton never rejected a genuine bottom-up view of the world. What he rejected was the distortion of America's party traditions that blocked the Democrats from fighting for the common person and the American dream. His formulation of the forgotten middle class recalls the imagery and remembrances that remain alive in people's heads—despite the decades of distortion and the sense of betrayal. He seeks to create something grounded in the past but modern and relevant as well.

To restore the credibility and relevance of these historic traditions, the Democrats will have to engage in a profound renewal of the bottom-up idea. The United States has changed radically over the course of the twentieth century. The country has little appetite for a modern-day Bryanism, for some backward-looking and protectionist philosophy or for some new round of social welfare spending. People understand that the new challenges threatening the standards of the common person will require something new, not warmed-over populism, not warmed-over New Deal policies, not the Great Society.

Through the glare of day-to-day events, one can see Bill Clinton struggling to forge a modern, middle-class-centered bottom-up party: a broad-based party encompassing the needs of the disadvantaged and working Americans and focusing on the values and interests of the middle class, a party that can help people prosper in a rapidly changing economy, a party that can break down bureaucracy and gridlock so that ordinary people can reclaim the country's government and politics.

The starting point is the middle class as the center of our politics. The concept is no doubt idealized and imperfect: not every middle-class citizen is honorable and worthy of such attention and not everybody who respects middle-class values is materially middle class. But the affirmation says that political meaning, political motivation, the public agenda, and our values are grounded in the lives of the common person. If that was true—if people came to believe the middle class is genuinely at the center of the Democratic discourse—that alone would constitute a major upheaval.

Bill Clinton has always understood America's ambivalence about government and has always linked his activist vision with a reformist determination. Today, any party aspiring to national leadership, but particularly the Democrats, will have to establish its bona fides as hostile to bureaucracy and the special-interest politics that have crowded out ordinary people. The explosion of distrust has changed the political discussion forever: people believe that the government wastes their money, ignores their interests and values, and caters to the powerful. Thus bottom-up politics at this political moment is necessarily reformist: prepared to change the way government spends money, delivers services, and listens to people. It must confront the federal deficits that symbolize a government out of control and out of touch.

The reformist agenda makes possible new Democratic initiatives that enlarge the capacity of people to prosper in a modern economy. That is the context for Clinton's initiatives on early-childhood education, higher school standards, job training, college loans, and programs that reward and empower the working poor, as the earned income tax credit does. These broad investments represent a break from the past. Instead of constructing safety nets that protect people falling on hard times, the Democrats are attempting to advance broad-based initiatives that empower both the lower and middle classes. Safety nets, however fiscally appealing, represent bad politics and a moral trap that ultimately separates the poor, as well as the Democrats, from the majority. Theda Skocpol posed the right question: "Why should people just above the poverty line, struggling without benefit of health coverage, child care, or adequate unemployment insurance pay for programs that go exclusively to people below the poverty line?"[23]

The Clinton initiative to make health care universal and affordable has become one of the primary battlegrounds for the parties. In his 1994 State of the Union Address, Clinton made clear that the audience for reform was middle America. Some say "there's no health care crisis," he noted and then proclaimed:

> Tell it to the 58 million Americans who have no coverage at all for some time each year. Tell it to the 81 million Americans with those pre-existing conditions; those folks are paying more or they can't get insurance at all or they can't ever change their jobs. . . . Or tell it to the 76 percent of insured Americans . . . whose policies have lifetime limits, and that means they can find themselves without any coverage at all just when they need it the most.[24]

For a middle class frustrated by stagnant living standards and by an increasingly competitive employment situation, this initiative offered the prospect of renewed confidence in this political community's capacity to promote both the individual welfare and the nation's growth. Some Republicans understood the risk. That is why William Kristol, one of the conservative movement's leading intellectuals, urged Republicans to "kill"—not amend—the Clinton health care plan: "It will relegitimize middle-class dependence for 'security' on government spending and regulation. It will revive the reputation of the party that spends and regulates, the Democrats, as the generous protector of middle-class interests. And it will at the same time strike a punishing blow against Republican claims to defend the middle class by restraining government."[25] Kristol's advice helped steel the Republicans for a year-long attack on big government that sidetracked the initiative and helped create the impression that Clinton is partial to big government solutions.

The Democratic commitment to invest in people and promote security in a market economy risks becoming parochial and backward looking unless it is embedded in an expansive view of the American economy. Protection of the people without a strategy for growth and jobs will seem like no protection at all. Roosevelt, Truman, and Kennedy understood that to succeed they had to find a way to join people and prosperity; support for the common person had to be combined with the promotion of American economic hegemony in a growing world economy. Since the world economy has become more competitive, the bottom-up principle of protecting the people will have to combine with an optimistic and credible assertion of American economic ascendance if it is to capture the public imagination.

The bottom-up worldview will also ring hollow if it fails to respect and honor the values of middle-class life. Political meaning begins in the neighborhoods, families, and churches across America, where reward for work, discipline, and the moral value of a strong family are first principles. These seem like simple affirmations, but not so for the Democrats of the old party order. The starting point on values is work—as it was for all those in the last century who spoke for the United States from the bottom up. The broad middle class hungers for a society and leaders who will again honor their work.

Democrats have hesitated to identify fully with all working- and middle-class communities because they fear that the values of those segments of society would clash with the dominant values of America's disadvantaged communities that so faithfully elected Democrats to office. But Democrats have been painfully wrong on the question of values. The great majority of black men and women of working age are working, frequently in the face of considerable odds—high bus fares, unaffordable child care and health insurance—and frequently for wages so low they barely make this a "rational" economic choice. Black women have always participated in the labor force at rates greater than white women, a reflection both of economic necessity and assumptions about their work lives. And we now know from Christopher Jencks and others that those on welfare not only are willing to work but are already working illegally in large numbers to supplement their checks and support their children.[26]

A politics grounded in the neighborhoods and families of America will as a matter of course promote work and discourage welfare; it will abhor criminality and the breakdown of the family; it will accept as common sense tough measures to jail criminals and prevent crime. These are universal instincts that unite black and white and allow Democrats to identify with the values and interests of bottom-up America.

WAITING IN MACOMB

Macomb County, Michigan, is not just a place. It represents the ordinary citizenry of America trying to make a better life and hold on to its dreams. Over the course of the last century, the different compacts offered by America's leaders have allowed them to work and raise their families while being hopeful about the future. That all broke down, however, and a sense of betrayal simmered in the country. The Macomb Counties across the land fell into revolt.

Yet the people of Macomb are not in search of a rebellion. They want a new contract, one they can trust and rely on, one that binds both the leaders and the citizenry, one that ensures a rising prosperity. They know little of what is happening in Canada, Europe, and Asia. They know something about corporate restructuring and a new world economy. They still want to know that America can create its own moment for its own people.

In one of the national focus-group projects discussed earlier, we asked people to draw one line representing America's history since 1950 and then another line representing America's future from the present to the end of the century. Given their extraordinary bleakness about the past couple of decades, it was striking that they were unwilling to give up on the future. Nearly everyone expected things to slide further or remain stagnant, perhaps for a number of years, but most believed that the United States would come together again for something better. For many, that was a matter of faith. One participant described his faith, despite the evidence, that some leaders somewhere would wake up to make things better in America: "My line bottomed out in '91. And then it goes up. I can't afford to be pessimistic. You have to look at it that way. Eventually somebody somewhere is going to wake up and say, 'You know, the S and L, we've gotta stop it. It's gotta be done.' And God knows who's going to do it, but the only way you get the strength to get your head off the pillow is to think there's going to be a better day, and that's it."

These voters are waiting for a new contract and a better day.

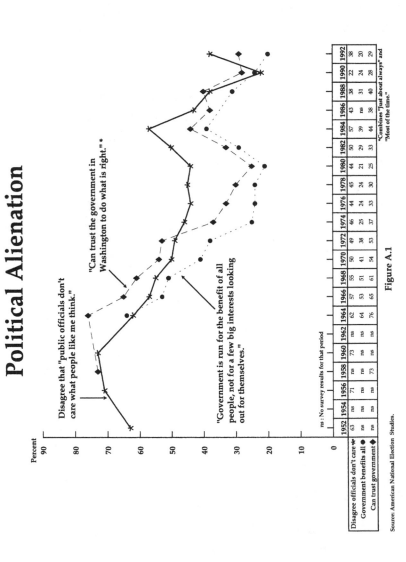

Political Alienation

Percent

Disagree that "public officials don't care what people think."

"Can trust the government in Washington to do what is right." *

"Government is run for the benefit of all people, not for a few big interests looking out for themselves."

ns : No survey results for that period

	1952	1954	1956	1958	1960	1962	1964	1966	1968	1970	1972	1974	1976	1978	1980	1982	1984	1986	1988	1990	1992
Disagree officials don't care ✳	63	ns	71	ns	73	ns	62	57	55	50	49	46	44	45	44	50	57	43	38	22	38
Government benefits all ●	ns	ns	ns	ns	ns	ns	64	53	51	41	38	25	24	24	21	29	39	ns	31	24	20
Can trust government ◆	ns	ns	ns	73	ns	ns	76	65	61	54	53	37	33	30	25	33	44	38	40	28	29

*Combines "just about always" and "Most of the time."

Figure A.1

Source: American National Election Studies.

Confidence in Institutions

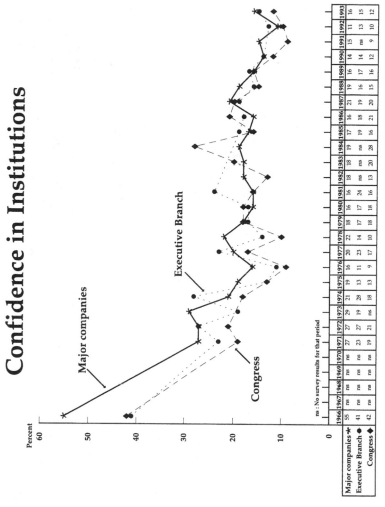

	1966	1967	1968	1969	1970	1971	1972	1973	1974	1975	1976	1977	1978	1979	1980	1981	1982	1983	1984	1985	1986	1987	1988	1989	1990	1991	1992	1993
Major companies ✳	55	ns	ns	ns	ns	27	27	29	21	19	16	20	22	18	16	16	ns	18	19	17	16	21	19	16	14	15	11	16
Executive Branch ●	41	ns	ns	ns	ns	23	27	19	28	13	11	23	14	17	17	24	ns	ns	ns	19	18	19	16	17	14	ns	13	15
Congress ◆	42	ns	ns	ns	ns	19	21	ns	18	13	9	17	10	18	18	16	13	20	28	16	21	20	15	16	12	9	10	12

ns : No survey results for that period

Figure A.2

Source: Louis Harris.

The State of the Country

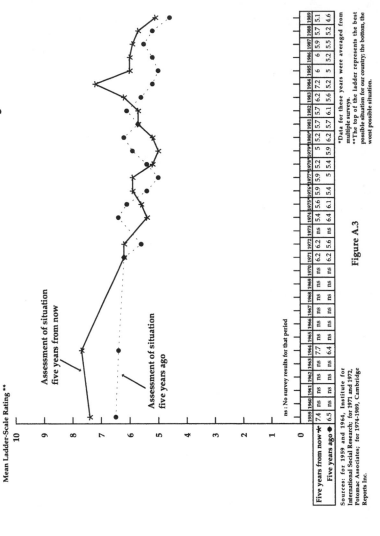

Mean Ladder-Scale Rating**

Assessment of situation five years from now

Assessment of situation five years ago

ns : No survey results for that period

	1959	1960	1961	1962	1963	1964	1965	1966	1967	1968	1969	1970	1971	1972	1973	1974	1975	1976	1977	1978	1979	1980*	1981	1982	1983	1984	1985	1986	1987	1988	1989
Five years from now ✳	7.4	ns	ns	ns	ns	7.7	ns	ns	ns	ns	ns	6.2	6.2	6.2	ns	5.4	5.6	5.9	5.9	5.2	5	5.2	5.7	5.7	6.2	7.2	6	6	5.9	5.7	5.1
Five years ago ●	6.5	ns	ns	ns	ns	6.4	ns	ns	ns	ns	ns	6.2	6.2	5.6	ns	6.4	6.1	5.4	5	5.4	5.9	6.2	5.7	6.1	5.6	5.2	5	5.2	5.5	5.2	4.6

Sources: for 1959 and 1964, Institute for International Social Research; for 1971 and 1972, Potomac Associates; for 1974-1989, Cambridge Reports Inc.

*Data for these years were averaged from multiple surveys.

**The top of the ladder represents the best possible situation for our country; the bottom, the worst possible situation.

Figure A.3

The Political Parties

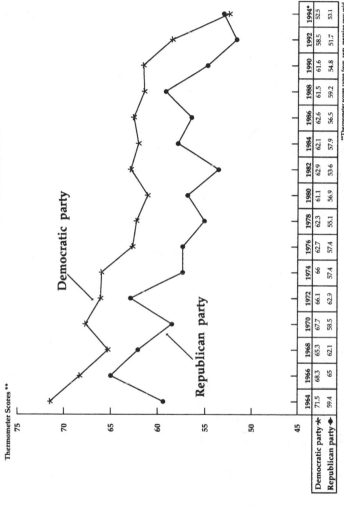

Thermometer Scores **

	1964	1966	1968	1970	1972	1974	1976	1978	1980	1982	1984	1986	1988	1990	1992	1994*
Democratic party ✶	71.5	68.3	65.3	67.7	66.1	66	62.7	62.3	61.1	62.9	62.1	62.6	61.5	61.6	58.5	52.5
Republican party ◆	59.4	65	62.1	58.5	62.9	57.4	57.4	55.1	56.9	53.6	57.9	56.5	59.2	54.8	51.7	53.1

Figure A.4

** Thermometer scores range from zero, meaning very cold and unfavorable, to 100 degrees, meaning hot and very favorable; 50 degrees means neutral, neither hot nor cold. Between 1964 and 1976, the survey referred to "Democratic" and "Republican"; after 1976, to "Democratic party" and "Republican party."

Source: American National Election Studies.
* Source: Democratic Leadership Council, Post-Election Survey, 1994

TABLE A.1

POLITICAL CULTURE: UNDERLYING ATTITUDES

	Factor Score*
Dimension 1: Middle-Class Consciousness	
Too many of the poor are trying to get something for nothing.**	.661
It's the middle class, *not* the poor, who really get a raw deal today.	.659
Too often equal rights is just used as an excuse for not being good enough to succeed.	.652
We have gone too far in pushing equal rights for different groups in this country.	.525
People who work hard for a living and don't make a lot of noise never seem to get a break.	.446
People have bad values today.	.359
Dimension 2: Anti-government	
You really can't trust the government to do the right thing.	.777
Government always manages to mess things up.	.747
Most politicians are corrupt.	.730
Individual freedom has got out of hand.	.404
Dimension 3: Financial Pressure	
I often don't have enough money to make ends meet.	.758
It is almost impossible to keep up with the cost of living.	.743
Things always seem to turn out pretty good for me.	−.545

Dimension 4: Secularism Tolerance

Abortion should be legal and generally available
and subject to only limited regulation.   .726

We should be more tolerant of people who choose
to live according to their own moral standards and
lifestyles, even if they are very different from our own.   .706

The government should do more to reinforce
moral and family values.   −.503

Dimension 5: Anti-establishment

Business corporations generally strike a fair balance
between making profits and serving the public.   −.644

Public officials usually care what people
like me think.   −.616

The system favors people who try to get around
the rules.   .540

The special interests, not the people, get their
way in government.   .378

---

*A factor score is the item's correlation with the underlying dimension. Items with higher factor score play a bigger role in defining the dimension.

**Respondents were asked whether they strongly agree, somewhat agree, somewhat disagree, or strongly disagree with each statement.

TABLE A.2

THE MESS IN WASHINGTON:
INDEPENDENT VOTERS*

Open-ended Responses	Percent
Politics as Usual	**48**
Politicians, too much partisan politics, parties don't work together, no cooperation, gridlock	20
Washington insulated, out of touch, doesn't listen to the people	12
Corruption, too much money, crooked politicians, no honesty, themselves, not the people	13
Lobbyists, special interests	3
Government	**21**
Overspending, too much spending, wasteful spending, government waste	10
Too much government, too much bureaucracy, too much red tape, not run like a business	8
National debt, budget	3
Bill Clinton	**8**
Clinton, Clinton lacks direction, Clinton leadership, White House	8

*Democratic Leadership Council, Post-election Survey, November 1994.

NOTES

Chapter 1. The Crash

1. Walter Lippmann, *Public Opinion* (New York: The Free Press, 1965), 226.

2. *New Republic,* November 14, 1964, 5; James Reston, "What Goldwater Lost," *New York Times,* November 4, 1964.

3. Jimmy Carter, Inaugural Address, in *Historic Documents of 1977* (Washington, D.C.: Congressional Quarterly, 1978), 91.

4. *U.S. News and World Report,* March 11, 1991, 56.

5. Gingrich and Gramm quoted in *The Washington Post,* November 10, 1994; Dole quoted in *The New York Times,* November 10, 1994; Broder quoted in *The Washington Post,* November 13, 1994.

6. I owe the concepts of "top down" and "bottom up" to Thomas Byrne Edsall with Mary Edsall, *Chain Reaction: The Impact of Race, Rights, and Taxes on American Politics* (New York: W. W. Norton, 1991), though I suspect all three of us are in debt to Franklin Roosevelt, who used the concept in his Forgotten Man Speech (Franklin D. Roosevelt, *The Public Papers and Addresses of Franklin D. Roosevelt: The Genesis of the New Deal, 1928–1932* [New York: Random House, 1938], 1:624–27).

7. These observations about the parties rely on extensive group discussions conducted with voters across the country between 1987 and 1993. Voters speak of these party images as "known," "just the way it is," an "illusion you have," "just an image thing" or "sort of stereotype." They have "always heard that," and they say, "That's always been my impression."

8. Walter Dean Burnham, "The Politics of Repudiation, 1992: Edging Toward Upheaval," *American Prospect* (Winter 1993): 24–27.

9. These results are based on an analysis of the exit polls conducted by Voter Research and Surveys (VRS), the exit polls for the national television networks.

10. Susan E. Howell, "The New Christian Right Issues, Ideology, and the Republican Party Image" (paper presented to the American Political Science Association, September 1993).

11. These results are based on calculations by VRS.

12. Peter Brown, *Minority Party: Why the Democrats Face Defeat in 1992 and Beyond* (Washington, D.C.: Regnery Gateway, 1991); for the Edsalls' volume, see note 6.

13. Edsall and Edsall, *Chain Reaction,* 3–4, 142, 154–55, 286.

14. E. J. Dionne Jr., *Why Americans Hate Politics* (New York: Simon and Schuster, 1991), 12.

15. Times Mirror Center for the People and the Press, *The New Political Landscape: The People, the Press and Politics* (October 1994), 22.

16. This discussion with voters derives from focus-group research conducted in the suburbs of Atlanta and Minneapolis–St. Paul for the Advocacy Institute and a range of organizations concerned with campaign-finance reform, including Common Cause, Public Citizen, ARCA Foundation, and the Philip M. Stern Family Fund.

17. University of Michigan, Survey Research Center (Ann Arbor, Mich., 1964), and *New York Times*/CBS News poll, October 8–10, 1990, as reported in "Public Opinion and Demographic Report," *American Enterprise,* November–December 1992, 83; ABC News/ *Washington Post* Poll, October 24, 1994.

18. Seymour Martin Lipset and William Schneider, *The Confidence Gap: Business, Labor, and Government in the Public Mind,* rev. ed. (Baltimore: Johns Hopkins University Press, 1987), 6–7; Rush Limbaugh, *The Way Things Ought to Be* (New York: Pocket Books, 1993), 91; Martin L. Gross, *The Government Racket: Washington Waste from A to Z* (New York: Bantam Books, 1992), 2. See also Kevin Phillips, *Boiling Point: Republicans, Democrats, and the Decline*

of Middle-Class Prosperity (New York: Random House, 1993), xvii; Jack W. Germond and Jules Witcover, *Mad as Hell: Revolt at the Ballot Box, 1992* (New York: Warner Books, 1993).

19. See Stanley B. Greenberg, "The Revolt Against Politics," a report based on a national survey conducted for the Democratic Leadership Council, November 17, 1994; also see NBC/*Wall Street Journal* poll, November 9, 1994. (See Appendix, Table A.2.)

20. Exit poll results based on 1994 data collected by Mitofsky International and for previous years by Voter Research and Surveys.

21. "National Political Environment/Impact on Your Race," memorandum from Public Opinion Strategies (October 18, 1994); *Los Angeles Times* Survey, October 17-19, 1994.

22. The term "middle class" has a broad meaning in this work, referring imperfectly to people who work for a living, receive wages or salary but who do not own a business or play an executive role. Obviously, the concept carries over to the household and into retirement. While I do not attempt to impose strict income brackets on the concept, I am thinking of people who fall in the bottom 60 percent of the income scale; in 1993, that included families earning under about $45,000. But all of that is subject to a great deal of regional variation, suggesting a higher top limit in places like Connecticut, Michigan, and California, where incomes are generally higher. Many of the voters meeting these criteria will think of themselves as "middle class," since almost half the populace (45 percent) does, but many will call themselves "working class," since an identical number (45 percent) choose that designation (U.S. Bureau of the Census, Current Population Reports, *Consumer Income 1992*, U.S. Government Printing Office [Washington, D.C., 1993]; General Social Survey, National Opinion Research Center, National Survey, Chicago, Illinois, April 1993).

But the term "middle class" belongs to almost all these voters, even if they think of themselves as lower or working class. In that sense, the term is an ideal more than a firm grouping of people. In chapter 6, we shall see that these voters think of the middle class as working people who are able to get ahead, to own something, but who are now embattled financially and on the verge of extinction. Richard Trumka, president of the United Mine Workers—leader of men who have symbolized laboring people's struggle for dignity—said, "you're middle class if you work for a living, if you don't clip coupons, if you depend on your own personal skills to make a living. And, if you work hard, if you play by the rules, then you deserve a chance to own your own home, have a nice car, send your kids to college, and feel you've achieved something in this life" (Trumka quoted in David Kusnet, *Speaking American: How the Democrats Can Win in the Nineties* [New York: Thunder's Mouth Press, 1992], 133).

Chapter 2. Macomb County in the American Mind

1. See accounts in David McCullough, *Truman* (New York: Simon and Schuster, 1992), 657; *Detroit Free Press,* September 6, 1960; Theodore H. White, *The Making of the President 1968: A Narrative History of American Politics in Action* (New York: Atheneum, 1969), 373–74; *Justice* (publication of the International Ladies Garment Workers Union), November 1, 1960, and October 15, 1968; H. Wayne Morgan, *William McKinley and His America* (Syracuse, N.Y.: Syracuse University Press, 1963), 219, 233–35.

2. *Chicago Tribune,* April 15, 1992, and October 26, 1992; *Dallas Morning News,* October 30, 1992; *Los Angeles Times,* October 30, 1992, and November 3, 1992; *Facts on File World News Digest,* November 5, 1992; *New York Times,* September 24, 1992; *Atlanta Journal and Constitution,* September 23, 1992; *USA Today,* September 10, 1992; Associated Press, November 5, 1988, and April 15, 1992; United Press International, November 6, 1988; *New York Newsday,* March 17, 1992; *Washington Post,* November 10, 1988.

3. Because of rounding, the sum total of these percentages is sometimes greater and sometimes lower than 100 percent. If we chose not to round, in all cases the sum total would be exactly 100 percent.

4. The story of Macomb can be replicated with somewhat less drama in white home-owning, working- and middle-class enclaves across the United States—places, mostly in suburbia, where the Democrats emerged as the home team, then lost ground because of Democratic defection, particularly to Reagan, but where the Republican hold has given way to a new competitive politics. In suburban Delaware County west of Philadelphia, places like Ridley, Upper Chichester, and Upper Darby Townships gave majorities to Kennedy in 1960, but then shifted Republican—over 60 percent for Reagan in 1984 and Bush in 1988—only to split evenly between Clinton and Bush in 1992. East Haven, Connecticut, a middle-class, heavily Italian suburb of New Haven, gave almost 60 percent of its votes to Kennedy before casting over 60 percent for Reagan, only to give Clinton a healthy, 41 to 35 percent margin. In the Chicago area, places like Cicero and Berwyn offer a similar drama. These traditional ethnic strongholds voted almost 70 percent for Reagan in 1984, but in 1992, split their votes evenly between Clinton and Bush. In newer growth areas, like Clearwater near Saint Petersburg, a near 70 percent vote for Reagan and a near 60 percent vote for Bush dissolved into a dead heat in 1992.

The story of Macomb is about a community experiencing our modern political history, and it is no doubt reflected in these areas discussed above. But it is also an individual drama: people who believed in the Democratic compact who grew disillusioned, defected, and then grew disillusioned again. The "Macomb state of mind" is probably evident among many of those who have moved into politically volatile, rapid growth suburban areas, like Riverside and San Bernadino in California.

5. Thomas R. Brooks, *Toil and Trouble: A History of American Labor* (New York: Delta, 1964), 212–18, 221–22, 271–72.

6. Macomb County Department of Planning and Economic Development, selected tables based on the 1990 U.S. Census (Mount Clemens, Mich., 1990); U.S. Bureau of the Census, *Census of Population and Housing, 1990: Population and Housing Units for Michigan* (Washington, D.C., 1993), table 4—Land, Area, Population, and Housing Units, 1990; Detroit Area Study, "Detroit: A

Metropolis Divided by Race? Report to Respondents" (Ann
Arbor: University of Michigan, Detroit Area Study, 1993); U.S.
Bureau of the Census, *County and City Data Book* (Washington,
D.C., 1947–88); U.S. Department of Labor, Bureau of Labor Sta-
tistics, Local Area Unemployment Statistics, *Unemployment in
States and Local Areas,* Washington, D.C. 1989–1993; U.S. Depart-
ment of Commerce, Economic Statistics Administration, Bureau
of Economic Analysis, *Regional Economic Information System* (Wash-
ington, D.C., 1993), table CA-05; U.S. Department of Labor,
Bureau of Labor Statistics, Local Area Unemployment Statistics,
Unemployment in States and Local Areas (Washington, D.C.,
1989–93).

7. National Advisory Commission on Civil Disorders, *Report of
the National Advisory Commission on Civil Disorders* (New York:
Bantam Books, 1968), 84–107.

8. The discussion of this period is based in part on interviews
with congressional staff and members of Congress from the area,
particularly Congressmen John Dingell and David Bonior.

9. George Wallace quoted in the *Detroit Free Press,* May 7, 10–12,
1972.

10. This electoral history of Macomb County was constructed by
Mark Gersh and Andrew Bechhoefer of the National Committee
for an Effective Congress.

11. Lawrence Mishel and David M. Frankel, *The State of Working
America, 1990–91* (Armonk, N.Y.: M. E. Sharpe, 1991), 70, 74, 104;
Bennett Harrison and Barry Bluestone, *The Great U-Turn: Corpo-
rate Restructuring and the Polarizing of America* (New York: Basic
Books, 1988), 115, 149.

12. David Kusnet, *Speaking American: How the Democrats Can Win
in the Nineties* (New York: Thunder's Mouth Press, 1992), 20.

13. Quoted in the *Macomb County Daily,* November 7, 1984.

14. The primary focus groups were conducted on March 20 and
21, 1985, in Sterling Heights, a city in Macomb, though participants were from all over the county. All the participants were former Democratic voters who had supported Reagan in 1984. The

sessions lasted two hours and involved about ten people each. The demographic composition of the groups are set out below:

Group 1   union men, 30–45 years of age

Group 2   non-union men, 30–45 years of age

Group 3   both union and non-union men, 46–60 years of age

Group 4   housewives, 30–45 years of age from both union and non-union households

Other groups were conducted May 21 and 22, 1985, in Waterford Township in neighboring Oakland County and were used to supplement the Macomb analysis:

Group 1   housewives, 30–45 years of age

Group 2   housewives, 46–60 years

Group 3   non-union men, 30–45 years of age

Group 4   both union and non-union men, under 30

15. Ronald Reagan quoted by the Associated Press and United Press International, November 5, 1988.

16. I conducted follow-up focus groups in March 1989, again supported by the House Democrats and the Michigan Democratic party.

17. VRS exit poll conducted in Michigan for the national television networks.

Chapter 3. The Great-Party Eras

1. Thomas Byrne Edsall with Mary Edsall, *Chain Reaction: The Impact of Race, Rights, and Taxes on American Politics* (New York: W. W. Norton, 1991), 181.

2. Arthur M. Schlesinger Jr., *The Age of Jackson* (Boston: Little, Brown, 1945), 6–8, 91–93, 346–47; Richard P. McCormick, *The Second American Party System: Party Formation in the Jacksonian Era* (Chapel Hill: University of North Carolina Press, 1966), 342–53;

Robert V. Remini, "The Democratic Party in the Jacksonian Era" in *Democrats and the American Idea: A Bicentennial Appraisal,* Peter B. Kovler, ed. (Washington, D.C.: Center for National Policy Press, 1992), 40–41, 54, 63; James Parton, *The Presidency of Andrew Jackson,* ed. Robert V. Remini (New York: Harper Torchbooks, 1967), 1–3.

3. See Barrington Moore Jr., *Social Origins of Dictatorship and Democracy: Lord and Peasant in the Making of the Modern World* (Boston: Beacon Press, 1967), 111–55, 420–29.

4. Frederick Lewis Allen, *The Big Change: America Transforms Itself, 1900–1960* (New Brunswick, N.J.: Transaction, 1993), 88.

5. Discussion of the period from 1880 to 1990 relies on the following works: Charles Hoffman, *The Depression of the Nineties: An Economic History* (Westport, Conn.: Greenwood Publishing, 1970), 271, 279–81; W. Elliot Brownlee, *Dynamics of Ascent: A History of the American Economy,* 2d ed. (Chicago: Dorsey Press, 1988), 274–86, 305–37; Allen, *The Big Change,* 7–14, 22–26; Sidney Lens, *Strikemakers and Strikebreakers* (New York: E. P. Dutton, 1985), 40–41, 64–65.

6. Hoffman, *The Depression of the Nineties,* 9–10, 57–68, 106–10, 258, 271, 279–81; Brownlee, *Dynamics of Ascent,* 330, 339; Matthew Josephson, *The Politicos, 1850–1896* (New York: Harcourt, Brace, 1938), 560–61.

7. This discussion draws upon James L. Sundquist, *Dynamics of the Party System: Alignment and Realignment of Political Parties in the United States,* rev. ed. (Washington, D.C.: Brookings Institution, 1983), 106–9, 123–25, 154; Robert Kelley, "The Democracy of Tilden and Cleveland," in *Democrats and the American Idea,* ed. Kovler, 154–55, 162–64; Josephson, *The Politicos,* 102–07.

8. Grover Cleveland quoted in Sundquist, *Dynamics of the Party System,* 124–27, 148.

9. Ben Tillman quoted in Josephson, *The Politicos,* 618.

10. R. Hal Williams, *Years of Decision: American Politics in the 1890s* (New York: John Wiley and Sons, 1978), 5, 11–12, 19–20, 44–51, 93–94; Robert W. Cherny, "The Democratic Party in the Era of William Jennings Bryan" in *Democrats and the American Idea,* ed.

Kovler, 174; Sundquist, *Dynamics of the Party System,* 154, 158; Walter Dean Burnham, "Party Systems and the Political Process" in *The American Party Systems: Stages of Political Development,* ed. William Nisbet Chambers and Walter Dean Burnham (New York: Oxford University Press, 1967), 297–98.

11. This discussion is based primarily on Theda Skocpol, *Protecting Soldiers and Mothers: The Political Origins of Social Policy in the United States* (Cambridge, Mass.: Harvard University Press, 1992), 64–65, 109–12, 124–29, 149–51. See also Allan Nevins, *Grover Cleveland: A Study in Courage* (New York: Dodd, Mead, 1933), 326–32; Richard E. Welch Jr., *The Presidencies of Grover Cleveland* (Lawrence: University of Kansas Press, 1988), 62–67.

12. William Jennings Bryan, *The First Battle: A Story of the Campaign of 1896* (Chicago: W. B. Conkey, 1898), 123, 203, 205.

13. Ibid., 81, 83, 110.

14. Sundquist, *Dynamics of the Party System,* 106–66.

15. William Jennings Bryan quoted ibid., 138.

16. Bryan, *The First Battle,* 206. Also see Donald K. Springen, *William Jennings Bryan: Orator of Small-Town America* (New York: Greenwood Press, 1991), 15–23.

17. This account of William McKinley depends substantially on H. Wayne Morgan's *William McKinley and His America* (Syracuse, New York: Syracuse University Press, 1963).

18. William McKinley quoted ibid., 61–62.

19. McKinley quoted ibid., 131.

20. Sundquist, *Dynamics of the Party System,* 156–57; Morgan, *William McKinley and His America,* 228, 233; Josephson, *The Politicos,* 647–57.

21. McKinley quoted in Morgan, *William McKinley and His America,* 235; Williams, *Years of Decision,* 122–23.

22. See Williams, *Years of Decision,* 104–5, 119; Sundquist, *Dynamics of the Party System,* 162–67.

23. Sundquist, *Dynamics of the Party System,* 163, 167; Walter Dean Burnham, *Critical Elections and the Mainsprings of American Politics* (New York: W. W. Norton, 1970), 38–41, 44, 48–50.

24. V. O. Key Jr., "A Theory of Critical Elections," in *Electoral Change and Stability in American Political History,* ed. Jerome M. Clubb and Howard W. Allen (New York: Free Press, 1971), 43; Sundquist, *Dynamics of the Party System,* 161.

25. Morgan, *William McKinley and His America,* 476–507; Williams, *Years of Decision,* 136, 151–55.

26. Brownlee, *Dynamics of Ascent,* 384–88; Allen, *The Big Change,* 124–25, 140; Allan J. Lichtman, "They Endured: Democrats Between World War I and the Depression," in *Democrats and the American Idea,* ed. Kovler, 229–34; William Allen White, *A Puritan in Babylon: The Story of Calvin Coolidge* (New York: Macmillan, 1938), 342.

27. White, *A Puritan in Babylon,* 293.

28. Andrew Mellon, *The New York Times,* and Robert M. La Follette quoted in Harry O'Connor, *Mellon's Millions: The Biography of a Fortune. The Life and Times of Andrew Mellon* (New York: John Day, 1933), 127–28, 132–33, 142, 310.

29. Walter Lippmann, "Puritanism de Luxe," in *Meet Calvin Coolidge: The Man Behind the Myth,* ed. Edward Connery Lathem (Brattleboro, Vt.: Stephen Greene Press, 1960), 52.

30. Brownlee, *Dynamics of Ascent,* 409; Alonzo L. Hamby, "The Democratic Moment: FDR to LBJ," in *Democrats and the American Idea,* ed. Kovler, 250; Allen, *The Big Change,* 147–49; Robert Higgs, *Crisis and Leviathan: Critical Episodes in the Growth of American Government* (New York: Oxford University Press, 1987), 161.

31. Sundquist, *Dynamics of the Party System,* 200–202; Hoover quoted in Arthur M. Schlesinger Jr., *The Age of Roosevelt: The Crisis of the Old Order* (Boston: Houghton Mifflin, 1956), 242; Hoover also quoted in Jordan A. Schwarz, *The New Dealers: Power Politics in the Age of Roosevelt* (New York: Alfred A. Knopf, 1993), 45–51.

32. Franklin D. Roosevelt, The Forgotten Man Speech, in *The Public Papers and Addresses: The Genesis of the New Deal, 1928–1932* (New York: Random House, 1938), 1:624–27.

33. Alfred E. Smith quoted in James MacGregor Burns, *Roosevelt: The Lion and the Fox.* (New York: Harcourt, Brace and World, 1956), 133; Schlesinger, *The Age of Roosevelt,* 416.

34. Roosevelt, Address at Oglethorpe University, in *The Public Papers and Addresses,* 1:639–47.

35. Higgs, *Crisis and Leviathan,* 176–80; Schwarz, *The New Dealers,* 71–72, 86.

36. Ann Shola Orloff, "The Political Origins of America's Belated Welfare State" in *The Politics of Social Policy in the United States,* ed. Margaret Weir, Ann Shola Orloff, and Theda Skocpol (Princeton, N.J.: Princeton University Press, 1988), 70–78; Theodore R. Marmor, Jerry L. Mashaw, and Phillip L. Harvey, *America's Misunderstood Welfare State: Persistent Myths, Enduring Realities* (New York: Basic Books, 1990), 33–35; Franklin Roosevelt, "The Election: An Interpretation," *Liberty,* December 10, 1932, 8.

37. Roosevelt quoted in Schlesinger, *The Age of Roosevelt,* 503, 584, 631–32. Also see Hamby, "The Democratic Moment," 256.

38. Brownlee, *Dynamics of Ascent,* 420; Edwina Amenta and Theda Skocpol, "Redefining the New Deal: World War II and the Development of Social Provision in the United States," in *The Politics of Social Policy,* ed. Weir, Orloff, and Skocpol, 83–84.

39. David McCullough, *Truman* (New York: Simon and Schuster, 1992), 63.

40. Truman quoted ibid., 232–33.

41. Truman quoted ibid., 658–59.

42. Thomas Dewey quoted ibid., 485, 621, 669; Amenta and Skocpol, "Redefining the New Deal," 92–94; Margaret Weir, "The Federal Government and Unemployment," in *The Politics of Social Policy,* ed. Weir, Orloff, and Skocpol, 153–56; Hamby, "The Democratic Moment," 268–69.

43. Hamby, "The Democratic Moment," 276–77; Weir, "The Federal Government and Unemployment," 168–73; Richard Reeves, *President Kennedy: Profile of Power* (New York: Simon and Schuster, 1993), 456–54.

44. Schwarz, *The New Dealers,* 195–97, 253–255, 280.

45. Samuel Lubell, "Revolt of the City," in *Electoral Change and Stability in American Political History,* ed. Jerome M. Clubb and Howard W. Allen (New York: Free Press, 1971), 3–4, 10–15, 23–24; Kevin Phillips, *The Emerging Republican Majority* (Garden City,

N.Y.: Anchor Books, 1970), 58, 65–67, 150, 336–38; Sundquist, *Dynamics of the Party System,* 240–51, 347.

46. Phillips, *The Emerging Republican Majority,* 151, 154–56.

47. Sundquist, *Dynamics of the Party System,* 271–77, 281–83; Phillips, *The Emerging Republican Majority,* 199.

48. The foregoing discussion of the Eisenhower and Kennedy period draws upon Phillips, *The Emerging Republican Majority,* 30, 69–74, 87, 99, 157–59, 344–45; Sundquist, *Dynamics of the Party System,* 337, 347, 351.

49. Phillips, *The Emerging Republican Majority,* 346.

Chapter 4. Failed Renewal: The Great Society

1. See George C. Edwards III with Alec M. Gallup, *Presidential Approval: A Sourcebook* (Baltimore: Johns Hopkins University Press, 1990).

2. Arthur H. Miller, "Political Issues and Trust in Government: 1964–1970," *American Political Science Review* 68 (September 1974): 953.

3. Lyndon Johnson quoted in Edward G. Carmines and James A. Stimson, *Issue Evolution: Race and the Transformation of American Politics* (Princeton, N.J.: Princeton University Press, 1989), 42–43, 50.

4. See David R. Mayhew, *Divided We Govern: Party Control, Lawmaking, and Investigations, 1946–1990* (New Haven, Conn.: Yale University Press, 1991).

5. See Thomas Byrne Edsall with Mary Edsall, *Chain Reaction: The Impact of Race, Rights, and Taxes on American Politics* (New York: W. W. Norton, 1991), 47–48, 51–52; Edwards, *Presidential Approval;* National Advisory Commission on Civil Disorders, Report, 114–15; U.S. Department of Justice, Federal Bureau of Investigation, *Uniform Crime Reports for the United States* (Washington, D.C., 1970), 2–14; Gallup Surveys, August–October 1968.

6. Lyndon Johnson, Address to the Nation, *Public Papers of the Presidents: Lyndon B. Johnson, 1967,* Vol. 2. U.S. Government Printing Office, Washington, D.C., 1968. July 27, 1967.

7. Stephen Skowronek, *The Politics Presidents Make: Leadership from John Adams to George Bush* (Cambridge, Mass.: Harvard University Press, 1993), 331–37.

8. Edsall and Edsall, *Chain Reaction,* 57, 87–88.

9. C. Vann Woodward, *The Strange Career of Jim Crow* (New York: Oxford University Press, 1966), 67–109; Hanes Walton Jr., "The Democrats and African Americans: The American Idea," in *Democrats and the American Idea: A Bicentennial Appraisal,* ed. Peter B. Kovler (Washington, D.C.: Center for National Policy Press, 1992), 333–47.

10. Theda Skocpol, "The Limits of the New Deal System and Roots of Contemporary Welfare Dilemmas," in *The Politics of Social Policy in the United States,* ed. Margaret Weir, Ann Shola Orloff, and Theda Skocpol (New York: Basic Books, 1990), 302–03; Carmines and Stimson, *Issue Evolution,* 31–32.

11. Adlai Stevenson quoted in Carmines and Stimson, *Issue Evolution,* 35–40; James L. Sundquist, *Dynamics of the Party System,* 355–56.

12. See Carmines and Stimson, *Issue Evolution,* 55–56, 63–64, 116–17.

13. John Kennedy and Martha Griffiths quoted in Richard Reeves, *President Kennedy: Profile of Power* (New York: Simon and Schuster, 1993), 39, 126–33, 353–57.

14. Lyndon B. Johnson, "To Fulfill These Rights," Commencement Address at Howard University, June 4, 1965, in *Public Papers of the Presidents of the United States: Lyndon Baines Johnson, 1965* (Washington, D.C.: U.S. Government Printing Office, 1966), 2:636.

15. Carmines and Stimson, *Issue Evolution,* 50–52.

16. James L. Sundquist, *Dynamics of the Party System: Alignment and Realignment of Political Parties in the United States,* rev. ed. (Washington, D.C.: Brookings Institution, 1983), 357–58; A. James Reichley, *Conservatives in an Age of Change: The Nixon and Ford Administrations* (Washington, D.C.: Brookings Institution, 1981), 176–86, 196–98.

17. Lewis Chester, Godfrey Hodgson, and Bruce Page, *An American Melodrama: The Presidential Campaign of 1968* (New York: Viking Press, 1969), 280–81; Theodore H. White, *The Making of the President 1968: A Narrative History of American Politics in Action* (New York: Atheneum, 1969), 344–49.

18. Kevin Phillips, *The Emerging Republican Majority* (Garden City, N.Y.: Anchor Books, 1970), 37–38, 205–06, 291–92, 464, 470.

19. Spiro Agnew quoted in Sundquist, *Dynamics of the Party System,* 386–87.

20. Carmines and Stimson, *Issue Evolution,* 132–37.

21. Theodore R. Marmor, Jerry L. Mashaw, and Phillip L. Harvey, *America's Misunderstood Welfare State: Persistent Myths, Enduring Realities* (New York: Basic Books, 1990), 33–35, 40–41.

22. Lawrence R. Jacobs, *The Health of Nations: Public Opinion and the Making of American and British Health Policy* (Ithaca, N.Y.: Cornell University Press, 1993), 138–43.

23. Johnson, "To Fulfill These Rights," 637–39; Robert X. Browning, *Politics and Social Welfare Policy in the United States* (Knoxville: University of Tennessee Press, 1986), 105–8; Margaret Weir, *Politics and Jobs: The Boundaries of Employment Policy in the United States* (Princeton, N.J.: Princeton University Press, 1992), 74–78, 84–88.

24. See Weir, *Politics and Jobs,* 83.

25. Phillips, *The Emerging Republican Majority,* 206.

26. Mario M. Cuomo, Keynote Address Before the 1984 Democratic National Convention, in *Official Report of the Proceedings of the Democratic National Convention* (Washington, D.C.: Democratic National Committee, 1984), 230.

27. For a discussion of this identity, see Stanley Greenberg, "Looking Toward '88: The Politics of American Identity," *World Policy Journal* (Fall 1987): 695–722.

28. Gallup Surveys.

29. Weir, *Politics and Jobs,* 74–75; Mayhew, *Divided We Govern,* table 4.1; Browning, *Politics and Social Welfare Policy,* 77.

30. For a discussion of state spending, inflation, taxes, and the impact on working-class voters, see Fred L. Block, *Revising State Theory: Essays in Politics and Postindustrialism* (Philadelphia: Temple University Press, 1987), and Adam Przeworski, *Capitalism and Social Democracy* (Cambridge, England: Cambridge University Press, 1985).

31. Phillips, *The Emerging Republican Majority,* 1, 30, 206–7; Walter Dean Burnham, *Critical Elections and the Mainsprings of American Politics* (New York: W. W. Norton, 1970), 146–47; John R. Petrocik, "Realignment: New Party Coalitions and the Nationalization of the South," *Journal of Politics,* May 1987, 366; Center for Political Studies, *American National Election Study, 1968* (Ann Arbor: University of Michigan, 1969).

32. Gary Orfield, "Race and the Liberal Agenda," in *The Politics of Social Policy,* ed. Weir, Orloff, and Skocpol, 336; Sundquist, *Dynamics of the Party System,* 291; William A. Rusher, *The Making of the New Majority Party* (New York: Sheed and Ward, 1975), 57–58; Edsall and Edsall, *Chain Reaction,* 60–61.

33. Chester, Hodgson, and Page, *An American Melodrama,* 651, 661, 705–8; White, *The Making of the President 1968,* 365–66; Petrocik, "Realignment," 48. Additional calculations are based on the University of Michigan's postelection American survey, Center for Political Studies *American National Election Studies* (Ann Arbor, Mich., 1968).

34. David E. Apter, *Choice and the Politics of Allocation* (New Haven, Conn.: Yale University Press, 1971).

35. E. J. Dionne Jr., *Why Americans Hate Politics* (New York: Simon and Schuster, 1991), 10–12; Kevin Phillips, *Post-Conservative America: People, Politics, and Ideology in a Time of Crisis* (New York: Random House, 1982), 18.

36. Arthur H. Miller, "Political Issues and Trust in Government: 1964–1970," *American Political Science Review* (September 1974): 951–53. The country, until the last few years, had never seen anything quite like this. Nixon's actions in Watergate and Jimmy Carter's in the Iran hostage crisis led more Americans to wonder whether government in Washington could be trusted to do the

"right" thing. But on most measures—including whether government is wasteful, run for a few big interests, or indifferent to ordinary people—the deterioration of confidence steadied after 1972, highlighting the upheaval that had transformed the relationship between the citizenry and politics.

37. Turnout began dropping after 1968, when 62.3 percent of Americans voted, hitting bottom in 1988, when 52.8 percent voted. That withdrawal from politics, according to an important study by Ruy A. Teixeira, is rooted first in the growing isolation of people from organizations like churches and second in a growing belief that politics is remote from the ordinary person, that public officials are uninterested in their needs and views. See Ruy A. Teixeira, *The Disappearing American Voter* (Washington, D.C.: Brookings Institution, 1992), 9, 42–47, 57.

38. Based on research sponsored by the Vietnam Veterans Foundation, June 1990.

39. Miller, "Political Issues and Trust in Government," 958–60, 970; Gallup Surveys, August 1968 (a majority seeing the war as a "mistake").

40. Miller, "Political Issues and Trust in Government," 958–60, 970.

41. Edward M. Kennedy, Speech Before the 1980 Democratic National Convention, in *Official Report of the Proceedings of the Democratic National Convention,* ed. Dorothy Bush (Washington, D.C.: Democratic National Committee, 1980), 349–56.

Chapter 5. Failed Renewal: The Reagan Revolution

1. Kevin Phillips, *The Emerging Republican Majority* (Garden City, N.Y.: Anchor Books, 1970); Theodore H. White, *The Making of the President 1968: A Narrative History of American Politics in Action* (New York: Atheneum, 1969), 396.

2. Richard Nixon quoted in Lewis Chester, Godfrey Hodgson, and Bruce Page, *An American Melodrama: The Presidential Campaign of 1968* (New York: Viking Press, 1969), 496; Richard Nixon presi-

dential materials, Nixon-Agnew television spots, 1968 campaign, National Archives and Records Administration, Washington, D.C.

3. Chester, Hodgson, and Page, *An American Melodrama,* 682. Also see Nixon presidential materials, Nixon-Agnew television spots.

4. Barry Goldwater, *The Conscience of a Conservative* (Washington, D.C.: Regnery Gateway, 1990), 6–7, 18–19, 28, 32–35, 39, 56, 64; Phillips, *The Emerging Republican Majority,* 236.

5. Nixon quoted in A. James Reichley, *Conservatives in an Age of Change: The Presidential Campaign of 1968* (New York: Viking Press, 1969), 174, 197, 174–202.

6. H. R. Haldeman, *The Haldeman Diaries: Inside the Nixon White House* (New York: G. P. Putnam's Sons, 1994), 117–19, 132, 183–86, 208.

7. Richard Nixon, Remarks on Accepting the Presidential Nomination of the Republican National Convention, August 23, 1972, in *Public Papers of the Presidents of the United States: Richard Nixon, 1972* (Washington, D.C.: U.S. Government Printing Office, 1974), 788.

8. White, *The Making of the President 1968,* 626–29; Reichley, *Conservatives in an Age of Change,* 61; David R. Mayhew, *Divided We Govern: Party Control, Lawmaking, and Investigations, 1946–1990* (New Haven, Conn.: Yale University Press, 1991), 90.

9. William A. Rusher, *The Making of the New Majority Party* (New York: Sheed and Ward, 1975), 75; Richard Whalen, quoted in Sidney Blumenthal, *The Rise of the Counter-Establishment: From Conservative Ideology to Political Power* (New York: Harper Collins, 1988), 60–61.

10. Reichley, *Conservatives in an Age of Change,* 165–67; Haldeman, *The Haldeman Diaries,* 181.

11. Reichley, *Conservatives in an Age of Change,* 137–44, 155–58; Richard G. Niemi, John Mueller, and Tom W. Smith, *Trends in Public Opinion: A Compendium of Survey Data* (New York: Greenwood Press, 1989), 76.

12. Norbert Goldfield, "The Nixon Years: Failed National Health Reform from Both Parties," *Physician Executive,* May 1992; Carole Gentry, "National Health Care: The Long Fight," *St. Petersburg Times,* July 24, 1989.

13. Reichley, *Conservatives in an Age of Change,* 172, 206–26;
Stephen E. Ambrose, *Nixon: The Triumph of a Politician, 1962–1972*
(New York: Simon and Schuster, 1989), 2:572–73; Mayhew,
Divided We Govern, 82–88.

14. Walter Dean Burnham, *The Current Crisis in American Politics*
(New York: Oxford University Press, 1982), 252; James L.
Sundquist, *Dynamics of the Party System: Alignment and Realignment
of Political Parties in the United States,* rev. ed. (Washington, D.C.:
Brookings Institution, 1983), 394–411; Warren E. Miller and Santa
A. Traugott, *American National Election Studies Data Sourcebook,
1952–1986* (Cambridge, Mass.: Harvard University Press, 1989), 81;
Kathleen Knight, "Partisan Differences in the Understanding of
Partisan Differences" (paper presented to the Midwest Political
Science Association, Chicago, April 1987), table 1; Warren E.
Miller, "Party Identification Re-examined: The Reagan Era"
(paper presented to the International Political Science Associa-
tion, Paris, July 1985), 27; Jerome M. Clubb, William H. Flanigan,
and Nancy H. Zingale, *Partisan Realignment: Voters, Parties, and Gov-
ernment in American History* (Beverly Hills, Calif.: Sage Publica-
tions, 1980), 309–11; Harold W. Stanley, William T. Bianco, and
Richard G. Niemi, "A New Perspective on Partisanship and
Group Support Over Time" (paper presented to the American
Political Science Association, New Orleans, 1985), table 3.

15. Jimmy Carter, "Energy and National Goals," Address to the
Nation, July 15, 1979, in *Public Papers of the Presidents of the United
States: Jimmy Carter, 1979* (Washington, D.C.: U.S. Government
Printing Office, 1980), 1237–38. In Carter's last year, 1980, the real
GDP grew −0.5 percent; inflation was 12.5 percent (U.S. Depart-
ment of Commerce, Economic Statistics Administration, Bureau
of Economic Analysis, *National Income and Product Accounts, 1959–88*
[Washington, D.C., 1992], vol. 2, table 8.1; U.S. Bureau of Labor
Statistics, Office of Consumer Pricing, *Consumer Price Index*
[Washington, D.C., 1980]).

16. Niemi, Mueller, and Smith, *Trends in Public Opinion,* 76;
Thomas Byrne Edsall with Mary Edsall, *Chain Reaction: The Impact
of Race, Rights, and Taxes on American Politics* (New York: W. W.
Norton, 1991), 105–6, 130–31.

17. Haynes Johnson, *Sleepwalking Through History: America in the Reagan Years* (New York: Doubleday, 1992), 94; Harry O'Connor, *Mellon's Millions: The Biography of a Fortune. The Life and Times of Andrew Mellon* (New York: John Day, 1933), 316; Ronald Reagan quoted in Kevin Phillips, *Post-Conservative America: People, Politics, and Ideology in a Time of Crisis* (New York, Random House, 1982), 9; also see 133–34.

18. Gary Wills, *Reagan's America: Innocents at Home* (New York: Penguin Books, 1988), 332–39.

19. Blumenthal, *The Rise of the Counter-Establishment,* 55–56, 62–63.

20. George Gilder, *Wealth and Poverty* (New York: Basic Books, 1981), 5–6, 8, 20, 27–28, 35.

21. David Stockman quoted in William Greider, "The Education of David Stockman," *Atlantic,* December 1981, 47; Gilder, *Wealth and Poverty,* 28, 63.

22. David M. Ricci, *The Transformation of American Politics: The New Washington and the Rise of Think Tanks* (New Haven, Conn.: Yale University Press, 1993), 155–62.

23. Benjamin M. Friedman, *Day of Reckoning: The Consequences of American Economic Policy Under Reagan and After* (New York: Vintage Books, 1989), 135–39, 149; Bureau of Labor Statistics, "Employment and Earnings," Washington, D.C., January 1994, 182.

24. See Blumenthal, *The Rise of the Counter-Establishment,* 280.

25. Peggy Noonan, *What I Saw at the Revolution: A Political Life in the Reagan Era* (New York: Random House, 1990), 270; Burnham, *The Current Crisis in American Politics,* 236–39, 282–89, 301.

26. Quoted in Sidney Blumenthal, *Our Long National Daydream: A Political Pageant of the Reagan Era* (New York: HarperCollins, 1990), 121–23.

27. Lou Cannon, *President Reagan: The Role of a Lifetime* (New York: Simon and Schuster, 1992), 40–41. Also see Noonan, *What I Saw at the Revolution,* 149–51, 267; Wills, *Reagan's America.*

28. Cannon, *President Reagan,* 88–94.

29. Reagan quoted in Noonan, *What I Saw at the Revolution,* 125–28.

30. Thomas Byrne Edsall, "The Reagan Legacy," in *The Reagan Legacy,* ed. Sidney Blumenthal and Thomas Byrne Edsall (New York: Pantheon Books, 1988), 25–27; Reagan quoted in Edsall and Edsall, *Chain Reaction,* 141; Phillips, *Post-Conservative America,* 15–22; Sundquist, *Dynamics of the Party System,* 422.

31. Cannon, *President Reagan,* 243–44; Greider, "The Education of David Stockman," 44–45.

32. Reagan quoted in Noonan, *What I Saw at the Revolution,* 127–28.

33. Jonathan Rieder, *Canarsie: The Jews and Italians of Brooklyn Against Liberalism* (Cambridge, Mass.: Harvard University Press, 1985).

34. David Halle, *America's Working Man: Work, Home, and Politics Among Blue-Collar Property Owners* (Chicago: University of Chicago Press, 1984). Also see Jonathan Schell, *History in Sherman Park: An American Family and the Reagan-Mondale Election* (New York: Alfred A. Knopf, 1987).

35. Reagan quoted in Blumenthal, *The Rise of the Counter-Establishment,* 282.

36. Barbara G. Farah and Helmut Norpoth, "Trends in Partisan Realignment, 1976–1986: A Decade of Waiting" (paper presented to the American Political Science Association, Washington, D.C., August 29, 1986), table 1; Knight, "Partisan Differences in the Understanding of Partisan Differences," table 1; Miller, "Party Identification Re-examined," 27.

37. Arthur H. Miller, "Realigning Forces in the United States Elections of 1984" (paper presented to the International Political Science Association, Paris, July 1985), 20–21, table 5; David J. Lanoue, "The Democrats' Dilemma" (paper presented at the American Political Science Association, Chicago, 1987), 19–20; see Figure 6.2.

38. Miller and Traugott, *American National Election Studies Data Sourcebook, 1952–1986,* 153.

39. See Appendix, Figure A.2.; Gallup Surveys, 1983, 1985; Opinion Research Corporation, National Surveys, 1981, 1983, 1985, and 1987.

40. Walter Dean Burnham, "The Reagan Heritage," in *The Election of 1988: Reports and Interpretations,* ed. Gerald M. Pomper (Chatham, N.J.: Chatham House Publishers, 1989), 26.

41. This study, "Liberalism Reconstructed: Survey on Liberalism in the 1988 Election," was directed by Celinda Lake with whom I collaborated (February 1989).

42. Confidence is based on the percentage saying "very high" or "high," in surveys conducted by Gallup, reported by CNN, July 19–21, 1993. Also see Lake and Greenberg, "Liberalism Reconstructed."

43. Kevin Phillips, *Boiling Point: Republicans, Democrats, and the Decline of Middle-Class Prosperity* (New York: Random House, 1993), 44, 49, 55–56; Friedman, *Day of Reckoning,* 152–53, 264–68.

44. Lee Atwater quoted in Bill Greider, "The Power of Negative Thinking," *Rolling Stone,* January 12, 1989, 51–53.

45. U.S. Bureau of the Census, *Money Income of Households, Families, and Persons in the United States: 1992,* Current Population Reports, Series P60-184 (Washington, D.C., 1993), table B-6; Lawrence Mishel and Jared Bernstein, *The State of Working America, 1992–93* (Armonk, N.Y.: M. E. Sharpe, 1993), 48.

46. I developed this line of argument in my work in 1988 for the Academy of Florida Trial Lawyers, who sponsored important research on values and the law.

47. Walter Dean Burnham, "The Reagan Heritage," 20–25.

Chapter 6. The End of Growth

1. This research was sponsored by the Center for National Policy and formed part of its report, *The Real Story of the U.S. Economy, 1950–1990* (Washington, D.C.: Center for National Policy, 1992).

2. Contemporary research supports this confident remembrance of prosperity. People in the late 1950s—indeed, right up to 1964—

rated the current situation of the country as strong (6.5 on a 10-rung ladder), a rating more positive than anything we have seen since but, more important, modest compared with the even greater optimism about what lay five years ahead (7.7 in 1964). In the graph, this good feeling and optimism are poised at the top, the future 1.2 points above the present, reflecting a faith that America was organized to bring prosperity. (See Appendix, Figure A.3.)

3. This chapter is based primarily on the Center for National Policy focus groups. In certain sections, like this one, I have supplemented that material with the results of additional focus groups conducted between 1987 and 1990 with swing voters from around the country. Most of the additional research was supported by the World Policy Institute, though various candidates have allowed me to include selected material without specific attribution.

4. A national survey at the start of the '90s showed that these reflections on prices are rooted in a statistical reality. Overall, 57 percent of the voters mentioned as their first or second most pressing *personal* economic problem the prices for things people need—well above any other economic concern, including kids having trouble getting started and getting ahead (34 percent), higher taxes (30 percent), the prospect of unemployment (19 percent), jobs not paying enough (14 percent), high interest rates (16 percent), and not enough opportunity (9 percent). When the economic focus was elevated to economic problems facing the country, price for health care and housing remained the primary concern (38 percent on first or second mention), even when compared with such weighty problems as the federal budget deficits (28 percent), poverty (23 percent), the growing gap between the rich and the poor (21 percent), the trade deficits (17 percent), high taxes (17 percent), and the United States falling behind other countries (16 percent). The survey was conducted jointly by me and Geoffrey Garin for Democrats for the '90s, March 1990. Pamela Harriman raised the funds to support the survey and encouraged its public dissemination.

The focus on children as a way to express concerns about the economy was first raised by Peter Hart in a study for Kidspac

(August 1987). I raised similar issues in an essay entitled, "Kids as Politics" (September 1987).

5. This study is based primarily on the March 1990 national survey of American opinion sponsored by Democrats for the '90s.

6. Reported by a campaign aide to the author.

7. Survey conducted for the World Policy Institute, October 1987; Roper Survey, in *US News and World Report,* March 30, 1988; Americans Talk Security, national survey, February 1988.

8. Americans Talk Security, February 1988.

9. Americans Talk Security, February 1988. Tom Kiley and John Marttila spoke of their views in a number of publications: *Wall Street Journal,* January 15, 1988; *National Journal,* April 9, 1988; and *Boston Globe,* May 3, 1988. For a more extended discussion of this issue, see my article, "The '88 Election: The Struggle for a Democratic Vision," *World Policy Journal* (Summer 1988): 553–57.

10. These results are from the Democrats for the '90s national survey (March 1990). The findings for each group are based on a sample of more than one hundred cases, except for white Catholics (74 cases), liberal Democrats (34 cases), and blacks (31 cases).

Chapter 7. The Clinton Solution

1. *New York Times,* October 4, 1991; Bill Clinton, Presidential Announcement Address, Little Rock, Arkansas, October 3, 1991.

2. David Maraniss, "A Political Life: William Jefferson Clinton," Part 1, *Washington Post,* July 13, 1992; *Arkansas Gazette,* March 21, 1976, and May 10, 1978.

3. Industrial Research and Extension Center, "Natural Increase Differentials, 1960–1975" (Fayetteville: University of Arkansas, 1976), 5; Phil Duncan, ed., *Politics in America: 1994* (Washington, D.C.: Congressional Quarterly Press, 1993), 93–94; U.S. Bureau of the Census, *Characteristics of the Population,* vol. 1 of *Census of Population: 1970* (Washington, D.C., 1972), table 57 State Data; Richard M. Scammon, *America Votes,* vol. 8 (Washington, D.C.: Congressional Quarterly, 1970), 25–26, and vol. 10 (Washington, D.C.: Con-

gressional Quarterly, 1973), 41–42; Secretary of State of Arkansas, *1974 General Election, United States Congress* (Little Rock, 1974). If one uses median income instead of per capita income, South Carolina whites were somewhat poorer than whites in Arkansas.

4. See V. O. Key Jr., *Southern Politics: In State and Nation* (New York: Vintage Books, 1949), 183–85; Diane D. Blair, *Arkansas Politics and Government: Do the People Rule?* (Lincoln: University of Nebraska Press, 1988), 33–35, 44–46.

5. For state comparisons, see David Osborne, *Laboratories of Democracy* (Boston: Harvard Business School Press, 1990), 88.

6. John Robert Starr, *Yellow Dogs and Dark Horses: Thirty Years on the Campaign Beat with John Robert Starr* (Little Rock, Ark.: August House, 1987), 156–57; Clinton's Farewell Address quoted in Jim Moore, *Clinton: Young Man in a Hurry* (Fort Worth, Tex.: Summit Group, 1992), 66.

7. Charles F. Allen and Jonathan Portis, *The Comeback Kid: The Life and Career of Bill Clinton* (New York: Birch Lane Press, 1992), 41–42; *Arkansas Gazette,* May 19, 1974.

8. Blair, *Arkansas Politics and Government,* 65.

9. *Arkansas Gazette,* July 12, 1974; Bill Clinton quoted in Stephen A. Smith, "Compromise, Consensus, and Consistency," in *The Clintons of Arkansas: An Introduction by Those Who Knew Them Best,* ed. Ernest Dumas (Fayetteville: University of Arkansas Press, 1993), 7.

10. Bill Clinton quoted in the *Arkansas Gazette,* May 19, July 2, July 26, September 25, September 29, and October 8, 1974.

11. Bill Clinton quoted ibid., May 12, May 19, August 21, October 3, and October 6–7, 1974.

12. Bill Clinton quoted ibid., October 7, 1974; Clinton quoted in Smith, "Compromise, Consensus, and Consistency," 7.

13. Bill Clinton quoted in the *Arkansas Gazette,* April 17, May 12, and October 1, 1974.

14. Bill Clinton quoted ibid., April 17, May 19, July 26, September 17, September 25, and October 27–29, 1974.

15. Ibid., November 3, 1974.

16. Bill Clinton quoted ibid., March 18 and May 11, 1976; February 25, March 7, April 25, April 29, and May 20, 1978.

17. Steve Smith quoted in Osborne, *Laboratories of Democracy,* 88–89; *Arkansas Gazette,* March 7, May 28 and May 31, 1978.

18. *Arkansas Gazette,* December 14, 1978; Phyllis Finton Johnston, *Bill Clinton's Public Policy for Arkansas: 1979–1980* (Little Rock, Ark.: August House, 1982), 57–58.

19. Bill Clinton quoted in the *Arkansas Gazette,* May 3 and November 21, 1978.

20. Bill Clinton quoted in Johnston, *Bill Clinton's Public Policy,* 57–60.

21. Frank White and Bill Clinton quoted in the *Arkansas Gazette,* October 23 and October 27, 1980.

22. Bill Clinton, Speech Before the Democratic State Convention, Hartford, July 18, 1980 (mimeograph), 3–5, 7–8.

23. Bill Clinton, Address Before the 1980 Democratic National Convention, in *Official Report of the Proceedings of the Democratic National Convention,* ed. Dorothy Bush (Washington, D.C.: Democratic National Committee), 585–89.

24. Bill Clinton quoted in *Arkansas Gazette,* November 21, 1980; Clinton quoted in Rudy Moore Jr., "They're Killing Me Out There," in *The Clintons of Arkansas,* ed. Dumas, p. 90. Johnston, *Bill Clinton's Public Policy,* 51; Osborne, *Laboratories of Democracy,* 89–91; Allen and Portis, *The Comeback Kid,* 67–68; Starr, *Yellow Dogs and Dark Horses,* 180–81.

25. See Blair, *Arkansas Politics and Government,* 84–87.

26. *Arkansas Gazette,* November 15, 1980.

27. Moore, "They're Killing Me Out There," 90; *Arkansas Gazette,* November 21, 1980; Bill Clinton quoted in *Arkansas Gazette,* November 23, 1980.

28. Blair, *Arkansas Politics and Government,* 86–87; Bill Clinton quoted in Maraniss, "A Political Life: William Jefferson Clinton," *Washington Post,* July 14, 1992. This section also draws on an interview with Dick Morris, Clinton's pollster and media adviser in

the 1982 race. David Watkins provided the commercials produced on behalf of the 1982 Clinton campaign.

29. *Arkansas Gazette,* November 7, 1982; Diane D. Blair, "Two Transitions in Arkansas, 1978 and 1982," in *Gubernatorial Transitions: The 1982 Election,* ed. Thad L. Beyle (Durham, N.C.: Duke University Press, 1985), 96–103.

30. Bill Clinton quoted in Allen and Portis, *The Comeback Kid,* 76–77; *Arkansas Gazette,* April 18, September 17; Clinton quoted in ibid., September 18, September 25, October 14, and October 17–20, 1982.

31. Clinton 1982 commercials provided by David Watkins.

32. Bill Clinton quoted in the *Arkansas Gazette,* October 17 and October 29, 1982.

33. Hillary Clinton quoted in the *Arkansas Gazette,* September 7, 1983; November 2, 1982.

34. *Arkansas Gazette,* November 20 and December 10, 1983; Dan Durning, "Education Reform in Arkansas: The Governor's Role in Policymaking," in *Gubernatorial Leadership and State Policy,* ed. Eric Herzik and Brent Brown (New York: Greenwood Press, 1991), 628, 632–34.

35. Paul Root, "Lessons from the Students," in *The Clintons of Arkansas,* ed. Dumas, 108; Osborne, *Laboratories of Democracy,* 92–100, 109; Starr, *Yellow Dogs and Dark Horses,* 192–96; Bill McAllister and David Maraniss, "Clinton: An Instinctive Deal-maker," *Washington Post,* March 28, 1992.

36. Richard M. Scammon and Alice V. McGillivray, *America Votes: 1984* (Washington, D.C.: Elections Research Center, Congressional Quarterly, 1985), 91–92.

37. Blair, *Arkansas Politics and Government,* 75, 85–87, 93.

38. Michael Dukakis quoted in *New York Times,* October 31, 1988; Lake and Greenberg, "Liberalism Reconstructed"; ABC News, *The '88 Vote* (New York: ABC News, 1988), 18–20.

39. Al From memorandum, November 3, 1989.

40. Al From memoranda to Bill Clinton, February 25, April 15, and September 5, 1990.

41. This material is based in part on an interview with Al From. Also see Al From memoranda to Bill Clinton, January 8 and February 23, 1990.

42. Bill Clinton quoted in *The New York Times,* March 25, 1990.

43. Robert J. Shapiro, "A Progressive Blueprint for Tax Equity," *Economic Outlook* (publication of the Progressive Policy Institute), May 21, 1990.

44. Bill Clinton, Address to the Democratic Leadership Council, New Orleans, March 24, 1990; Democratic Leadership Council, "The New Orleans Declaration. A Democratic Agenda for the 1990s." National Conference, March 22–25, 1990. The directors of the organization, among them Will Marshall and Al From, situated their support for responsibility and civic obligation in a well-developed critique of the Republicans' "gilded age" and "moral complacency," though these themes were not featured in New Orleans. (Will Marshall, *Citizenship and National Service: A Blueprint for Civic Enterprise* [Washington, D.C.: Democratic Leadership Council, 1988], 2.)

45. Bill Clinton, Keynote Address, Democratic Leadership Council, Cleveland, May 6, 1991.

46. Democratic Leadership Council, "The New American Choice. Opportunity, Responsibility, Community." National Convention, Cleveland, May 5–7, 1991.

47. Bill Clinton, Keynote Address, DLC, Cleveland, May 6, 1991.

48. Bill Clinton, Address to Tri-State Democrats Unity Dinner, Sioux City, Iowa, September 6, 1991.

49. Bill Clinton, Address to Democratic National Committee, Los Angeles, September 20, 1991.

50. Bill Clinton, "A New Covenant for Economic Change," Georgetown University, Washington, D.C., October 23, 1991.

Chapter 8. The Battle for Macomb

1. Lawrence Mishel and Jared Bernstein, *The State of Working America, 1992–93* (Armonk, N.Y.: M. E. Sharpe, 1993), 34, 66, 74, 132, 162, 166.

2. U.S. Bureau of Labor Statistics, *Local Area Unemployment Statistics* (Washington, D.C., 1989–94) figures for Macomb County, Mich.; U.S. Department of Commerce, Economic Statistics Administration, Bureau of Economic Analysis, *Regional Economic Information System* (Washington, D.C., 1993), table CA-05.

3. George Bush, State of the Union Address, January 28, 1992.

4. NBC News/*Wall Street Journal* poll, May 20, 1992; ABC News/*Washington Post* poll, June 8, 1992.

5. The reporters who had helped make Macomb County a bellwether were there in force: Tom Edsall of *The Washington Post* and author of *Chain Reaction,* Gwen Ifill of *The New York Times,* and Ron Brownstein of the *Los Angeles Times.*

6. Bill Clinton, speech at Macomb County Community College South, Warren, Mich., March 12, 1992.

7. Bill Clinton, speech at Pleasant Grove Baptist Church, Detroit, March 13, 1992.

8. This account is based on my own notes from these meetings.

9. Linda Bloodworth-Thomason and Mandy Grunwald argued that Bill Clinton needed to break free of the conventional media by barnstorming the popular culture shows—from Arsenio Hall and Rush Limbaugh to MTV. Only in those settings would Clinton get the opportunity to talk about his beliefs and his life's work.

10. Professor Samuel L. Popkin, author of *The Reasoning Voter,* had posed the question that structured the exercise: What three "facts" about Bill Clinton's life allow people to construct their own profile of Clinton the person and to infer what he believes deep inside and what he would be like as president?

11. George Bush, Address to the Knights of Columbus, New York, August 5, 1992; Speech Before the Republican National Convention, Houston, Tex., August 21, 1992.

12. George Bush, Speech Before the Republican National Convention; Address to the Detroit Economic Club, September 10, 1992.

13. George Bush, "Agenda for American Renewal," 1992, 2.

14. This headline appeared after Bush's speech before the Republican convention and encouraged Bill Clinton to speak out against Reaganism at the Detroit Economic Club that same day (*Detroit Free Press,* August 21, 1992).

Chapter 9. The Perot Dissolution

1. Antonio Gramsci, *Selections From the Prison Notebooks of Antonio Gramsci,* ed., Quintin Hoare and Geoffrey Nowell Smith (New York: International Publishers, 1971), 276.

2. Ross Perot, *United We Stand: How We Can Take Back Our Country* (New York: Hyperion, 1992), 4.

3. Ibid., 15–16.

4. Ibid., 8, 57–72.

5. Ibid., 13, 21–22, 24, 30–31.

6. Ibid., 75–81.

7. Ibid., 58, 61–62, 66.

8. Kevin Phillips, *Boiling Point: Republicans, Democrats, and the Decline of Middle-Class Prosperity* (New York: Random House, 1993), 243–44.

9. Ibid., 234.

10. This report is based on the largest national survey yet of Perot voters, twelve hundred interviews conducted across the country in proportion to the Perot vote in 1992. The survey was supplemented by a national sampling of Bush and Clinton voters (eight hundred interviews) and by a series of six focus groups with key segments of the Perot bloc: under-thirty voters in San Bernardino, California; older, non-college-educated Perot voters in Bangor, Maine; and under-fifty, non-college-educated voters in Akron, Ohio (where one group consisted of just union workers). The national survey was conducted from April 12 to April 19, 1993, and the focus groups were conducted between May 13 and May 18. (Democratic Leadership Council, "The Road to Realignment. The Democrats and the Perot Voters," 1993.)

11. In the survey described in note 10, Perot voters split fairly evenly between Clinton (36 percent) and Bush (39 percent) in a race without Perot. But given the Perot voters' predominant Republican past, an even split represents a major gain for the Democrats. Had Perot voters split evenly nationally, as the exit polls indicated they would have, Clinton would have won with 53 percent of the vote.

12. These attitudes reflect measurements on a number of dimensions discussed in the next section.

13. Martin P. Wattenberg, "The 1992 Election: Ross Perot and the Independent Voter" (paper prepared for the American Political Science Association, Washington, D.C., August–September 1993), 6; VRS, 1992. See also the discussion of attitudinal dimensions in the next section.

14. Respondents were asked to give a "temperature score" (ranging between zero and one hundred degrees) to a list of individuals and institutions, with zero meaning very cold and unfavorable and one hundred meaning very hot and favorable. The relationships among the responses (that is, the extent of dissimilarity) can be seen graphically on the matrix (statistically, a series of coordinates) that forms a "perceptual map"—in effect, a map of the Perot voters' political world.

  The feelings about Perot, not surprisingly, form a distinctive point on the matrix—positioned away from other political figures and institutions. Almost directly opposite Perot is Congress—the institution Perot voters felt very negatively about. That is the defining polarity in the matrix. The other polarity is formed by the cluster of Republican figures and institutions to the right and the cluster of Democratic ones to the left. In the world of Perot voters, small business is on the "Republican side" yet is close to Perot and therefore somewhat positive. Truman is on the "Democratic side," also close to Perot and very positive.

  Congress falls on an "unfavorable" line at the farthest point from Perot. Congress and government cluster close together and are therefore viewed similarly. On that same "unfavorable" line, to the Republican side, is big business and, to the Democratic side, labor unions. The most partisan Republican figure on the matrix

is Ronald Reagan—positioned the farthest away from Perot to
the right. On the Democratic side, the most partisan position is
shared by liberals and Clinton, who are clustered together
(though Clinton is somewhat closer to Perot and somewhat more
positive).

15. Albert O. Hirschman, *Rhetoric of Reaction: Perversity, Futility, Jeopardy* (Cambridge, Mass.: Harvard University Press, 1991).

16. A national survey of 1,250 voters conducted November 8
and 9, 1994, for the Democratic Leadership Council. The survey,
which included an oversample of independent voters, also
included 244 1992 Perot voters.

Chapter 10. New Contract

1. Craig R. Whitney, "Little Big Men," *New York Times,* April 3,
1994; Michael Barone, "Getting the Bum's Rush Everywhere," *US
News and World Report,* November 22, 1993; Chalmers Johnson,
"The Tremor: Japan's Post-Cold-War Identity," *New Republic,*
August 9, 1993; *Economist,* March 26, 1994; Doug Saunders and
Carl Wilson, "The Collapse of Canada's N.D.P.," *Nation,* Novem-
ber 29, 1993; *Maclean's,* April 11, 1994; William Schneider, "Time
to Take Italian Politics Seriously," *National Journal,* April 9, 1994.

2. Michael K. Brown, "Remaking the Welfare State: A Compara-
tive Perspective," in *Remaking the Welfare State: Retrenchment and
Social Policy in America and Europe,* ed. Michael K. Brown
(Philadelphia: Temple University Press, 1988), 8–14; Richard C.
Morais, "Les Miserables," *Forbes,* February 28, 1994; Charles A.
Radin, "Malaise Hits Japanese As Economy Dims," *Boston Globe,*
May 9, 1994; *Wall Street Journal,* November 1, 1993.

3. David Harvey, *The Condition of Post Modernity: An Enquiry into
the Origins of Cultural Change* (Cambridge, Mass.: Blackwell, 1990),
125–45, 167–72.

4. Times Mirror Center for the People and the Press, *The New
Political Landscape: The People, the Press and Politics* (October 1994), 3.

5. A national survey of 1,250 respondents conducted for the
Democratic Leadership Council on November 8 and 9, 1994. The

survey concentrated on independent voters, reflected in a 751-person oversample.

6. These focus group discussions with independent voters were sponsored by the Democratic Leadership Council and held on November 9 and 10, 1994. The Macomb groups included older independent voters (between the ages of 40 and 64) without a college degree. In Riverside, the participants were younger (ages 30 to 50) and had some post–high school education, including many with a college degree. Men and women participated in separate groups.

7. Stephen J. Rosenstone, John Mark Hansen, Paul Freedman, and Marguerite Grabarek, "Voter Turnout: Myth and Reality in the 1992 Election" (paper presented to the American Political Science Association, Washington, D.C., September 1993), figure 1, tables 6 and 7.

8. *New York Times*/CBS News poll, January 19, 1993.

9. Everett Carll Ladd, "The 1992 Vote for President Clinton: Another Brittle Mandate?" *Political Science Quarterly* 108, no. 1 (1993), 1–2, 13–15, 20, 22, 25.

10. John Podhoretz, *Hell of a Ride: Backstage at the White House Follies, 1989–1993* (New York: Simon and Schuster, 1993), 172; Grover G. Norquist, "The Unmaking of the President: Why George Bush Lost," *Policy Review* (Winter 1993), 12–14.

11. Ladd, "The 1992 Vote for President Clinton," 25; Grover G. Norquist, "GOP Hat Trick," *American Spectator,* January 1994.

12. The discussion of the religious right and abortion relies on the VRS exit polls as well as on the following articles based on the National Election Study, University of Michigan: Lyman A. Kellstedt, John C. Green, James L. Guth, and Corwin E. Smidt, "Religious Voting Blocs in the 1992 Election: The Year of the Evangelical?" *Sociology of Religion* 1994, vol. 55, no. 3; David C. Leege, "The Decomposition of the Religious Vote: A Comparison of White, Non-Hispanic Catholics with Other Ethnoreligious Groups, 1960–1992" (paper presented to the American Political Science Association, Washington D.C., September 1993); Alan I.

Abramowitz, "It's Abortion, Stupid: Policy Voting in the 1992 Presidential Election" (paper presented to the American Political Science Association, Washington, D.C., September 1993).

13. U.S. Department of Commerce, Economic and Statistics Administration, Bureau of the Census, "Income, Poverty, and Health Insurance, 1993," October 1994; Frank Levy, "The Future Path and Consequences of U.S. Earnings-Education Gap" (paper presented to the Federal Reserve Bank of New York, New York, November 1994), 3.

14. Walter Dean Burnham, "American Politics in the 1990s," in *The American Prospect Reader in American Politics,* ed. Walter Dean Burnham (Chatham, N.J.: Chatham House Publishers, 1995).

15. Stephen Skowronek, *The Politics Presidents Make: Leadership from John Adams to George Bush* (Cambridge, Mass.: Harvard University Press), 409–46.

16. Bill Clinton, Address to the Democratic Leadership Council, Cleveland, May 6, 1991.

17. E. J. Dionne, Jr., *Why Americans Hate Politics* (New York: Simon and Schuster, 1991), 11–12, 345.

18. The DLC post-election survey asked independent voters to choose among the following pairs of statements:

Bill Clinton has tried to move the country in the right direction.	64 percent
Bill Clinton has tried to move the country in the wrong direction.	32 percent
Clinton is a traditional liberal Democrat.	37 percent
Clinton is a new kind of Democrat.	56 percent
He is part of the Washington establishment.	35 percent
He is trying to change the Washington establishment.	59 percent

19. Michael C. Dawson, "Demonization and Silence: Preliminary Thoughts on the 1992 Presidential Election, the New Consensus

on Race, and African-American Public Opinion," April 1993, 1–2, 7–9. Also see Andrew Hacker, "The Blacks and Clinton," *New York Review of Books,* January 28, 1993.

20. Paul M. Sniderman and Thomas Piazza, *The Scar of Race* (Cambridge, Mass.: Harvard University Press, 1993), 28–33, 150–51.

21. William Julius Wilson, *The Truly Disadvantaged: The Inner City, the Underclass, and Public Policy* (Chicago: University of Chicago Press, 1987), 112–18.

22. Jesse Jackson quoted in William Raspberry, "The Black Dilemma," *Washington Post,* July 12, 1991.

23. Theda Skocpol, "Sustainable Social Policy: Fighting Poverty Without Poverty Programs," *American Prospect,* Summer 1990, 59.

24. Bill Clinton, State of the Union Address, January 25, 1994.

25. William Kristol, "Defeating President Clinton's Health Care Proposal," Project for the Republican Future, memorandum to Republican leaders, December 2, 1993.

26. Christopher Jencks and Kathryn Edin, "The Real Welfare Problem," *American Prospect,* Spring 1990; Wilson, *The Truly Disadvantaged,* 76.

INDEX